Entrepreneurial Small Businesses

To Suzie, Jack and Meg Shepherd, and
Maria, Elin and Nils Wiklund

Entrepreneurial Small Businesses

A Resource-based Perspective

Dean A. Shepherd

Indiana University, USA

Johan Wiklund

Jonkoping International Business School, Sweden

Edward Elgar

Cheltenham, UK • Northampton, MA, USA

Published by
Edward Elgar Publishing Limited
Glensanda House
Montpellier Parade
Cheltenham
Glos GL50 1UA
UK

Edward Elgar Publishing, Inc.
136 West Street
Suite 202
Northampton
Massachusetts 01060
USA

A catalogue record for this book
is available from the British Library

Library of Congress Cataloguing in Publication Data
Shepherd, Dean A.
  Entrepreneurial small businesses : a resource-based perspective / Dean Shepherd,
    Johan Wilkund.
        p. cm.
  Includes bibliographical references.
    1. Small business. 2. Entrepreneurship. 3. New business enterprises.
  I. Wiklund, Johan. II Title.

  HD62.7.S5257 2005
  338.6'42–dc22   2004063602

ISBN 1 84542 018 7

Printed and bound in Great Britain by MPG Books Ltd, Bodmin, Cornwall

Contents

Figures

Tables

1. An introduction to entrepreneurial small businesses

Academic interest in small business is relatively recent. Whether the previous lack of interest reflected real-world dominance of big business or simply unawareness of small business by researchers could be debated. More important, however, is that scholars now recognize that small businesses are essential for entrepreneurial activity, innovation, job creation and industry dynamics (Acs, 1992; Thurik and Wennekers, 2001). Evidence from a range of countries shows that since the 1970s, economic activity has moved away from large firms to small firms and at present the majority of new jobs are created by small firms (Davidsson et al., 1994; Thurik and Wennekers, 2001). As a consequence, over the past 25 years, researchers in several academic fields have increasingly become interested in various issues related to small business.

This book is concerned with the growth, performance and entrepreneurial activities of small businesses. While small businesses are not necessarily entrepreneurial, and entrepreneurship also takes place outside of the small business sector, it is clear that the entrepreneurial activities of small businesses are related to outcomes of individual small businesses as well as the economy at large. Small businesses make a substantial entrepreneurial contribution because they are a source of considerable innovative activity, in particular of radical innovation, and are important change agents in the economy (Acs, 1992; Baumol, 1993).

There is also a close relationship between the entrepreneurial activities, growth and performance of small businesses. For a healthy economic development, it is essential that old ideas are replaced by new ones and that old products, services and processes are substituted by those which are better and more effective. New ideas and innovations are often created by new and small businesses that grow rapidly and sometimes even create new industries. Many of the best known and most successful Swedish companies such as IKEA, SKF, Tetra Pak, AGA and Electrolux, were founded and developed upon individual innovations. More recent examples outside of Sweden are Apple, Microsoft and Netscape; all relatively young companies that have grown extremely rapidly and have changed the computer industry. Most people would regard these as examples of exceptional entrepreneurship.

The above discussion implies that entrepreneurship is a key to economic development and also illustrates how closely connected entrepreneurship is to small business growth. In his classic definition of entrepreneurship Schumpeter (1934) stressed that entrepreneurship has to do with combining resources in new ways that create disequilibrium in the economic system. In other words, entrepreneurial firms are innovative to such an extent that they have a substantial impact on the market.

In another well recognized definition of entrepreneurship, Stevenson advocates that pursuit of opportunity is the most important component of entrepreneurship (Stevenson, 1984; Stevenson and Jarillo, 1986; 1990). This definition concerns the business's relation to, and success in, the market place, and realizing what the wants and needs are, and will be in the future. These two definitions complement each other. When combined, entrepreneurship is defined as *taking advantage of opportunity by novel combinations of resources in ways which have impact on the market*. This is the view of entrepreneurship held throughout this book.

It is hard to imagine a small business taking advantage of an opportunity and having considerable impact on the market place without growing. Let us consider Microsoft for a moment. If Microsoft sold 100 licenses a year, it would neither have any considerable impact on the market, nor would Microsoft take advantage of the opportunity that apparently exists in the computer software market. If we accept the view that entrepreneurship is a matter of degree and not a dichotomous yes or no variable (for example, Stevenson, 1984), expanding Microsoft is at least more entrepreneurial than refraining from doing so. Thus, it seems that growth is an important manifestation of entrepreneurial behavior in small businesses.

THE NEED FOR SYSTEMATIC KNOWLEDGE

As we mention above, there is now considerable academic interest in small business. At the aggregate level, scholars have started to accumulate evidence of the importance of small businesses. Whereas small businesses appear to be a vital part of the economy, the prospect for any individual business is uncertain. Many small businesses die during their first years of operation, or struggle to survive. The number of small businesses that achieve large economic returns for their owners and grow substantially is limited.

Research has revealed that the majority of small firms do not grow, and that many are not even interested in pursuing growth (Storey, 1994; Wiklund et al., 2003). Rapid growth firms are not concentrated in specific industries. Contrary to common belief, these firms may be found in labor as well as knowledge intensive industries; in manufacturing as well as the service sector (Smallbone et al., 1995; Storey, 1996).

This raises some challenging questions. Is it at all possible to predict which firms will grow, or is firm growth haphazard? Do high performing small businesses share any common characteristics that distinguish them from low performing small businesses? What is the role of entrepreneurship in the growth and performance of small businesses? If we wish to take policy measures to stimulate the development of small businesses, which groups should be stimulated and what type of measures should be taken?

It is important to find out which factors affect the growth and performance of individual small firms. Of particular importance is to identify those factors that could be influenced by small businesses themselves and/or society in general. Knowledge of these factors could form the basis for activities to improve small business performance. It is, for instance, of little or no use to a small business manager to know that the firm would perform better if he or she had a different personality. For the same reason, it is important to find factors that have a sustainable rather than temporary influence on growth and performance.

Unfortunately, our knowledge about these issues is still limited. In recent years several comprehensive lists of studies have been compiled and reviewed. Storey (1994) identified more than 25 growth studies. Delmar (1997) scrutinized the operationalizations of growth used in 55 studies. One of the authors of this book reviewed and classified close to 70 studies for his dissertation work (Wiklund, 1998), while Ardishvili et al. (1998) included in their classification a full 105 published and unpublished studies focusing on new and/or small firm growth.

However, rather than presenting a set of solid generalizations on the causes and effects of growth, these reviewers all tend to come up with relatively critical accounts. These criticisms concern both theoretical and methodological shortcomings. Storey (1994: 5, 125) holds that small firm growth is one of the areas where theorists so far have not made major contributions. As to empirical studies he notes that these have been conducted independently of each other, and that they frequently address issues of specific interest to the researcher in a way that makes comparability with other studies difficult. Cooper (1995; 120) agrees that we need better theoretical frameworks and more theory driven empirical research.

Because the research is so scattered, providing a review of previous findings is likely to provide a mosaic rather than one coherent picture. Therefore, we have instead chosen to address a number of related small business issues in one book. By utilizing a similar theoretical and methodological logic across all chapters and by interpreting our results in a similar fashion we believe that we are able to present a coherent picture of pertinent small business issues. Empirically, we analyse a number of different samples, thus ensuring that the results obtained are not specific to any particular sample but have greater generality. Most of the research presented in the book has been through the peer review process where other academics judge the scientific quality of the work. This should ensure that the results presented are scientifically valid.

BUILDING OUR UNDERSTANDING OF ENTREPRENEURIAL SMALL BUSINESSES

Definition of a Small Business

When trying to define what a small firm is, it becomes evident that the concept of smallness varies and that there is no single suitable definition of a small firm. It is particularly clear that smallness varies from industry to industry since the size of a company is most often compared to the size of its competitors (Bolton, 1971; Stanworth and Grey, 1991; Storey, 1994). The auto manufacturer SAAB is perceived as being a small company within that industry, whereas not even the largest hairdresser comes close to the size of SAAB.

Basically, there are two different ways of defining small firms. The first type of definition could be labeled theoretical. Criteria for defining a small firm would typically include small market share, personalized management, vulnerability to environmental conditions and non-economic objectives of the manager. These types of definitions are theoretical in the sense that they, based on previous research, presume that small firms are fundamentally different from large firms concerning these dimensions. These fundamental differences provide the rationale for studying small firms as a separate group. One major problem in selecting a sample of small firms based on these criteria is that we do not know if small firms really are fundamentally different until we compare them to large firms, which means that we need a large firm sample for comparison. The other problem is that we would need to do some initial research just to find out whether a particular firm really meets the criteria of smallness and should be included in the sample for further research. Thus, theoretical definitions of small firms lead to very time and resource consuming sample selection.

The second type of definition could be labeled as quantitative. In this case, size itself is the criterion for smallness, and quantitative size data regarding sales, employees or equity are usually used when classifying firms as large or small. The problem with these definitions of small firms is that they tend to disregard the fact that the small firm sector is heterogeneous and that smallness varies across industries.

The European Union has proposed a quantitative definition based on employment (and some additional requirements concerning sales). The term used is: 'small and medium enterprise' (SME). The SME sector is disaggregated into three components:

- Very small enterprises (sometimes referred to as micro-enterprises) (0 to 9 employees);
- Small enterprises (10 to 49 employees and annual sales of not more than ECU 7 million);
- Medium-sized enterprises (50 to 249 employees and annual sales of not more than ECU 27 million).

This is a quantitative definition that takes some of the theoretical aspects into consideration. According to Storey (1994), one of the advantages of the distinction of micro-enterprises from small enterprises is that there is a notable shift in the formality regarding organization and customers at around 10 to 20 employees which makes micro-enterprises different from small enterprises. In the research presented in this book, we mainly rely on this quantitative definition to define small businesses and to select the samples that we study.

The Role of Strategic Choice

The focus of this book is on the growth and performance of individual small businesses. Thus, we do not consider population ecology models, which focus on the death and survival of populations of organizations, or regional economics studies comparing aggregate performance levels of small businesses in different locations. Some streams of research (for example, industrial economics) take a relatively deterministic view of organizational design and performance outcomes, that is, there is little acknowledgement that the decisions of the individual can have impact on the phenomena being investigated. While we agree that there are always some constraints in any decision making situation, our view is that small business managers have substantial discretion to exercise choice in the business's course of action and therefore can substantially influence small business growth and performance. Therefore, our philosophy in writing this book is that the destiny of the small business is not completely determined by the characteristics of the environment and other factors outside the control of the small business but is highly dependent upon the decisions its management makes.

Furthermore, this book does not take a strict economic rationalist argument where the goal of the small business manager and his/her firm is to always maximize economic profits. Rather, given the attainment of some threshold level of performance, managers may choose to pursue various goals that are not necessarily the maximization of profit. Depending on personal goals, small firms may perform at levels far below their full potential. This view of a manager's discretion is central to the strategic choice approach to understanding growth and performance (Keats and Bracker, 1988).

The Roles of the Individual, Firm and Environment

While we do follow the tradition of small business and entrepreneurship research that focuses on the individual we also investigate and integrate other levels of analysis, namely, the firm and the environment. Such an approach has been called for by other scholars in the field (Low and MacMillan, 1988; Zahra, 1993b). Small firms are a particularly suitable area for conducting this type of research (Chandler and Hanks, 1994). Due to their small size, small businesses are not as well insulated from environmental impacts as are larger firms, which makes it all the more important to take into consideration environmental influences.

Due to the business's small size it typically has a relatively simple organizational structure and a relatively homogeneous organizational culture, both of which are dominated by the small business manager and his/her vision. In this sense, we can consider the business and its manager to be very much intertwined. For instance, the manager has a direct and crucial influence on the actions of the small business, whereas in the large firm more people are involved in the decision making process. It is not surprising then that researchers of small businesses focus primarily on the individual (for example, characteristics and decisions) while those that investigate large firms focus more on the firm (for example, corporate culture, organizational reputation, management team, board composition, and so on).

When businesses are new and/or very small, single individuals are responsible for important decisions and actions and there is little need to study entrepreneurial strategy: 'All revolves around the entrepreneur. Its goals are his goals, its strategy his vision of its place in the world' (Mintzberg, 1984; 534). After a firm is established and starts growing, a single individual typically has less influence on the firm and the management becomes more professional; the management *team* also becomes increasingly important (Stanworth and Grey, 1991). But, at what size does the organization become more interesting than the entrepreneur and vice versa? There is, of course, no such size. Instead, the dual focus on both the individual and the organization is needed in research on small businesses. Although we advocate the importance of strategic choice, the environment does play an important role in providing (or not) opportunities for growth and either rewarding or punishing entrepreneurial behavior. Therefore, in this book we consider individual, firm and environmental factors in our explanation of small business growth and performance.

The Resource-Based Perspective

This book is primarily influenced by streams of theory that we collectively label the 'resource-based perspective'. The most salient characteristic of the resource based perspective is the focus on the firm's internal strengths. The resource-based perspective can be traced back to the seminal work by Penrose (1959) on firm growth. However, the perspective has experienced a revival during the 1990s in the strategic management literature. To a great extent this has been a reaction to the analyses of the 1980s, where the focus of strategic management research was on market positioning (Grant, 1991).

The internal resource-based perspective may be particularly suitable when trying to understand why some small businesses perform better and grow more than others. Small businesses do not have the market power to dominate customers and competitors, and therefore market positioning appears less relevant for small businesses. Of course, the environment has profound impact on small businesses and it is essential for them to pursue the opportunities that arise in the environment. However, we argue that the way in which this is done is determined by internal characteristics. For example, as we show in Chapter 2, the human capital and motivation of the small business manager has profound effect on subsequent small business growth. Irrespectively of whether or not profitable opportunities arise in the environment, unless the small business manager has the capacity and aspirations to pursue these opportunities growth will not occur.

Further, previous studies have found that the resources that small businesses control or have access to are important for their capacity to grow and perform well (see Wiklund, 1998, Appendix 1, for a review of this literature). Several strands of resources have been studied such as financial capital, start-up experience, education level of the small business manager and of employees, and so forth. The resource-based perspective provides a solid theoretical embedment for such findings and offers explanations as to why those small businesses that can access particular resources acquire an advantage over other small businesses, which allows them to grow and perform well. In this book, we examine several strands of resources, that is, the human and social capital of the small business manager, the marketing and technological knowledge of staff, the access to financial capital (debt and equity) and how they contribute to the entrepreneurial activities, growth and performance of small businesses. The resource-based perspective provides us with an overarching theoretical framework for hypothesizing about these relationships and interpreting our empirical findings.

LAYOUT FOR THE REST OF THE BOOK

Chapter 2 focuses on 'The motivation to grow a small business'. This chapter takes an important step towards an increased understanding of a small business manager's growth aspirations and the actual growth achieved by his or her small business. While there is a positive relationship between the aspiration for, and the achievement of small business growth, the relationship is more complex – it depends on the resources of the small business manager and opportunities for growth that exist in the environment. Specifically, education, experience and environmental dynamism magnify the positive effect that growth aspirations have on the realization of small business growth. In this chapter we also acknowledge that 1) while some people have the motivation to grow their business they may not have the capability to do so and 2) while some people have the capability to grow their businesses they may not have the motivation to do so.

Chapter 3 focuses on 'Who grows small businesses and how they choose to do it'. This chapter explores differences in small business managers in terms of their own personal resources (human capital) and their access to resources (social capital) as a means of distinguishing those who engage in subsequent entrepreneurial activities from those who do not and also as a means of distinguishing between the modes used to exploit these subsequent entrepreneurial activities. We find that human capital (education and start-up experience), and social capital (business network and relational density) are important resources in explaining whether small business managers engage in subsequent entrepreneurial activities or not. We also find that one type of resource is associated with a particular mode for organizing the entrepreneurial activities.

Chapter 4 focuses on 'The small business's entrepreneurial orientation and knowledge-based resources'. We explore the performance implications of a small business's knowledge-based resources focusing on those that are applicable to the discovery and exploitation of opportunities. We also explore the performance implications of a small business entrepreneurial orientation, where entrepreneurial orientation represents how the numerous components of a small business are organized in order to discover and exploit opportunities. We find that the way that a small business is organized (its entrepreneurial orientation, or EO), can enhance the positive relationship between knowledge-based resources and small business performance. We argue that those small businesses with considerable knowledge-based resources know where to look for opportunities, can more accurately assess the value of potential opportunities, and have the ability to extract value from these opportunities, but unless the firm is organized to grasp and enthusiastically pursue these opportunities, then the knowledge-based resources are likely to be underutilized.

Chapter 5 focuses on 'The small business's entrepreneurial orientation, financial capital, and the environment'. This chapter further explores small business performance through the concomitant consideration of EO, resources internal to the small business (access to capital), and resources external to the small business (environmental dynamism). The nature of the configurations suggests that businesses that face performance constraints, in terms of a stable environment and limited access to capital, can be superior performers if they have a high entrepreneurial orientation (EO). This finding is consistent with the saying that 'necessity is the mother of invention'. It appears that a high EO provides businesses with the ability to find and/or discover new opportunities that can differentiate them from other firms and create a competitive advantage. When the environment is dynamic and the firm has considerable access to capital, it appears that small business performance might be improved by a more inwardly focused orientation that better capitalizes on these abundant opportunities by focusing on efficient exploitation.

Chapter 6 focuses on 'Venture capitalists' investment decision policies and maintaining a good relationship'. With the help of Andrew Zacharakis, we use theory from the resource-based view (RBV) of strategy to investigate venture capitalists' (VCs') decision policies when assessing the likely performance of potential portfolio companies. We find that venture capitalists value those businesses that 1) have a proprietary technology, 2) have a management team with market familiarity, 3) are in a fast growing market, and 4) have a management team that have considerable general leadership skills. Although venture capitalists always prefer greater general experience in leadership, they value it more highly in large markets, when there are many competitors, and when the competitors are relatively weak. We also find that previous start-up experience of the business's management team may substitute for leadership experience. Understanding venture capitalists' decision policies may help small businesses to access equity capital to pursue growth opportunities. There are numerous benefits to a business that can establish a long term relationship with a venture capitalist and in this chapter we explore how small business managers can better manage this relationship. The entrepreneur and the VC need to balance the level of control and trust building mechanisms so that the optimal level of confidence in partner cooperation can be achieved. We propose that the entrepreneur can build trust with the VC (and vice versa) by signaling commitment and consistency, being fair and just, obtaining a good fit with one's partner, and with frequent and open communication. Open and frequent communication acts as a catalyst for the other trust building mechanisms.

Chapter 7 focuses on 'Loan officers' decisions policies towards small businesses'. Loans from banks represent an important funding source for small businesses. Along with Volker Bruns, we investigate the decision policies of loan officers in their assessments of small business loan requests. We find that loan officers are more likely to provide a small business loan if that business's past performance had been high and/or the business's competence was related to the project for which funding was required. The findings also suggest that project risk decreased the likelihood of a loan officer granting a loan for those small businesses with weak financial standing, but had little or no impact on those small businesses with strong financial standing. Similarly, project risk decreased the likelihood of a loan officer granting a loan to those small businesses with collateral dependent on the success of the project, but had little or no impact on those small businesses that were able to offer collateral independent of project success. We also explore differences in loan officers' human capital to explain differences in their decision policies.

Chapter 8 focuses on 'Learning from small business failure'. In the pursuit of entrepreneurial outcomes there is the risk that the business will fail. This chapter employs the psychological literature on grief to explore the emotions arising from business failure. It suggests that the loss of a business due to failure can cause the small business manager to feel grief, which is a negative emotional response interfering with the ability to learn from the events surrounding that loss. Recovering from grief involves dealing with the loss, avoiding thinking about the loss, or a dual process that iteratively combines these two approaches. A dual process provides the speediest path to grief recovery enabling small business managers to learn more from the events surrounding the loss of the business owing to a lack of emotional interference. But even in the presence of grief, a dual process minimizes emotional interference enhancing the ability of small business managers to learn from the loss of a business. An improved ability to learn from business failure is important for individuals and society. We then challenge educators to prepare students better so that if they do become small business managers and their small business fails they can recover more quickly from the negative emotions associated with the loss of the business.

Chapter 9 concludes the book.

APPROPRIATE AUDIENCE FOR THE BOOK

We hope the audience for the book is broad. We do not 'shy away' from its academic origin, with all chapters based on research articles that have been or will shortly be published in academic journals. We believe that this high-lights the cutting-edge nature of the information contained within the book. But we also realize that academic jargon, especially associated with research methods, can be off-putting and unnecessary for small business practitioners. To accommodate scholars and practitioners, we have included in the text of each chapter only a description of the sample and the results of the empirical study with other aspects of the research method contained within an appendix at the end of the chapter. This provides scholars the opportunity to delve deeper into the scientific aspects of the study and allows the practitioner to either learn about the sample and the results (written in a less academic tone) or skip the section completely. Following each section of 'sample and results', we present the results again in the form of general rules of thumb that will be of interest to both prac-titioners and scholars. Therefore, to practitioners, professors, PhD stu-dents, MBA students and senior undergraduates this book offers cutting-edge material about entrepreneurial small businesses. They may focus on the practical implications of the chapters, the literature reviewed, or the possibilities for future research.

We hope they enjoy the book as much as we did researching and writing it.

2. The motivation to grow a small business[1]

INTRODUCTION

Traditionally, business research in general and research on firm growth in particular have taken an economics perspective. Inherent in this perspective is an assumption that people are motivated by money and this motivation drives behavior. For example, managers of small businesses are assumed to be motivated by money and therefore make decisions in the running of those businesses with the goal to maximize firm profitability. While money and profits are often a motivating influence, they are not the only factor that motivates the decisions and behaviors of small business managers. Indeed, financial rewards may not even be the most important motivator.

A psychological perspective on why people act takes a broader view of motivation than an economics one. This perspective appears highly appropriate to the small business context, because there is ample evidence that small business managers are motivated by factors other than simply the promise of financial reward. We know that people start and operate their own firms for a variety of reasons other than maximizing economic returns (Davidsson, 1989a; Delmar, 1996; Kolvereid, 1992; Storey, 1994). Some entrepreneurs are 'pulled' into self-employment by the promise of rewards not available to them by any other means and some can be considered to be 'pushed' into self-employment in an attempt to avoid an undesirable situation. The pull of self-employment can come from a number of sources. Individuals are often lured to self-employment because it offers the utility that comes from greater autonomy and control over one's own life rather than the constant supervision and orders from a boss (Bird, 1989; Douglas and Shepherd, 2000; Katz, 1994). One small business manager commented that:

> The main reason that I have persisted working in small business is that I now have two kids in high school, and they have sport on the weekends, or they have certain things first thing in the morning, or in the afternoon, and I can watch. If I'm working for a big organization, sure there's a steady income, but in return I get a whole raft of expectations that I will be a certain place at this time and

I'll do these things. I have more control working in a small business environment. (Cameron, 2003)

Similarly, another small business manager referred to the greater autonomy that being self-employed provided him: 'We can work our own hours. We can work when we want. Plus being your own boss is a bonus. No-one else can tell you what to do' (Cameron, 2003).

Another one suggested that, 'It is a dream among people to handle one's own stuff. I worked for Volvo for nine months but there I was just a small part of a large complex' (a Swedish entrepreneur).

Some choose self-employment because it is the best way to fulfill a sense of loyalty that they have to a product and/or loyalty to a market and customers (Bruno et al., 1992). For example, having worked for many years in developing a specific new product, an R&D manager finds out that the project is to be terminated and the product will never reach the market unless he or she is willing to create a new business and finalize product design and launch it him/herself. Another illustration is provided by this quote from a small business manager: 'Success for me is probably patient driven – if my patients succeed then I probably regard myself as successful. I don't really think a lot of business success; I think more of patient success' (Cameron, 2003). Others find that running their own business is a way to satisfy a need to prove oneself – to show others and even oneself that they can successfully take on this entrepreneurial task (Bruno et al., 1992).

Finally, there may even be more philosophical motivations for becoming a small business manager. Cova and Svanfeldt (1993: 297) propose that entrepreneurs '. . . create a product that flows from their own internal desires and needs. They create primarily to express subjective conceptions of beauty, emotion, or some aesthetic ideal'. One small business manager commented that 'I want the work I produce to be absolutely cutting edge' (Cameron, 2003). Similarly, for members of a family business, the firm may not only be a source of income but also a context for family activity and the embodiment of family pride and identity (Meyer and Zucker, 1989: 78). The business identity and that of the family are so intertwined that they are inseparable. The business provides a means of communicating about family issues and the family provides a sense of cohesion for the business, and vice versa.

Whether or not running a small business actually leads to the fulfillment of these personal goals is an open question. It depends on whether there is a strong link between the small business manager's motivations on the one hand and business outcomes on the other. That is, if the outcome is within one's control then highly motivated behavior will likely lead to the desired outcomes. But being highly motivated to achieve something that is beyond one's sphere of influence is not likely to make the desired outcome more likely. For example, to be highly motivated for a big swell and a north wind to improve surf conditions will not make that desired outcome more likely – weather conditions are beyond our control.

Small business growth is an area where control is of particular interest. Do small business managers have control over whether the business grows? If the answer is yes, then motivation is likely to be an important predictor of small business growth, but if small business growth is like the weather and outside the control of its management, then individuals' motivations will not provide any insight into growth outcomes. In order to investigate such a question empirically, there must exist differences in the motivations of managers to grow their small businesses. In fact, most small business managers are not motivated to grow their businesses at all. Growth implies radical changes of the business's characteristics. These changes may run counter to the founder's initial goals. Indeed, previous research indicates that expectations of changed work conditions (e.g. as the business grows, more formal structures need to be put in place, capital raised, and/or requirements for more formal financial reporting) are a primary concern for small business managers, which in turn reduces their motivation to expand their businesses (Wiklund et al., 2003). Given that people differ in their reasons for becoming a small business manager and in the concerns they have over the changed circumstances of the business that result from growth, it is reasonable to expect that they differ in their motivations for growth. To the extent that small business growth is, at least in part, within the control of its manager, then these motivational differences are likely to provide an explanation for differences in business growth.

While small business managers likely differ in their motivations to expand the business, they likely also differ in their ability to control the outcome. That is, if two individuals are equally motivated to achieve growth but one has greater ability than the other, we would expect that the one with greater ability has greater control over outcomes and is more able to achieve the desired outcome. Michael Jordan and a ten-year-old might be equally motivated to dunk a basketball but given that Michael Jordan is 6' 7" and the ten-year-old maybe 5'1", then Michael Jordan is more likely to achieve the desired outcome. In fact, it does not matter how motivated the ten-year-old is, the desired outcome is not within his or her control (for reasons of genetics). So motivation may be important in explaining small business growth but it only represents half the story: we must also consider ability.

Concerning small businesses, the ability of top management is regarded one of the key capabilities (Jennings and Beaver, 1997). In order to expand his or her business, the small business manager must have the ability to secure the resources needed for growth as well as the capability of developing the organization (Covin and Slevin, 1997; Sexton and Bowman-Upton, 1991). Thus, personal ability also plays an important role in small business growth. Therefore, to gain a deeper understanding into the role of an individual's motivation in small business growth, we must also consider the ability of the individual and the ability of the firm. In this chapter we take a first step in this direction by investigating the motivations and the ability of the individual. In the next chapter (Chapter 3) we continue our focus on the ability of the individual, which shifts to the firm level of analysis in Chapters 4 and 5.

Relatively few studies have empirically investigated the link between motivation on the one hand, and small business growth on the other. The relative scarcity of such studies may be attributed to research design requirements. That is, in order to study small business growth we need to measure motivation at one point in time and then small business growth some period after. This temporal separation of motivation and growth outcomes is necessary because business growth is not instantaneous. The motivations and behaviors of today will take some time to have an impact before they result in growth. For example, the motivation to grow may result in greater investment in R&D, marketing promotions, and an alliance with a foreign firm, but it takes (1) time for R&D to generate new products or new features for existing products, (2) time for marketing promotions to be developed, implemented, and absorbed by the target market, and (3) time for an alliance partner to be selected, the relationship organized, and products to be sold in that country.

Not only must we consider the time separation of the small business manager's motivation and the business's subsequent growth, we must also consider the possible direct or moderating influence of other factors. As mentioned above, small business growth may be influenced by the decisions and actions of the small business manager, but it is unlikely to be under his or her total control. In other words, a range of factors in addition to motivation, probably affect growth outcomes. For example, the conditions of the market could help or hinder small business growth; access to resources could be limited stalling any attempts to grow the business, as well as the skills and knowledge of the small business manager being insufficient to select the appropriate growth strategies (Covin and Slevin, 1997; Sexton and Bowman-Upton, 1991).

So how can we build an understanding of the relationship between the small business manager's motivation and growth? Several psychological theories deal with behavior that is under the limited control of individuals. They share the common feature that the outcome (such as small business growth) is modeled as a joint function of motivation and individual ability (Ajzen, 1991). There is strong theoretical reason to believe that individual ability (that is, access to the resources and opportunities necessary to exert the behavior) affects the relationship between motivation and outcomes (Ajzen, 1991). More specifically, the theory of planned behavior has been successful in predicting other behaviors under limited volitional control (Ajzen, 1991; Bagozzi and Warshaw, 1992; Doll and Ajzen, 1992): for example, consumer behavior in willingness to pay (Ajzen and Driver, 1992), driver compliance with speed limits (Elliot et al., 2003), and choice of travel (Bamberg et al., 2003).

In this chapter, we apply the theory of planned behavior to small business growth to gain a deeper understanding of the role of an individual's motivation in achieving this outcome. First, we present the theory of planned behavior, which leads to proposed relationships concerning how growth aspirations and variables pertaining to resources and opportunities interact with these aspirations, in explaining small business growth. Second, we introduce the sample and the results of our empirical test of these proposed relationships. Finally, we discuss the results and implications of this chapter for both scholars and practitioners.

THE THEORY OF PLANNED BEHAVIOR AND SMALL BUSINESS GROWTH

A General Framework of Motivation

The theory of planned behavior developed by Icek Ajzen (Ajzen, 1988; Ajzen, 1991) is a well-established (Olson and Zana, 1993; Petty et al., 1997) and validated (Locke, 1991) psychological theory that explains specific actions in specific contexts where individuals have some, but incomplete, control over the outcome. Central to this approach to understanding motivation is the role of intentions: 'Intentions are assumed to capture the motivational factors that influence a behavior; they are indications of how hard people are willing to try, of how much of an effort they are planning to exert in order to perform the behavior. As a general rule, the stronger the intention to engage in a behavior, the more likely should be its performance' (Ajzen, 1991: 181). Intentions have successfully predicted a range of behaviors. For example, Schifter and Ajzen (1985) found that intentions to lose weight were accurately predicted on the basis of attitudes, subjective norms and perceived control; perceived control and intentions were together moderately successful in predicting the amount of weight that a subject actually lost over a six-week period.

The theory of planned behavior is a 'pure' psychological theory in the sense that it relates a number of psychological constructs to each other. Therefore, perceived behavioral control rather than actual behavior control is included in the theory. Ajzen argues: 'The resources and opportunities available to a person must to some extent dictate the likelihood of behavioral achievement. Of greater psychological interest than actual control, however, is the *perception* of behavioral control and its impact on intentions and actions' (Ajzen 1991: 183, emphasis original). He then recognizes that: 'prediction of behavior from perceived behavior control should improve to the extent that perceptions of behavioral control realistically reflect actual control' (Azjen, 1991: 185). As our intention is the explanation of growth and there is reason to believe that actual control plays a role in firm growth (see Ajzen's logic and the introduction), we model the influence of actual control on small business growth. As Ajzen (1991: 188) notes, 'past theory as well as intuition would lead us to expect an interaction between motivation and control' – control is likely to moderate the relationship between growth aspirations and the achievement of growth.

A Framework of Motivation Specific to Small Business Growth

In the entrepreneurship literature, Sexton and Bowman-Upton (1991) criticize growth models that do not consider the motivation of the individuals making the strategic decisions in a small business and argue that the growth aspirations of the small business manager sets limits to the growth a business will achieve. That is, that while some small businesses have the potential for substantial growth, the motivations of their managers may not be to achieve that level of growth and 'hold the business back' at a slower growth rate. Of course the motivations of the small business manager are not the only factor that constrains the growth of small businesses. Small business growth can be limited: (1) sometimes the environment does not offer attractive opportunities for growth (for example, the economy is in a recession), (2) the abilities of the small business manager are insufficient to match his or her enthusiasm for growth and he does not 'see the opportunities that exist' or is unable to 'make' the right opportunities happen, and (3) the small business cannot access the resources necessary to implement its growth strategies. Refining this argument, Covin and Slevin (1997) suggest a model where growth is a function of growth aspirations, moderated by market constraints, entrepreneurial capability and organizational resources. Based on the theory of planned behavior and acknowledging the contribution of these entrepreneurship scholars we propose and empirically test a motivation-based model of small business growth, which is shown in Figure 2.1.

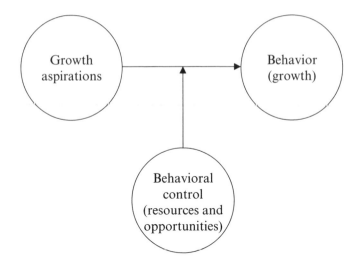

Source: Wiklund and Shepherd (2003a).

Figure 2.1   *Theory of planned behavior for studying how growth
aspirations influence actual growth*

Growth aspirations and growth realized

Previous empirical research has found a direct positive relationship between
motivation and growth (Bellu and Sherman, 1995; Kolvereid and Bullvåg,
1996; Miner et al., 1994; Mok and van den Tillaart, 1990). Studying a
sample of small business founder-managers in the USA, Bellu and Sherman
(1995) find that certain motivational patterns are associated with growth for
entrepreneurial organizations. Ambition, the desire to achieve by experiencing personal success, is particularly important. Also, those who attribute
success to their own ability and failure to causes beyond their control appear
to do better. These factors seem to interact with the dynamism of the environment, so that entrepreneurs with these motivational attributes are more
likely to succeed in environments where opportunities more often arise.

Miner et al. (1994) examine the same motivational factors as Bellu and
Sherman (1995) comparing the managers of high-growth small business to
low-growth businesses with a five-year lag between motivations and growth
outcomes. In addition to finding support for self-achievement, they also
find that those who are motivated to plan for the future, receive feedback
on results, and to innovate, are more likely to manage high-growth firms.

Kolvereid and Bullvåg (1996) study a large sample of owners of four-
year-old Norwegian businesses. They found that those small business managers who stated that they intended to expand their businesses indeed

expanded their business more over the following two years than those who had no growth intentions. Similarly, Mok and van den Tillaart (1990) found that future expectations among small business managers were strong predictors of performance six years into the future, stronger than indicators of past performance such as net profits or sales. Thus:

Proposed relationship 2.1: *Small business managers with higher growth aspirations achieve greater small business growth than for those with lower growth aspirations.*

The moderating effect of resources and opportunities
However, to proposed relationship 2.1 above (small business managers with higher growth aspirations achieve greater small business growth) we offer a big *but*. But the effect of aspirations on a specific outcome is dependent upon (a) the extent to which the individual can decide at will to attempt to perform the behavior and (b) the probability that attempting to perform the behavior will lead to a successful outcome. That is, the strength of the relationship between growth aspirations and the growth actually achieved varies depending upon whether the small business manager is free to go for growth and upon the desirability of taking the action that may (or may not) lead to the desired outcome. For example, a small business manager may aspire to double the business's sales within the next three years, but other stakeholders of the business (other owners, employees, banks and so on) may exert influences that ensure the pursuit of a more modest growth strategy. Even with the support of these stakeholders, the small business manager might not pursue the ambitious growth strategy because there is a high probability that it will place such a strain on cash flows that even a minor change in the environment might result in bankruptcy. So therefore, when the extent to which the individual can decide at will to attempt to perform the behavior is high and the probability that attempting to perform the behavior will lead to a successful outcome is high, then the more likely it is that high growth aspirations will lead to actual small business growth. That is, the more control that the small business manager has over his or her activities and over the growth outcome, the stronger will be the relationship of 2.1 (the more likely to explain small business growth).[2]

But what gives the small business manager such control? Small business managers have greater control when they have greater access to resources and a greater number, and/or more attractive opportunities for growth. Therefore, we now turn to these control factors to gain a deeper understanding of this relationship between the small business manager's aspirations toward growth and the actual business growth achieved – the specific resources and opportunities that may affect growth.

Resources and Opportunities for Small Business Growth

The growth of a small business is dependent upon the small business manager's capacity to manage growth (Sexton and Bowman-Upton, 1991). This involves the ability to conduct internal reorganizations in response to the increased size of the business as well as the ability to discover and exploit new growth opportunities (Covin and Slevin, 1997). For example, life-cycle stage models support the idea that the managerial challenges change as organizations mature and grow. In their review of the life-cycle construct, Hanks et al. (1993) provide a synthesis of ten different life-cycle models. All of these models propose that certain key dimensions of organizations will change with respect to age and size, such as an increase in the formalization of communications, an increase in the layers of organizational structure, and an increase in the level of bureaucracy. But to grow, the manager needs to find or create opportunities for growth. Some small business managers are better at one or both of these tasks than are others. Whether it is meeting the changing managerial challenges associated with growth and/or finding/creating opportunities for growth, small business managers differ in their ability to deliver on these important aspects of control. We now explain such differences.

The role of human capital

The human capital of a small business manager gives him or her the ability to make decisions and take the actions necessary to achieve growth. It consists of skills and knowledge that assists in running the business successfully (Snell and Dean, 1992). Such skills and knowledge can be obtained through education and experience. At this point it is important to acknowledge the distinction between general and specific human capital (Becker, 1975). General human capital is not related to the ability of conducting a specific job and typically refers to years of education or years of work experience (Rauch and Frese, 2000). A consistent finding for general human capital is that educated individuals are more likely to run faster-growing small businesses than those who are less educated (Sapienza and Grimm, 1997; Storey, 1994).

While there has been support for the benefit of education, previous research has not found that general work experience has a positive affect on small business growth. Unlike general human capital, specific human capital in the small business context is specific to the domain of operating a small business and consists of skills and knowledge of conditions, internal and external to the small business, that help organize the business successfully, thus facilitating growth (Rauch and Freese, 2000). Specific human capital, such as start-up experience, management experience, and experience of working in rapidly growing organizations, has been found to explain, in part, the growth of small businesses (Birley and Westhead, 1994; Macrae, 1992; Van de Ven et al., 1984). For example, Van de Ven et al. (1984: 94) found that: 'startup success and company stage development are positively related to a broad set of skills and expertise exhibited by the entrepreneur. This is due to the fact that, in a small business, the entrepreneur must often act as the central brain and agent: differentiation and specialization are not possible.'

Business growth creates considerable challenges for management and it is difficult to foresee what these challenges will be (Hambrick and Crozier, 1985). Therefore, the specific human capital obtained from previously experiencing rapid growth is of great value. Similarly, managing a growing, and thereby larger, business is different from managing a smaller one. Those who have experienced the management of businesses of other types and sizes may therefore have an advantage over those who have only managed their own business because they have been exposed to a wider variety of managerial challenges. Another way to gain the broad expertise valuable to expand a business could be through the start-up of other businesses. Starting a business requires resource acquisition and matching these resources with the opportunity, which is similar to the requirements of expanding a business. This leads us to formulate the following proposition:

Proposed relationship 2.2: *Growth aspirations are more closely related to actual business growth for those small business managers who are (a) more highly educated and (b) have more related experience (experience with start-up, management, and rapidly growing organizations) than those small business managers with less education and less related experience.*

The role of financial capital
The growth of a small business also depends on the type and amount of resources controlled by, or made available to it (Covin and Slevin, 1997). Securing funding may be particularly important in achieving the growth objectives of the firm (Sexton and Bowman-Upton, 1991). It is probable that lack of financial capital would restrict a small business manager's opportunities to take action. Many small business managers experience shortages of financial capital that limit their ability to pursue various initiatives (McGrath, forthcoming). For example, access to more financial capital facilitates the pursuit of resource-intensive growth strategies (Cooper et al., 1994) because slack resources can be used for experimentation with new strategies and practices, allowing the business to pursue new growth opportunities (Bourgeois, 1981; Penrose, 1959). For example, entry into a new foreign market requires slack resources to conduct initial market

research, make minor changes to product and packaging, conduct a promotion campaign, and cope with unforeseeable issues that arise. A recent review of the literature indicated that several studies have found that access to financial capital affects small business growth (Storey, 1994). For example, in a longitudinal study, Cooper et al. (1994) confirmed that access to financial capital predicted growth. Thus:

Proposed Relationship 2.3: *Growth aspirations are more closely related to actual business growth for those small business managers that have superior access to financial resources than for those with less access to financial resources.*[3]

The role of environmental dynamism

While access to financial capital can provide the small business manager with the means to conduct a range of activities, the growth of the firm will to some extent be determined by the growth opportunities in the business's market niche. For any given product in any given niche, factors such as competition, the growth of overall demand, and changes in customer preferences, set limits to growth (Covin and Slevin, 1997; Sexton and Bowman-Upton, 1991). For example, strategies to achieve growth such as product variations, promotional campaigns, and lower prices, can typically be matched by competitors such that the net gain in sales from such strategies are limited and can have a negative impact on profitability. Even if these strategies were to work such that the small business was able to gain a greater market share, they may not result in business growth if the market is declining in overall sales – the amount of pie one has for dessert does not necessarily increase with the slice of the pie if the size of the pie has decreased. A decrease in overall market demand for a particular market (a smaller pie) may result from competition, from the introduction of a substitute product (a product from another industry that can be used instead of the products offered by the industry of which the small business is a member), and an overall decline in most markets due to a world-wide recession.

Changes in the business environment do not always constrain small business growth; the environment can be the source of new growth opportunities (Drucker, 1985). For example, as the demand for products and services changes, this could represent a growth opportunity for those businesses that can deliver products and services attuned to this new demand. Such environmental characteristics, as described above, can be expressed as high in environmental dynamism. More specifically, dynamic environments are associated with high unpredictability of customers and competitors, and high rates of change in market trends and industry innovation (Miller, 1987b).

The shifts in demand and conditions typical of a dynamic environment are likely to generate opportunities from which the growth oriented business can take advantage (Chandler and Hanks, 1994; Covin and Slevin, 1991; Zahra, 1993a). The less growth oriented businesses, however, are less alert to opportunities in the dynamic environment and will therefore benefit less, and even face negative growth in such environments. Thus:

Proposed relationship 2.4: *Growth aspirations are more closely related to actual business growth for those small business managers that are in more dynamic environments than for those in more static environments.*

In sum, the relationships stated above propose that small business managers with a higher aspiration for growth achieve higher levels of business growth but more human capital (higher educational level and greater specific experience), access to financial capital, and environmental dynamism enhance the effect of a small business manager's growth aspirations on the level of business growth achieved. Although there is theoretical support for these relationships and some empirical support, it is important to conduct a thorough empirical analysis of these relationships. In the next section we will summarize our sample and report the results of our study. We realize that some readers will be less interested in this academic side of the book, and to them we suggest that they skip the next section of the book. Other readers might be interested in more details about the research method. We refer these readers to the appendix of this chapter, which contains a description of the variables and their measures. A more technical description of the sample and results can be found in Wiklund and Shepherd (2003a).

SAMPLE AND RESULTS

Sample

Although the balance of the research methods are contained in the appendix to this chapter, we want to briefly summarize our sample to which the results can be attributed. Our sample selection began with a list of all limited companies registered in Sweden. We then randomly selected more than 200 independent small businesses from each of four sectors – knowledge intensive manufacturing, labor intensive manufacturing, professional services and retailing. Our first survey collected data on business size (sales and employees), the independent variables, control variables, and characteristics of the business and the small business manager. Three years later we collected data on size (sales and employees). We excluded from our sample those businesses where the small business manager had been replaced during the period between the first and second data collections and excluded those whose small business manager did not have control over the business's strategic decisions (for example, where the manager was subservient to directions from the head office of a parent company). The final sample was 326. These small businesses had, on average, 22 employees and were 30 years old. The managers of these small businesses were on average 48 years old and had over 12 years of schooling.

Analysis and Results

The proposed relationships were tested using hierarchical regression analysis. That is, we ran three models of increasing level of complexity to provide a conservative test of the proposed relationships. The results are displayed in Table 2.1. Column two of the table represents the base model which used only the control variables to explain small business growth, that is, variables for business size, business age, manufacturing, and service. This model fails to explain a statistically significant share of the variance in small business growth.

In the next step, we entered the variables of growth aspiration, human capital (education and experience) and access to financial capital as our 'main-effects-only' model. Together these four variables make a significant contribution over and above the base model in offering an explanation of small business growth. Within this model, the findings suggest that growth aspirations and financial capital have a statistically significant influence on growth. The positive sign of the regression coefficients suggests that small business growth was higher for those individuals with greater growth aspirations and for those that had greater access to financial capital. The finding for growth aspiration provides support for proposed relationship 2.1, namely, 'Small business managers with higher growth aspirations achieve greater growth than those with lower growth aspirations.'

Based on this main-effects-only model, it appears that experience, education or environmental dynamism did not have a relationship with small business growth. However, such a conclusion could be wrong because a non-significant finding does not necessarily mean that the relationship does not exist, only that we were unable to detect it. This is where the third model comes in, which investigates greater complexity in the relationships. As displayed in the right column of Table 2.1, the addition of the interaction terms (growth aspirations with each of education, experience, and financial capital) provides a deeper explanation of small business

Table 2.1   Hierarchical regression analysis: independent and interaction effects on actual growth

	Base model	Independent effects only	Interaction effects
Manufacturing	−0.08	−0.06	0.04
Service	0.00	0.00	0.16
Business size	0.06	0.03	0.01
Business age	−0.08	−0.06	−0.03
Age of respondent	−0.15*	−0.13	−0.09
Growth aspiration		0.15*	1.55***a
Education		0.04	−0.36a
Experience		−0.06	0.45*a
Financial capital		0.17*	0.32a
Environmental dynamism		0.13	1.36***a
Aspiration education			0.85*
Aspiration experience			0.45*
Aspiration financial capital			−0.18
Aspiration environmental dynamism			2.35***
R^2	0.04	0.11*	0.24***
Adj. R^2	0.02	0.06*	0.19***
ΔR^2		0.06*	0.13***

Notes:
Standardized regression coefficients are displayed in the Table.
a = in the presence of interactions, the coefficients for independent terms making up the interactions convey no meaningful, but possibly misleading information (Cohen and Cohen, 1983).
* $=p<0.05$; ** $=p<0.01$; *** $=p<0.001$; n $=326$.

growth over and above that of the main-effects-only model. Examining the regression coefficients of the interaction terms, it is evident that education, experience and environmental dynamism moderate the relationship between growth aspirations and growth. This means that these variables magnify the strength of the relationship between growth aspirations and growth.

To determine the nature of these interactions, each relationship was plotted on a *y*-axis of growth and an *x*-axis of growth aspirations for high and low levels of the moderator terms. These plots are displayed in Figures 2.2, 2.3. and 2.4. The first plot, Figure 2.2, indicates that growth increases with aspiration but at a greater rate for those with higher education. The second plot, Figure 2.3, indicates that growth increases with aspiration but at a greater rate for those with more experience. These findings provide

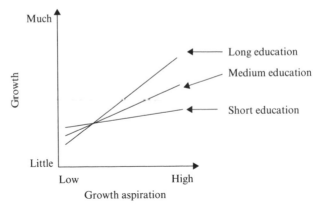

Figure 2.2   Interaction of aspiration and education on growth

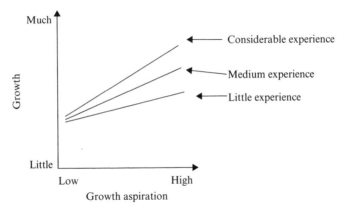

Figure 2.3   Interaction of aspiration and experience on growth

support for proposed relationship 2.2, that is, we found that 'Growth aspirations are more closely related to actual business growth for those small business managers who are more highly educated and have more related experience (experience with start-up, management, and rapidly growing organizations) than for those with less education and less related experience.'

The third plot, Figure 2.4, indicates that growth increases with aspiration but at a greater rate for those in more dynamic environments. This finding provides support for proposed relationship 2.4, that is, we found that 'Growth aspirations are more closely related to actual growth for those small business managers that are in more dynamic environments.'

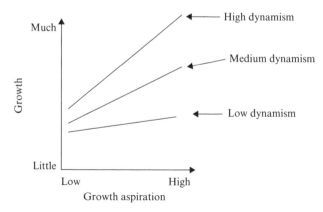

Figure 2.4   Interaction of aspiration and dynamism on growth

The interaction with access to capital was not statistically significant and therefore proposed relationship 2.3 is not supported, that is we *did not find* that 'growth aspirations are more closely related to actual growth for those small business managers that have superior access to financial resources.' Rather we found (from the main-effect-only model) that 'Those small business managers that have superior access to financial resources are more likely to achieve actual business growth than those with less access to financial resources.'

A Summary of Key Findings

This chapter's proposed relationships and those that were found in our study are reported in Table 2.2. While we can say that the stronger the aspirations for growth the more likely it occurs, this general statement appears a little too simplistic or at least ignores some of the deeper relationships at play here. Aspirations are more likely to result in the desired growth outcome for those small business managers who have more education and more experience, and for those small business managers who are in dynamic environments. It appears that, to the extent that education captures general human capital and our measures of experience capture specific human capital, those small business managers with superior human capital have greater control over the achievement of those outcomes they are motivated to achieve than those with less human capital. That is, highly educated and highly experienced small business managers appear to have greater control over their destiny, at least in terms of small business growth. Similarly, aspirations for growth are more likely to lead to actual small business growth when the small businesses are in dynamic environments.

Table 2.2   A summary of proposed relationships, levels of support and the relationships found

Proposed relationship	Support?	Relationship found
2.1: Small business managers with higher growth aspirations achieve greater business growth.	Yes	Small business managers with higher growth aspirations achieve greater business growth.
2.2: Growth aspirations are more closely related to actual business growth for those small business managers who are (a) more highly educated and (b) have more related experience (experience with start-up, management and rapidly growing organizations).	Yes	Growth aspirations are more closely related to actual business growth for those small business managers who are (a) more highly educated and (b) have more related experience (experience with start-up, management and rapidly growing organizations).
2.3: Growth aspirations are more closely related to actual business growth for those small business managers who have superior access to financial resources.	No	Those small business managers who have superior access to financial resources are more likely to achieve actual business growth.
2.4: Growth aspirations are more closely related to actual business growth for those small business managers who are in more dynamic environments.	Yes	Growth aspirations are more closely related to actual business growth for those small business managers who are in more dynamic environments.

It appears that dynamic environments provide small business managers opportunities to act on, and achieve, their desired growth outcomes.

IMPLICATIONS OF THE ROLE OF MANAGERS' MOTIVATIONS ON SMALL BUSINESS GROWTH

Practical Implications

This chapter's proposed relationships and those that were found in our study (reported in Table 2.2) can be thought of as rules for explaining the relationship that motivation (in this case small business manager's growth aspirations) has with the actual growth of their small businesses. There is a general rule of thumb and three qualifying rules that specify when the general rule of the thumb is most applicable.

General rule of thumb 2.1: *Small business managers with higher growth aspirations achieve greater business growth than those with lower growth aspirations.*

The more motivated the manager is to expand his or her business the more likely it is to happen. The flipside is also apparent: the more motivated the small business manager is to maintain the current size of the firm the more likely their desires will be met. This positive relationship between the motivation of small business managers and the growth of their businesses has been found across a number of different studies (Bellu and Sherman, 1995; Kolvereid and Bullvåg, 1996; Miner et al., 1994; Mok and van den Tillaart, 1990). But the relationship is stronger or weaker depending on the characteristics of the small business manager and the nature of the business's environment. It is these variations that are captured in the following qualifying rules.

Qualifying rule 2.1: *Growth aspirations are more closely related to actual growth for those small business managers who are more highly educated than for those who are less educated.*

Interestingly, we found that there was no significant direct effect of education on small business growth. This could lead one to the false impression that education has little to do with small business growth, but this qualifying rule suggests that education has a significant role in understanding small business growth. The role of education may not be direct, but it does have a moderating influence on the relationship between the small business manager's growth aspirations and business growth realized. By moderating, we mean that education magnifies the strength of the relationship between growth aspirations and small business growth. It appears that small business managers who are more highly educated have greater control over their own destiny, at least in terms of growth.

What gives them that control is still an open question. It might be that better educated people generally formulate better decisions toward the achievement of their goals, are more effective at implementing strategies that satisfy their motivations, or it could be that better educated people have a more effective social network that can help them obtain the resources needed to achieve desired outcomes. It is clear however, that more highly educated small business managers do not necessarily achieve small business growth, but they do appear more successful at achieving their desired outcomes and therefore those who desire growth are more likely to achieve it than is someone who has equal desire but is less educated.

There is a flipside to this qualifying rule, and that is, that small business managers with less education, to a certain extent can compensate for less education with considerable motivation. That is, although less education may lead to less 'perfect' growth strategies or less effective means of strategy implementation, when these deficiencies are minor they may be overcome by the sheer enthusiasm and strength of will to succeed. The old saying that 'it is better to have 100 per cent commitment behind a strategy of 80 per cent quality than have 80 per cent commitment behind a perfect strategy' is highly relevant here. A word of caution is also necessary. The small business manager with minimal education and a high motivation to achieve growth may become highly frustrated to the extent that the outcome may not be within his or her sphere of influence and may even put the survival of the business at risk. In fact, a seminal work on small businesses in England found that growing small businesses are more likely to be managed by more highly educated individuals (Storey, 1994).

Qualifying rule 2.2: *Growth aspirations are more closely related to actual growth for those small business managers that have more related experience (experience with start-up, management and rapidly growing organizations) than those with less related experience.*

This qualifying rule is similar to the previous one; although rather than the more general human capital aspect of education this one focuses on specific experience to managing a growing small business. Again, if one were to consider only the main-effects-only model the experience of the small business manager would not appear to be related to small business growth. Such a conclusion would be simplistic and premature. Experience does play a role indirectly through magnifying the positive relationship between growth aspirations and small business growth. To investigate the impact of managers' motivations on small business growth without taking into account this moderating influence of experience, we would be underestimating the role of both motivation and experience in explaining small business growth. Similar to education, experience appears to provide small business managers with specific human capital that helps them achieve outcomes consistent with their motivations.

It is likely that experience enables the small business manager to acquire knowledge and skills that are specifically relevant for managing a growing organization. For example, as the business grows, each new stage offers a number of new challenges. Having experience in start-up, management, and managing a rapidly growing firm is likely to provide the small business manager with some insight into how these challenges can be addressed in the pursuit of desired growth. Such experiences are also likely to help the small business manager achieve non-growth related goals, that is, rather than expand the business the experienced manager is more capable of finding the desired size and fine-tuning the business to meet his or her aspirations for the business. More experience does not necessarily mean more small business growth. Rather, it means that small business managers are more capable of achieving their desired outcomes for the business.

Qualifying rule 2.3: *Growth aspirations are more closely related to actual growth for those small business managers that are in more dynamic environments than those that are in more static environments.*

To look at the main-effects-only model, one might be tempted to conclude that environmental dynamism does not have a significant relationship to small business growth but like the human capital variables reflected in the previous two qualifying rules, environmental dynamism does have an indirect relationship with small business growth in that it magnifies the relationship between growth aspiration and small business growth. That is, being motivated to achieve growth will help you achieve growth but you still need the opportunities to enact that motivation. The opposite also appears to be the case. It is no good having the opportunities to grow if you do not have the motivation to act on them. These are interesting notions and suggest to us that while our focus has been on the individual who runs the business (in terms of motivation and human capital) we must also consider the environment and whether it provides small business managers the opportunity to grow. Such an understanding has led leading experts in the field to argue that entrepreneurship occurs at the nexus of the individual and the opportunity (Shane and Venkataraman, 2000) and it may be misleading to investigate one without consideration of the other. Our findings reinforce these arguments.

One of the expected moderated relationships was not statistically significant. Although this relationship might exist and we merely failed to find it in this study, we did find a main-effects-only relationship that forms that basis of the following general rule of thumb on small business growth.

General rule of thumb 2.2: *Those small business managers that have superior access to financial resources are more likely to achieve actual growth than those with less access to financial resources.*

Necessity may be the mother of invention, but small businesses need financial capital to grow. We found that access to financial capital had a direct effect on small business growth. This suggests that small businesses with access to more financial capital grow more, aspirations aside. A plausible interpretation of this finding is that access to slack financial resources allows experimentation within the firm allowing it to generate and pursue new opportunities (March and Simon, 1963: 146) regardless of the small business manager's aspirations. It is important to note here that we are talking about access to financial capital rather than the specific case of access where the money is sitting in the bank. Access to financial capital could be higher for those small businesses that have a large bank overdraft from which to draw, can access further loans if necessary, and can raise capital from increased equity infusion. Issues relating to raising debt capital are addressed in Chapter 7 and those related to raising equity capital are addressed in Chapter 6.

Categorizing Small Business Growth Outcomes by the Motivation and the Ability of Managers

We conclude that, consistent with Sexton and Bowman-Upton (1991), attempts to explain growth in a way that does not take into consideration the growth motivation of the small business manager are likely to have little success. That is, without considering the motivation of the small business manager, we are likely to overestimate growth for those small businesses managers that have highly educated and experienced managers and for those small businesses in dynamic environments. In this case, there is the potential to grow but there is no desire. Furthermore, by not considering the motivation of small business managers, we are likely to underestimate growth for those small businesses managed by less educated and less experienced managers and who operate in relatively static industries.

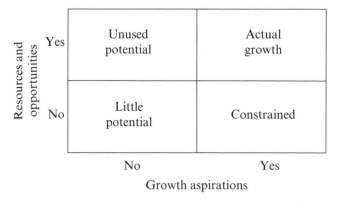

Source: Sexton and Bowman-Upton (1991); Wiklund (1998).

Figure 2.5   Four types of firms in terms of resources and opportunities for growth and growth aspirations

Motivation can compensate (although to a lesser extent) for lower levels of education, less experience and/or being located in a static environment.

Based on the information in this chapter, we present a categorization of small business growth outcomes based upon the small business managers' motivation to expand their businesses and the ability to do so. Specifically, Figure 2.3 categorizes small business growth along two dimensions; resources and opportunities for growth provide one dimension and growth aspirations the other. Depending on their position along these two dimensions, four types of small businesses are identified:

1. Starting with the small businesses in the upper right quadrant, which possess both the necessary opportunities and resources, *and* the aspiration to grow, we propose that these small businesses are the ones mostly likely to exhibit *actual growth*. To these small businesses we say good luck. They are pursuing a desired outcome that is within their reach. This is not to say that they will always achieve growth, there are other intervening factors that could lead to less growth than expected or even bankruptcy. It is possible that other chapters in this book might help them further in achieving their goal of small business growth or coping with the consequences of 'going for it' and not making it.

2. In the upper left quadrant are the small businesses which have an *unused potential* since they, if they were motivated, have the ability, resources and opportunity to expand. A relatively large proportion of all small businesses are probably in this situation. For example, one small business manager commented that:

> I enjoy doing what I'm doing. The minute I stop enjoying it I'll do something else. I'm not as well off as I'd like to be but I don't have that goal of having so much money in the bank . . . I think I've reached the stage of life where money's not that important. It's about lifestyle, it's being able to do a whole lot of things. You just need enough money to do what you want to do . . . So success for me is that the business runs at a profit – it doesn't have to be a huge profit, just a profit – that I make enough out of it to keep myself the way I want to be kept and that I get the satisfaction of client feedback saying, 'Hey, you're doing a good job'. (Cameron, 2003)

To these small business managers we say: 'if you are happy with the size of the business, then well done and we hope that you continue to enjoy'. The only proviso to this congratulatory statement is if there is dispute among the stakeholders of the business in terms of its growth outcomes, then the situation becomes a source of conflict. For example, the small business manager may have a non-active partner in the business who is looking to make his or her investment grow by increasing the size of the business. In such a situation, the motivations of others may also need to be considered. Although partners often have different objectives for a business, this is less often the case with small businesses where ownership is dominated by one individual or by a family where motivations are often relatively consistent.

3. Small businesses which strive for growth but lack certain skills, capital, other abilities, resources and opportunities, we call *constrained*. These small businesses are situated in the lower right quadrant. Although we have suggested earlier in the chapter that deficiencies in the ability to achieve growth can, to a certain extent, be compensated for by increased motivation (that is, increased enthusiasm and effort towards achieving the desired goal), the inconsistency between one's aspirations and one's ability is more than likely going to lead to disappointment, and possibly the failure of the business. To these small business managers, we suggest that they move out of this quadrant by changing their classification on either of the dimensions. That is, increase one's ability so that the desired growth outcome becomes more likely. This might occur simply through the passage of time as the manager accumulates more experience and this experience leads to knowledge and skills that are important in for-mulating and implementing growth strategies. Although we have focused on the human capital of the small business manager we suspect that his or her human capital can be complemented by human capital of the small business's other managers. For example, the small business manager's ability might be limited in managing cash flows in a way to fuel growth effectively, but he or she could hire a CFO (Chief Financial Officer) to undertake these activities. We believe that other members of the management team might be able to increase the ability of the small business to achieve growth but this should not understate the impor-tance of the human capital of its leader because in the end the leader is the one most responsible for the direction of the firm. The other change that could be made to move a small business out of this quadrant is to adjust the small business manager's motivation in a way that is more consistent with his or her abilities (the next category). For example, rather than being motivated to grow and make the company public, the small business manager with limited abilities might be better off focus-ing on using the business to generate a 'good' income without the loss of independence that would occur through employment.

4. Small businesses in the fourth category, finally, have neither motivation nor abilities or resources for growth, and thus have little potential for growth. Not all businesses are suited to expansion. Owing to limited management abilities, these businesses may actually perform better if they remain at a smaller scale. One small business manager commented

on his biggest problem with running a small business 'Probably for me I struggle with coming up with new ideas. That can be a bit of a problem, and then developing the whole thing to make it pay' (Cameron, 2003). This group still has an important role in society for creating employment. To these small business managers we use an American saying, 'Way to go'. We believe they are making an important contribution to society by utilizing their resources to the fullest to generate economic wealth for the nation and themselves, gain utility from other aspects of the business not related to money, but not overextending themselves that will likely lead to financial ruin and emotional heartache.

Implications for Policymakers

The practical implications of this chapter for policymakers are numerous. First, we find that small business managers with greater growth aspirations are more likely to realize growth. The importance of motivation has largely been overlooked in policy programs. So far there has been an overemphasis on implementing support programs that provide small businesses with resources or aim at increasing the ability for small businesses to grow, including training programs for small business managers and tax cuts. Implicit in most supportive programs is the assumption that if only small businesses had these resources and abilities, they would grow. We find that it is important to consider resources *and* motivation simultaneously, and this has consequences for public policy. Referring back to Figure 2.3, we are able to develop policy implications for each of the four groups identified in the figure.

1. The small businesses in the upper right quadrant (*actual growth*) are not in great need of policy programs. They are achieving their desired outcomes and simultaneously create wealth and employment for society. Appropriate policy measures include policies aimed at easing and simplifying government communications and operations, such as reducing bureaucratic red tape, as well as ensuring a flexible labor market such that these businesses are able to recruit the talent needed to maintain their growth trajectory.
2. Small businesses with *unused potential*, in the upper left quadrant, require different policy measures. The major factor limiting the growth of these small businesses is a lack of growth aspiration. The goals of society (for instance, creation of new jobs) do not necessarily conform to the goals of individual small business managers. In order to align these goals, it might be possible for policymakers to make growth more attractive to small business managers by reducing some of the barriers.

The following quotes from Australian small business managers (Cameron, 2003) indicate that government policies may in fact be a demotivating influence:

- '[The government should] . . . raise the GST (collection of sales tax by the small business) threshold, that would take a lot of people out of the net – little businesses that are caught up . . . because it works on your turnover, not on what you make. That makes it fairer for those businesses that are competing against the back-yarders too, who aren't paying GST.'
- 'I keep my business under [the threshold] so I don't have to worry about the GST because it was killing us.'
- 'We may have to employ someone in the next few years. And that concerns me. At the moment we have subcontractors and that's great because they, in a way, are self employed, even though they sort of work for us. But if we put them on as employees, we've got super, workcover, all of that. That will be a headache for me. And I don't want to do it. So if anything, I need something to help make it easier to employ.'
- 'And just help us to understand things in a clearer way. Take worker's comp [workers' compensation scheme]. If you want to understand it, you've got to read a 150 page document, and it's a minefield. Why can't it be simple – a checklist of the real core aspects of what my compliance is in that particular industry. Along SIC [standard industry classification] lines. They know what the SIC industries are, they could base it around that and send it out to all small businesses in that SIC classification.'
- 'There's difficulties in trying to work out whether some people are an employee or a contractor. But if you put them on as a contractor and they're not, you get caught for payroll tax, tax itself if they haven't paid, insurance, super, workers comp and all of a sudden it just flows through.'

3. Most small business policies are at present designed under the assumption that the majority of small firms belong to the *constrained* category. Prevalent advice and financial support services are probably most effective in relation to this group, provided they are appropriately designed. In particular, we found that education plays an important role in enabling growth aspirations to be realized. Governments and others wishing to expand an economy need to emphasize the importance of education which could increase the ability of small business managers to realize their growth aspirations.

4. Small businesses in the fourth category, *little potential* for growth, still have an important role in society for creating employment and so on.

These small businesses are unlikely to benefit greatly from policy changes other than those policies that more broadly improve the macroeconomic environment.

Realizing that the needs of different types of small businesses differ, there are still some policy measures that are generally positive. Considering the influence of dynamic environments on growth, general policies should be aimed at creating more munificent environments. Policy measures can help create more vibrant markets. Keeping in mind that most small firms operate in the private service and retail sector in the domestic market, measures aimed at increasing domestic *consumer* demand are likely to be most effective. This could involve measures to increase the purchasing-power of consumers, such as the reduction of income or sales tax.

Implications for Scholars

Although many of the finer details behind the research methods and statistical techniques behind the results reported in this chapter are not contained within but in the source article published in the *Journal of Management Studies* (Wiklund and Shepherd, 2003a), the concepts and relationships detailed in this chapter do have important implications for scholars interested in the role of motivation in explaining small business management. The most important implications of this chapter (and the book) for scholars is in generating future research. A number of the avenues for future research that we believe are likely to be highly fruitful and make important contributions to our understanding of small business growth are now outlined.

First, while we believe that the results are likely to be generalizable to small businesses outside Sweden, care must be taken in assessing country effects such as culture. Although evidence from several countries suggests that only a small fraction of all small businesses grow to substantial size, there are national differences suggesting that a greater share of businesses become larger in, for example, the UK (Storey, 1994) and the USA (Birch, 1977) than in Sweden (Davidsson et al., 1994). Such differences may stem from individual differences in growth aspirations, perceived opportunity, resource structures or some combination of these. Future research might be able to explain why nations differ in the extent to which small businesses grow by looking at national differences in the motivation of their small business managers. It might be that some countries provide incentives (or have fewer disincentives) for growing small businesses which result in managers with greater aspirations for growth. Based on this chapter, we would argue that such research could be enhanced if both the abilities of the small business manager and the availability of opportunities for growth were also assessed. That is, maybe countries differ not only in the motivations of their small business managers but also in the abilities of their small business managers and the abundance of opportunities for growth and together these national differences provide a more complete understanding of country differences along important economic indicators.

Second, we must point out that the measurement of resources and opportunities are relatively course-grained in the study summarized in this chapter. A more fine-grained assessment including direct measurement of the entrepreneur's ability to access resources and the actual opportunities available to the individual business rather than the general dynamics of the industry would probably strengthen the relationship between these variables and actual outcomes. More specifically, experience in management start-ups and with growing businesses is better captured as a continuous variable (that is, a number of years). While experience is often used as a proxy for expertise, operationalizations that consider both the number of years of experience and the quality of that experience would likely produce stronger and more significant results. The measurement of 'access to financial capital' should also be strengthened by a multi-item operationalization and resources other than financial also considered.

Third, as is often the case with survey research, there is a possibility of survivor bias. Six businesses in the sample had gone out of business before the first survey, and another 31 went out of business during the three years of the study. Many more had failed, of course, before the sampling frame was constructed. Therefore, we can only generalize our findings to *surviving* small businesses. It is possible that higher growth aspirations are also associated with greater risk-taking propensity. Risk-taking, in turn, may be associated with higher chances of failure. Owing to high failure rates among new and small firms, future research needs to address whether those characteristics that lead to higher growth among surviving businesses are also associated with a higher risk of failure. For example, does general rule of thumb 2.1 also apply to failure? That is, the higher the growth aspirations of the small business manager, the greater the likelihood that the business will fail.

Fourth, a natural extension of this study is to investigate heterogeneity of growth aspirations among small business managers. Why do some small business managers aspire to expand their businesses rapidly while others do not? The theory of planned behavior offers a theoretical framework for such an empirical investigation. It should be possible to build on previous work on the antecedents of growth motivation (for example Davidsson, 1989b; Kolvereid, 1992; Wiklund et al., 1997) in assessing how attitudes toward behavior and social norms influence growth aspirations and, in turn, how growth aspirations and perceived behavioral control influence intention.

Finally, a more detailed examination of the interplay between growth and growth aspirations may be particularly interesting. Ajzen (1991) admits that feedback loops probably are present in his model. Feedback from growth to growth aspirations is likely. Growth may be an 'acquired taste', that is, managers of expanding firms may experience the benefits of expansion and larger size and thus become more motivated to grow their firm(s). In other words, it appears plausible that the experience of realized growth affects future growth aspirations.

CONCLUSION

This chapter takes an important step towards an increased understanding of a small business manager's growth aspirations and the business growth actually realized. While there is a relationship between aspiration for and actual growth, the relationship is more complex – it depends on the educational level and experience of the small business manager as well as the level of environmental dynamism. Education, experience and environmental dynamism magnify the positive relationship that growth aspirations have on growth. This chapter highlights the importance of a small business manager's human capital, access to financial resources, and environmental dynamism in explaining the nature of the relationship between motivation and small business growth. In the next chapter we further explore the resources of the small business manager to explain which small business managers engage in the entrepreneurial activity of new entry and the mode used for its exploitation.

APPENDIX: VARIABLES AND MEASURES

In the text of this chapter we have summarized the sample and the results of the study. The section below details the variables and measures of the study and is directly from our paper published in the *Journal of Management Studies* (Wiklund and Shepherd, 2003a). This published paper provides some more details on the sample and results that are not included in the text of the chapter or in this appendix.

Variables and Measures

Growth
Four measures were used to capture small business growth. Growth in terms of sales and employment was calculated as the relative change in size

from 1996 to 1999 in all businesses controlled by the respondent. When assessing performance, comparisons with competing businesses in the market reveal important additional information (Birley and Westhead, 1994). Therefore, respondents were asked to rate their sales and employment growth compared to competitors on five-point scales. Each of the variables were standardized and summed to an index. The Cronbach's Alpha value of the scale was 0.91.

Growth aspirations
The scale measuring growth aspirations consisted of four questions that had been successfully used in two previous studies (Davidsson, 1989a; Delmar, 1996). Respondents were asked whether a 25 per cent increase in the number of employees in five years would be mainly negative or mainly positive.[4] A seven-point scale ranging from very negative to very positive was used to measure this item. A similar question was then asked where a 100 per cent employee increase replaced the 25 per cent of the previous question. At the extreme level of growth aspiration individuals would score higher on the 100 per cent than the 25 per cent increase item (9.2 per cent of the sample). These individuals' responses were manually recoded to the highest value (seven) on the 25 per cent scale. Two open-ended questions were also posed. Respondents were asked to report the ideal size of the business in five years in terms of both sales and the number of employees. These responses and the 1996 size figures were used to calculate ideal growth rates of both sales and employees and converted to two seven-point scales. The two items from the 25 per cent and the 100 per cent scale were summed with the two items created from the open-ended questions to form a global growth aspiration index. The Cronbach's Alpha value of the index is 0.72 and corrected item-total correlations range from 0.47 to 0.55 indicating that the index has acceptable reliability (Nunnally, 1967) and that all items share sufficient variance with the index (Nunnally and Bernstein, 1994).

In order to establish construct validity further, we followed the guidelines provided by Robinson et al. (1991). Convergent validity was established by correlating our index with another index aimed at measuring expected consequences of growth consisting of ten items with a Cronbach's Alpha value of 0.78 (the measures were derived from expectancy theory). The correlation between the two indices was 0.62, suggesting that the correlation between the two underlying theoretical constructs, corrected for measurement error, is 0.81 (Cohen and Cohen, 1983). To establish discriminant validity, we correlated the growth aspirations index with previous three-year growth rate in terms of employees and sales. None of these correlations were above 0.10. These analyses taken together warrant the construct's convergent and discriminant validity according to Robinson et al's. (1991) criteria.

General human capital (education level)
Respondents were asked to state their highest level of completed education. This variable was then recoded into years of education.

Specific human capital (experience)
To measure experience, three variables deemed to be important to growth in previous research were utilized: start-up experience, management experience and experience of working in rapidly growing organizations. As these three variables all represent different ways of gaining experience (that is, specific human capital) they all measure a common experience construct. Hence, they were summed to an index. It should be noted, however, that these indicators are formative, meaning that the construct is an effect of its indicators as opposed to reflective indicators where the underlying construct causes the empirical observations (Wold and Jöreskog, 1982). Therefore, reliability analysis, which is suitable for reflective indicators, conveys no relevant information.

Respondents were asked if they had started any other business. This variable was coded zero for those who had no start-up experience and one for those that did. The respondents were then asked if they had ever worked as a manager in another business or organization for more than a year. This variable was coded zero if they had no such experience and one if they did. If the respondent had worked as a manager in a rapid growth business (annual sales growth of at least 20 per cent) the rapid-growth experience variable was coded one, if not it was coded zero. The respondents' total score on these three variables was summed into the experience index.

Access to financial capital
A subjective measure of 'access to capital' was utilized and captured on a seven point scale anchored by 'insufficient and a great impediment for our development' and 'fully satisfactory for the business's development'.

Environmental dynamism
The construct 'environmental dynamism' captures industry growth rates as well as other dimensions of increased environmental dynamism. We used Miller's (1987) scale consisting of four items to capture this variable. The Cronbach's Alpha value of the scale is 0.69.

Control variables
As business size, business age, industry (whether manufacturing, service or retail), and the age of the small business manager have been frequently investigated in previous research and may influence growth (see Delmar, 1997 for a review of predictors of growth), they were included as control

variables. Initial analyses suggested that the Swedish equivalents of ISIC codes we used for stratification were not always updated or relevant. The interview included a question about the respondents' main line of business (manufacturing, retail or service). Cross-referencing these with the ISIC codes showed some deviations. We chose to rely on the respondents' self-report of their main activity as a better indictor of their main industry.

NOTES

1. This chapter is based on Wiklund, J. and Shepherd, D.A. (2003a).
2. In other words, the individual's control over the behavior affects the strength of the aspiration – behavior relationship (Ajzen, 1991; Bagozzi and Warshaw, 1992) by working as a moderator.
3. As we will describe below, this proposed relationship was not supported in our study. Rather we found that 'those small business managers that have superior access to financial resources are more likely to achieve actual growth.'
4. While it is unlikely to impact the results, it should be noted that a five-year time horizon was used to operationalize growth aspirations yet there is a three-year time difference from when aspirations and growth were measured.

3. Who grows small businesses and how they choose to do it[1]

INTRODUCTION

Growth and entrepreneurship are inextricably linked. The essential action of entrepreneurship is new entry (Lumpkin and Dess, 1996), and involves engaging in new, potentially income generating, activities. This includes entering a new or established market with a new or existing product. This can be done either by a new start-up firm or by an existing firm. This entrepreneurial act has two important implications for our understanding of entrepreneurial small businesses. First, new entry is the source of the new products and/or the new markets that can lead to growth. For example, by discovering a new technology, a small business can use that technology to generate new products that better satisfy customer's demand than existing products. This will likely increase a small business's sales. Similarly, a small business can grow by taking its existing products to new markets, whether those new markets are international or different segments (based on demographics or psychographics) of one's domestic market. Second, the small business manager has a choice of how they want their new entry to take place; either new entry can occur within the current business or can be 'housed' in a newly created organization. Each can have certain advantages. One Swedish entrepreneur emphasized the value of expanding through the creation of new organizations. 'It is more enjoyable to work in smaller units. It is more fun to work in a unit of five to fifteen individuals than expanding the company to 150 with one single boss.'

Our knowledge about new entry, in terms of opportunity discovery and exploitation, has been developed along two separate streams of research, with each stream representing one of the two organizational modes available for the exploitation of an opportunity by a small business manager. These two streams of research can be labeled 'internal' and 'external' entrepreneurship (Burgelman, 1983). Internal entrepreneurship focuses on entrepreneurial activities in existing organizations (internal mode) whereas external entrepreneurship (new organization mode) is concerned with entrepreneurial activities in new independent firms (Burgelman, 1983;

Sharma and Chrisman, 1999).[2] This has left a gap in our understanding of entrepreneurship in small businesses. Most of the research on internal entrepreneurship has focused on large organizations, which may or may not provide insight into entrepreneurial activities of small businesses. Conversely, external entrepreneurship focuses on the creation of new organizations, but small businesses can be entrepreneurial in many ways without the creation of a new organizational entity. For example, they can develop new products or enter new markets.

In order to fill this gap, in this chapter we explore which small business managers are more likely to discover and exploit subsequent opportunities. By subsequent opportunities we mean new entries pursued after the creation of the original small business. We also explore the choice of organizational mode: that is, of those small business managers that do discover and exploit a subsequent opportunity, why some of them choose to exploit it using their existing small business and others through the creation of a new organization. The answer to these issues is important for a number of reasons.

First, our knowledge of opportunity discovery and exploitation revolves around either the internal mode or the new organization mode to the exclusion of the other. In this chapter we increase our understanding of the discovery and exploitation of opportunities whether it is internal to an established small business or through the creation of a new independent organization. A model that has explanatory ability for this broader construct of entrepreneurial activity is more powerful and has greater generality than one that is specific to only one mode of organization.

Second, we highlight commonality between internal and external entrepreneurship suggesting where exchange between the two streams of research may be appropriate. In particular, our current knowledge about discovery and exploitation within existing organizations is built upon samples of *large* organizations. This chapter focuses on the discovery and exploitation of opportunities within existing *small* businesses.

Third, small business managers face a choice of how they want to grow their businesses, that is, the organizational mode to exploit subsequent opportunities. By making this choice an informed one, we hope that growth can be achieved more effectively.

Finally, we know that some small business managers may engage in multiple new entries (Wright et al., 1997). The term habitual entrepreneur has been coined to describe such individuals (Westhead and Wright, 1998). Over time, habitual entrepreneurs may choose different modes of organization for their new entries (Westhead and Wright, 1998); they can create a new independent business to carry them out, or use the framework of their existing small business. If we wish to understand why some individuals but not others engage in multiple new entries and do so by comparing those who start multiple new independent firms to those who do not, we are ignoring the possibility that some other individuals may conduct similar activities but do so within the framework of their existing organizations. A more appropriate approach to answer such a question would be to compare those who repeatedly engage in new entries and those who do not, irrespective of the organizational mode the former used for that activity.

The chapter proceeds as follows. First, based on a review of the resource-based and entrepreneurship literature, we propose that the levels of human and social capital can help distinguish those who pursue - multiple new entries from those who do not as well as distinguish those who use a new independent organization as the organizational mode from those who use an internal mode. Second, we introduce the sample and the results of our empirical test of these propositions. Finally, we discuss the results and implications of this chapter for both scholars and practitioners.

RESOURCES AND ENTREPRENEURSHIP

In order to build our understanding of those small business managers more likely to discover and exploit subsequent opportunities for growth and their choice of organizational mode for doing so, we rely on resource-based theory. We choose this resource-based approach primarily because recent research by organizational scholars has begun addressing issues of organizational mode with a resource-based theory of the firm, discussing the central question of when market contracting or firm organization is more likely and appropriate (for example, Conner, 1991; Conner and Prahalad, 1996; Madhok, 1996, 1997). That is, resource-based theory has provided considerable insight into the decision of whether to contract another firm to conduct a particular activity (for example, to sub-contract out customer service, manufacturing or debt collection) or to conduct the activity oneself, perhaps by reorganizing the business and hiring new employees, such as by creating a customer service department, building a new production facility, or better managing one's own accounts receivable. In essence, managers are expected to choose between these organizational forms (market contracting or firm reorganization) based on which yields the highest value to resources at the lowest cost (Conner and Prahalad, 1996; Madhok, 1997).

Although we are not interested in whether the manager engages in market contracting or not, from an entrepreneurial small business perspective the resource-based theory provides an avenue for an increased understanding of the organizational mode issue facing small business managers: 'do I exploit this discovered opportunity within my existing small business or do I create a new business for its exploitation?' This theory can also be used to understand who has the ability to discover and exploit a business opportunity. Therefore, we look to the characteristics of the resources to help us explain who discovers and exploits new opportunities and their choice of mode given that they have been discovered. In this chapter we follow the lead of these scholars of a resource-based theory of the firm by investigating the resources at the disposal of small business managers and their impact on the discovery and exploitation of growth opportunities and the organizational mode used to exploit those opportunities.

Resource-based theory is focused on the combination and deployment of a firm's resources in order to achieve a competitive advantage (Conner, 1991). Resources are simply inputs into the production process and include plant and equipment, knowledge, and a patented technology. When those resources are valuable, rare, and inimitable they can lead the small business to a competitive advantage. The nature of the business's resources is the topic of the next chapter (Chapter 4). In this chapter we are more interested in the resources of the individual (the small business manager). It has been suggested that resource-based theory can be important to understanding entrepreneurial outcomes by looking at the resources of individuals (Alvarez and Busenitz, 2001).

As we argued in the previous chapter, the human capital of the small business manager is essential to the small business's capacity to conduct its intended activities. Research suggests that human capital is indeed important for conducting entrepreneurial activities, that is for pursuing new entry (Carpenter et al., 2001; Coff, 1999). Over and above their own resources, small business managers can utilize their relationships with others (their human capital) in order to leverage their own resources (Granovetter, 1985; Alvarez and Busenitz, 2001).

Therefore, in this chapter we focus on human and social capital and (1) explore small business managers' human and social capital to explain why some small business managers discover and exploit subsequent opportunities while others do not, and (2) explore small business managers' human and social capital to explain choice of organizational mode. We now explore human and social capital in terms of explaining which small business managers are likely to discover and exploit opportunities for growth and which are not.

DISCOVERY AND EXPLOITATION OF SUBSEQUENT OPPORTUNITIES

Human Capital

Central to the concept of human capital is the notion that individuals with more or higher quality human capital achieve superior performance in executing relevant tasks (Becker, 1975). In the context of growth, human capital refers to the knowledge and skills that assist in successfully engaging in new entries (see Davidsson and Honig, 2003; Snell and Dean, 1992), such as the creation of new products or the targeting of new markets. As described in the previous chapter, human capital refers to the knowledge, skills and experience of an individual and is comprised of both general and specific human capital. General human capital is particularly important for small business managers to generate entrepreneurial activities because this stock of general knowledge provides a basis by which new information can be recognized, accessed and integrated into one's existing knowledge. That is, the more general human capital that a small business manager has, the faster he or she can learn new things, which in term increases his or her knowledge base (Cohen and Levinthal, 1990). For example, it is much faster and easier to learn calculus for someone who knows algebra than for someone who does not. Such a process is important in entrepreneurship because the small business manager with greater general human capital has an increased ability to 'see' new information and understand its significance. More general knowledge means that the small business manager has a greater array of fields in which he or she can integrate new information and therefore find more avenues to discover or generate growth opportunities. We can say that more general human capital equips the small business manager with a greater 'opportunity set' (see Gimeno et al., 1997).

The general human capital of an entrepreneur is typically operationalized as education (Rauch and Frese, 2000). However, the findings from empirical research on the relationship between education and entrepreneurial activities have been mixed. For example, Bates (1990) found that higher education was associated with business start-up in the service sector, but not in other sectors. Evans and Leighton (1989) found that education predicted start-up in only one of two samples being investigated. Davidsson and Honig (2003) found that while education had a positive influence on the chance that a person would discover new opportunities, education did not predict successful exploitation. Despite these mixed findings, we follow the logic of resource-based theory. Thus:

Proposed relationship 3.1: *Small business managers with more education are more likely to pursue subsequent opportunities than those with less education.*

While general human capital is generalizable across contexts, specific human capital is not and, in this context, refers to the knowledge, skills, and experience that are applicable to entrepreneurial activities, but have few applications outside of this domain (see Becker, 1975; Gimeno et al., 1997). In the entrepreneurship literature, the most frequently investigated aspect of specific human capital is previous start-up experience. Start-up experience may provide small business managers with expertise in creating and running a new independent business and it shows that he or she has the specific ability to discover and exploit opportunities.

Furthermore, start-up experience provides the basis for knowledge that allows managers to judge the relevance of new information (Cooper et al., 1995). It acts like a filter which allows the small business manager to focus on valuable information and not get over-loaded with information that is irrelevant or of little value. This 'information filter' can help the small business manager better assess the 'real' value of new opportunities, speed up the business creation process and enhance performance (Davidsson and Honig, 2003). While few studies have empirically tested the role of start-up experience on whether individuals pursue entrepreneurial activities across modes, some studies have examined how previous start-up experience is related to the likelihood of starting a new independent business. It appears that previous start-up experience is a relatively good predictor of starting subsequent businesses (Bates, 1995; Davidsson and Honig, 2003). Thus:

Proposed relationship 3.2: *Small business managers with more start-up experience are more likely to pursue subsequent opportunities than those with less start-up experience.*

Social Capital

A person's networks of interpersonal relationships forms the basis of his or her social capital (Granovetter, 1985; Coleman, 1988). Social capital can help small business managers to access resources that are difficult to find or buy and reduce the cost of otherwise expensive resources (Cromie et al., 1994; Portes, 1998; Lin et al., 1981). For example, if I need specialized equipment for a limited time it may be difficult to find a business partner who is willing and able to lend me this equipment and it will take time and money to work out a contract. If a friend has the same equipment these things will be much easier and cheaper to resolve. If I can access resources at a lower cost, then less return is needed to obtain a 'sufficient' return on investment; that is, when the investment is small the return can be small but still cover the cost and therefore entrepreneurial action is more likely for those who have substantial social capital (Burt, 1997; Shane and Venkataraman, 2000).

Social capital can enhance an individual's access to information about new opportunities as well as the equipment, financial capital, advice, information and reassurance necessary for opportunity exploitation (Birley, 1985; Johannisson, 2000). It has been found that social capital does indeed facilitate the discovery of opportunities (Burt, 1992) and assists in the creation of new independent ventures (Cooper and Dunkelberg, 1986).

Social capital is often described in terms of formal and informal networks. Business networks composed of independent firms linked by common interests, friendship and trust, as opposed to formal contracts, constitute important informal networks (Powell, 1990; Uzzi, 1996). These small business managers indicate the importance of informal business networks to the functioning of their businesses (Cameron, 2003):

- 'I find that I talk to a lot of other business owners – most of them in businesses totally different to mine – but you can relate to the problems that you're having and all of that stuff – whether it's staffing or funds or cash flow or whatever.'
- 'Most of us have sounding boards, or people that we can network with. Most of my customers are from the legal and accounting professions and if I've got an idea I can turn to them and ask advice. I've got friends in the same industry and I can speak with them.'

Membership in a business network is important because it facilitates the transfer of difficult-to-codify, knowledge-intensive skills that are expensive to obtain in other ways (Larson, 1992; Powell, 1990; Uzzi, 1996). By difficult-to-codify, we mean that this knowledge exists in the form of intuition and the person who possesses it has a difficult time in articulating exactly what it is. Thus, it is difficult to set a price for such skills and trade them on the market.

In addition to the knowledge and skills discussed above, the small business manager's informal network also allows the exchange of goods that would otherwise be difficult to exchange. The informal relationship that a small business manager has with a resource provider may mean that exchanges can take place without the need for contracts (where specificity is required, trust is low and monitoring is necessary) and this also facilitates the pursuit of opportunities (Uzzi, 1996) because the small business manager can get rapid and inexpensive access to the resources needed for pursuing an opportunity. Thus:

Proposed relationship 3.3: *Small business managers with more developed business networks are more likely to pursue subsequent new entries than those with less developed business networks.*

Small business managers can also utilize formal network structures including establishing contacts with support agencies or through membership of formal trade associations (Johannisson, 2000). Ties to such institutions are associated with enhanced resource accessibility and predictability; that is, these small businesses are more likely to have access to the resources they need and be able to predict more accurately issues related to such access such as the time it takes to transfer the resources, their cost, and so on (Baum and Oliver, 1996). As the examples in Table 3.1 demonstrate, different government and community agencies provide entrepreneurs with different types of resources: some provide access to information while others act as social network brokers by facilitating links with other important resource providers. As stated by some small business managers (Cameron, 2003):

- 'What I've found helpful is the industry associations, which we're members of. They probably haven't got the best calibre of people, but when it comes to things like superannuation, and award rates, and what you can and cannot do with enterprise agreements – anything of that nature – in other words the employment of your staff – and ensuring that you are abiding by the laws of the land – I've found them very good in that respect . . . If anybody is in business and has an association like that, my advice would be to join it.'
- 'The Guild has district meetings where you can meet over dinner, and there'll be a talk about issues we're facing with the Government . . . And it's great to hear the problems other pharmacists are talking about. You always pick up something.'
- 'I think it's good to get a feel for what's happening out there in the market – whether issues are just us or whether it's the market as a whole.'

Relationships with government agencies can also facilitate legitimacy and status, because they signal to other stakeholders that the small business manager conforms to what is expected by these agencies and more broadly to social expectations (Baum and Oliver, 1996). As suggested by

Table 3.1   *Examples of government agencies in the USA and Sweden*
            that provide resources to entrepreneurs

Government agency	Resources accessed by entrepreneur via agency
USA[a]	
SBA: Office of Entrepreneurial Development	Help small businesses start, grow and be competitive in global markets by providing quality training, counseling and other forms of management and technical assistance.
SBA: Office of Technology	Promotes programs to improve the competitive capability of small research and development businesses.
US business advisor	Provides one-stop access to federal government information, services, and transactions.
SWEDEN	
Employment office	Provides enterprise allowance funding to the unemployed for starting a business and start-up courses.
ALMI	Provides advice and venture capital for new ventures.
Start-line	Provides a free of charge telephone service giving advice to people starting a business.
Jobs and society	Provides a free of charge national network of agencies giving advice and contacts to people starting a business.
Municipality office for industry and commerce	Local office supporting industry and commerce present in most municipalities in Sweden.
County council	Provides funding, advice and other support to SMEs.
Chamber of Commerce	Promotes trade by assisting with market information, business contacts, introductions, etc.
Regional agency for female entrepreneurs	Provides special funding and advice to female business founders. Part of the county council.
Municipality office for female entrepreneurs	Provides special funding and advice to female business founders. Part of the local government.

Note: a = Information from www.sba.gov and www.business.gov.

Baum and Oliver (1992, 1996), relational density (the number of links to formal institutions) represents a source of legitimacy, which provides access to more resources for both the entrepreneur and the organization. For example, a bank will likely acknowledge the links a small business manager has made with various government agencies and perceive him or her to be less of a credit risk than a small business manager without such links (holding all other attributes of the small business manager constant). Therefore, relational density with government agencies can reduce the costs of acquiring the resources necessary for entrepreneurial activities. Thus:

> **Proposed relationship 3.4:** *Small business managers with higher relational density with government support agencies are more likely to pursue subsequent opportunities than those with lower relational density with government support agencies.*

RESOURCES AND MODE OF ORGANIZING

We have used a resource-based perspective above to investigate an essential act of entrepreneurship: new entry, which involves the discovery/generation of what are believed to be business opportunities. We expect that small business managers with more human and social capital are more likely to discover and exploit these opportunities. These same resources likely provide insight into which mode is used for this entrepreneurial activity (Conner, 1991; Conner and Prahalad, 1996; Madhok, 1996). That is, the human social capital of the small business manager can help explain whether he or she chooses to exploit an opportunity using their existing small business or by setting up a new separate company. Madhok and Tallman (1998) argue that individuals choose an organizational mode based on assessment of which mode is expected to yield the highest value from existing resources. For example, a small business manager who is good at managing an existing organization but is bad at setting up a new business will likely use the internal mode for opportunity exploitation.

Resources can be embedded or generic. Embedded resources provide the greatest benefits when applied in a context where these resources can act in concert with other complementary resources (Madhok, 1996), but the value to be generated from such resources would tend to be reduced if they were housed in another operating context (Madhok, 1997). We propose that a small business manager will favor the particular mode for new entry that best utilizes the value of available embedded resources. However, the value of generic resources is independent of the mode in which it will be housed and therefore we do not believe that generic resources distinguish between modes of organizing for new entry. We now classify human and social capital in terms of whether they are generic or embedded resources and for those that are embedded we propose the most appropriate mode to house these resources.

Embedded Resources

Consistent with Madhok's (1996) notion of embedded resources, individuals typically engage in the discovery and exploitation of opportunities that are related to the knowledge they already possess (Kogut and Zander, 1992; Shane, 2000; Venkataraman, 1997). By extension, we propose that individuals typically use a mode for new entry that is related to the human capital they already possess. We proposed above that the start-up experience of small business managers is positively associated with subsequent new entries. However, creating a new independent organization as the mode for new entry introduces some liabilities of newness not present for those using an established firm as their vehicle for its exploitation (see Singh et al., 1986). Stinchcombe (1965) introduced the concept of the liability of newness to describe the high mortality risk facing new organizations relative to their more mature counterparts. Sources of the liability of newness appear to be derived from the costs of learning new tasks; the strength of conflicts regarding new organizational roles; and the presence or absence of informal organizational structures (Stinchcombe, 1965; Singh et al., 1986).

Therefore, a chronic problem of creating a new independent organization is lack of organization: there is conflict and confusion in recognizing the tasks that need to be performed and in allocating people to those tasks and there is uncertainty for employees regarding how to perform their new role effectively and how to adjust to market changes (Stinchcombe 1965). Entrepreneurs who use a new independent organization as the mode for new entry must construct an organizational structure that specifies tasks, allocates people to those tasks and provides avenues of authority; develop informal communication channels within the organization; and create and foster relationships with key stakeholders (Shepherd et al., 2000).

Small business managers with start-up experience understand these issues and have likely developed strategies to resolve them. Although this experience is embedded in the small business manager and is therefore transferable from one mode to the other, start-up experience has greater value in one of the contexts. It appears that start-up experience is a resource embedded in the new independent organization mode for new entry and therefore represents greater value when housed in this mode relative to when new entry is pursued internal to an existing firm because these organization issues are of less (or no) concern. Thus:

Proposed relationship 3.5: *Of the small business managers pursuing subsequent opportunities, those with more start-up experience are more likely to use the new independent organization mode than those with less start-up experience.*

Generic Resources

Generic resources provide the same value regardless of organizational context (Madhok, 1996). Therefore, they have a general value and can be important in explaining the involvement in entrepreneurial activities, but will not distinguish between the modes chosen for pursuing the activity. Becker (1975) uses logic similar to Madhok's (1996) when defining general human capital – it can be widely applied retaining the same value. Because education represents general human capital, it is transferable from one context to another (is a generic rather than an embedded resource) and does not appear to represent more value to one mode over the other. Therefore, we do not expect education to distinguish between new entry modes. Similarly, social capital is tied to individuals because it is derived from interpersonal contacts (Granovetter, 1985). It assists individuals in obtaining relevant information and other resources needed for new entry. Although social capital is likely to influence chances of involvement in entrepreneurial activities, it should provide similar value to both modes of organizing the activity. Therefore, we expect neither membership in business networks nor relational density to distinguish between the modes.

Summary

The resource-based theory of the firm suggests that resources provide the basis for explaining entrepreneurial activities and the organizational mode chosen for these activities. We have followed this lead and investigated the resource endowments of small business managers to gain a deeper understanding of who is more likely to engage in entrepreneurial activities and the mode of organization used to pursue those activities. Specifically, we expect that those small business managers with more human and social capital to be more likely to engage in subsequent new entries than those with less human and social capital. We also expect that start-up experience is embedded in the new organization creation process and therefore is of most value if the new independent organization mode is used rather than exploited using the existing small business. General human capital (education) and social capital (business network and relational density with government support agencies) are generic resources that can be used equally as effectively through either mode. Although there is theoretical support for these relationships and some empirical support, it is important to conduct a thorough empirical analysis of these relationships. In the next section we will summarize our sample and report the results of our study.

We realize that some readers will be less interested in this academic side of the book, and to them we suggest that they skip the next section of the chapter. Other readers might be interested in more details about the research method or a more detailed description of the results. We refer these readers to the appendix which contains the relevant information on variables and measures, more details on the analysis and a post-hoc analysis.

SAMPLE AND RESULTS

Sample

Two factors were instrumental in designing the study. We needed a sample that would contain a sufficient share of individuals who were likely to engage in new entries and who had some freedom to choose between the two modes for this entrepreneurial act. For this reason, we chose a cohort of small business managers who created a new independent organization as a new entry. We then investigated whether these small business managers engaged in subsequent new entries and which mode was used for these subsequent new entries. We followed this cohort over six years, which provides a well-defined time span over which subsequent new entries could occur.

We started with all new businesses registered in Sweden during 1994. Cross-referencing of official national registers of VAT, income tax, and business registrations produced 74 600 new business registrations. Businesses in agriculture, fishing and forestry were excluded and a proportional stratified sample of 14 000 cases was constructed. Three stratification criteria were used: legal form (sole proprietor, partnership, incorporation); industry (manufacturing, service, retail); and geographical location by county. Business registrations that were takeovers of existing businesses, re-registrations of established businesses (those with a change in their legal form), or registrations of companies with no operations were excluded after the first wave of data collection. The number of small business managers to be included in our analysis was further reduced by non-responses to the mail questionnaires of 1995, 1998, and 2000 (see Table 3.2 for sample details).

The final sample size of 2253 represents useable responses from a cohort of individuals that pursued new entry through the creation of an independent business in 1994. Information on the independent and control variables was collected with mail questionnaires in 1995 and 1998, whereas data pertaining to the pursuit of subsequent new entries during the six-year period was collected with a mail questionnaire in 2000. Several of the founder managers in the sample closed their business during the six-year period studied and others did not complete all survey rounds; therefore we used a Heckman-type model to correct for attrition (cf. Heckman, 1979).

Entrepreneurial small businesses

Table 3.2   *Results distinguishing small business managers pursuing subsequent new entries from those who are not*

	Variables	Regression coeff.	Standard error	Regression coeff.	Standard error
		Base model		Full model	
Human capital	Education			0.07**	0.02
	Start-up experience			0.37***	0.08
Social capital	Relational density			0.27***	0.05
	Business network			0.18***	0.03
Controls	Access to debt capital	−0.09**		−0.14***	0.04
	Access to equity capital	0.00		0.01	0.04
	Performance	0.02		0.01	0.04
	High-tech-manu.	0.23	0.17	0.36	0.29
	Other manufacturing	0.30***	0.08	0.40**	0.13
	Professional services	0.35***	0.06	0.40***	0.09
	Service	0.09	0.08	0.06	0.12
	Retail	0.29	0.07	0.40***	0.11
	Corporation	−0.03	0.05	−0.04	0.08
	First year's sales	0.10***	0.01	0.05	0.04
	Number of employees	0.01	0.01	0.02*	0.01
	Female	−0.12***	0.04	−0.19**	0.07
Model	χ^2	125***	25	226***	
	$\Delta\chi^2$			101***	
	Log likelihood	5466		5317	
	Rho	0.96***	0.04	0.12	0.56
Selection model	Start-up experience	−0.16***	0.03	−0.08*	0.04
	First year's sales	0.09***	0.01	0.09***	0.01
	Immigrant	0.13***	0.03	0.19***	0.04
	Incorporation	−0.09*	0.04	−0.11*	0.04
	Constant			−0.71***	0.05

Notes:
* $= p < 0.05$;
** $= p < 0.01$;
*** $= p < 0.001$;
$n = 5993$; subsequent new entry $= 908$;
no new entry $= 1345$;
censored observations $= 3740$.

Analysis and Results

In our first model, we investigate differences in human and social capital between those small business managers who pursue subsequent new entries (908 small business managers) and those who do not (1345 small business managers), correcting for sample selection. The results are reported in Table 3.2. We first entered the control variables in a base model. The model is statistically significant and the significant coefficients indicate that there are financial capital, industry, size, and gender effects in explaining who pursues new entries and who does not.

The inclusion of the research variables in the full model significantly improves model fit. Analysis of the significant regression coefficients suggests that small business managers with more human capital in terms of more education and more start-up experience are more likely to pursue subsequent new entries than those with less education and less start-up experience. These findings provide support for proposed relationships 3.1 and 3.2 respectively, namely, *Small business managers with more education are more likely to pursue subsequent opportunities than those with less education* (3.1) and *Small business managers with more start-up experience are more likely to pursue subsequent opportunities than those with less start-up experience* (3.2). Small business managers who pursue subsequent new entries also have more social capital in terms of more developed business networks and greater relational density (coefficient $= 0.27$; $p < 0.001$). These findings provide support for proposed relationships 3.3 and 3.4, respectively, namely, *Small business managers with more developed business networks are more likely to pursue subsequent new entries than those with less developed business networks* (3.3) and *Small business managers with higher relational density with government support agencies are more likely to pursue subsequent opportunities than those with lower relational density with government support agencies* (3.4).

In the second model, we included in the analysis only those small business managers who pursued subsequent new entries and then investigated the differences in human and social capital between those who used a new independent organization mode (371 small business managers) and those who did not (535 small business managers). The results are reported in Table 3.3. We first entered the control variables in a base model. The model is statistically significant, with legal form and size affecting the choice of mode.

The inclusion of the research variables in the full model significantly improves the explanation of the choice of organizational mode. Analysis of the coefficients indicates that among small business managers who pursued subsequent new entries, those with more specific human capital in terms of greater start-up experience were more likely to use the new independent

Table 3.3   Results distinguishing those who use the independent new organizations mode for new entry from those who do not

Constructs	Variables	Regression coeff.	Standard error	Regression coeff.	Standard error
		Base model		Full model	
Human capital	Education			0.02	0.02
	Start-up experience			0.26***	0.06
Social capital	Relational density			−0.03	0.04
	Business network			0.00	0.02
Controls	Access to debt capital	−0.03	0.04	−0.06	0.03
	Access to equity capital	−0.02	0.04	−0.02	0.03
	Performance	0.09	0.05	0.10***	0.03
	High-tech-manu.	0.33	0.31	0.31	0.17
	Other manufacturing	−0.07	0.12	−0.08	0.12
	Professional services	0.09	0.10	0.09	0.09
	Service	0.00	0.11	−0.05	0.16
	Retail	0.06	0.10	0.08	0.09
	Corporation	0.14*	0.09	0.05	0.07
	First year's sales	−0.08*	0.03	0.09***	0.02
	Number of employees	0.00	0.00	0.00	0.00
	Female	−0.20	0.13	−0.22***	0.07
Model	χ^2	31**		136***	
	$\Delta\chi^2$			105***	
	Log likelihood	2860		2815	
	Rho	−0.93*	0.01	−1.00	0.02
Selection model	Start-up experience			0.13**	0.05
	First year's sales			0.11***	0.01
	Immigrant			0.13**	0.04
	Incorporation			−0.05	0.05

Notes:
* = $p < 0.05$;
** = $p < 0.01$;
*** = $p < 0.001$; $n = 4646$;
external mode = 371;
internal mode = 537;
censored observations = 3740.

organization mode than those with less start-up experience. This finding provides support for proposed relationship 3.5, namely, *Of the small business managers pursuing new opportunities; those with more start-up experience are more likely to use the new independent organization mode than those with less start-up experience.* As anticipated, education, business networks, and relational density did not appear to be associated with the mode used for subsequent new entries.

It is possible that those new entries that were more related to the existing activities of the organization were pursued using the internal mode whereas those unrelated in nature were pursued using a new independent organization. If human and social capital were also correlated to the 'relatedness' of the new entry, this would lead to spurious results in our prediction of mode of entry. To minimize such concerns we conducted a post-hoc analysis (reported in the appendix). We found that it is unlikely that the relatedness of the new entry to the existing activities of the firm leads to spurious results.

A Summary of Key Findings

This chapter's proposed relationships and those that were found in our study are reported in Table 3.4. In this chapter we set out to distinguish

Table 3.4 A summary of proposed relationships and levels of support

Proposed Relationship	Support?
3.1: Small business managers with more education are more likely to pursue subsequent opportunities than those with less education.	Yes
3.2: Small business managers with more start-up experience are more likely to pursue subsequent opportunities than those with less start-up experience.	Yes
3.3: Small business managers with more developed business networks are more likely to pursue subsequent new entries than those with less developed business networks.	Yes
3.4: Small business managers with higher relational density with government support agencies are more likely to pursue subsequent opportunities than those with lower relational density with government support agencies.	Yes
3.5: Of the small business managers pursuing new opportunities, those with more start-up experience are more likely to use the new independent organization mode than those with less start-up experience.	Yes

empirically the entrepreneurial activity from the organizational mode chosen for pursuing it. The separation of the act of entrepreneurship (new entry) from how it is undertaken (mode) is important (see Shane and Venkataraman, 2000), but not well understand (Venkataraman, 1997). As suggested by the resource-based literature, different types of resources play an important role for entrepreneurial activities as well as the mode for organizing the pursuit of these activities. Using the resource-based theory of the firm as our theoretical framework this chapter explored differences in small business managers in terms of their own personal resources (human capital) and their access to resources (social capital) as a means of distinguishing those who engage in subsequent entrepreneurial activities from those who do not and also as a means of distinguishing between the modes used for these subsequent entrepreneurial activities. We found that human capital (education and start-up experience), and social capital (business network and relational density) are important resources in explaining whether small business managers engage in subsequent new entries or not. We also found that embedded resources (start-up experience) are associated with a particular mode of entry. We now discuss these findings in greater detail.

DISCUSSION

Practical Implications

This chapter's proposed relationships and those that were found in our study (as reported in Table 3.4) can be thought of as rules for distinguishing those small business managers who engage in subsequent new entries from those who have not yet done so and for distinguishing between those who use their existing small business to pursue this subsequent new entry from those who create a new organization for this new entry.

General rule of thumb 3.1: *Small business managers with more education are more likely to pursue subsequent new entries than those with less education.*

Human capital theory posits that those individuals with more or better human capital will make better decisions and perform better than those with less human capital. Having established that the pursuit of new entries is an appropriate measure of an entrepreneurial outcome (Lumpkin and Dess, 1996) and education is an indication of the small business manager's general human capital, the above general rule makes the important connection between a small business manager's level of education and the pursuit of new entries. That is, higher education is positively associated with a greater likelihood of the pursuit of new entries (whether those new entries are exploited using the existing small business or involve the creation of a new independent organization).

The aim of education is to build a student's knowledge. That knowledge is likely to be relatively broad in scope and therefore not necessarily targeted at the small business manager's task of generating and exploiting opportunities. Even though this stock of knowledge built up through years of education (at least in part) is not specific to generating and exploiting new entries, it appears that education does provide a small business manager with some knowledge and skills that are useful in entrepreneurship. We know that individuals with more knowledge are better able to recognize signals as new, process the new information so that it now forms part of their stock of knowledge, and ascertain the value of this new information (Cohen and Levinthal, 1990). This is particularly relevant to small business managers wanting to expand their businesses (existing or new). Being able to better recognize, assimilate and assess new information means that these more educated individuals are more likely to recognize the opportunity for new entry and act on that recognition. This is what was meant by Gimeno et al. (1997) when they suggested that entrepreneurs with more general human capital have a larger opportunity set: more highly educated individuals will recognize/generate more possible opportunities from which they can select the one that they wish to pursue. Those with less education are likely to see/generate fewer such opportunities and from this smaller opportunity are less likely to find one that they believe is attractive.

Furthermore, this ability to learn is useful in the further development of the opportunity throughout exploitation. For example, the environment is likely to change in ways not previously expected, the ability to recognize and understand these changes early will help the small business manager make changes to his or her business strategy to react to, and capitalize upon these changes. Knowing that one has the ability to recognize and respond to currently unforeseeable opportunities also makes entrepreneurial action more likely.

This argument for the benefits of education in generating entrepreneurial outcomes makes sense and is consistent with the findings of the study summarized in this chapter. If it is so obvious, then why have so many studies in the past had trouble finding this relationship or found only mixed results? For example, Evans and Leighton (1989) found that education predicted start-up in only one of two samples being investigated. Davidsson and Honig (2003) found that while education had a positive influence on the chance that a person would discover new opportunities, education did not predict successful exploitation. It could be that individuals who are more educated have the ability to discover/generate entrepreneurial activities but choose not to exploit them. For example, highly educated individuals are likely to have higher opportunity costs than their less educated counterparts (Amit et al., 1995). Therefore, although there might be profits to be made by becoming self-employed and pursuing this discovered opportunity, these highly educated individuals have other opportunities that offer considerable income at less risk (such as to remain as an employee). Less educated individuals may be giving up less to pursue a discovered opportunity and are therefore more likely to exploit a discovered opportunity (even though they are less likely to discover one in the first place). Another possible explanation is that although highly educated individuals 'see' more clearly the benefits of a possible opportunity they may also have greater ability to 'see' the risks associated with the action than those with less education. Given that our focus is individuals who have already created a new independent organization, these possible explanations for non-findings in previous entrepreneurship research on education are less applicable to the study summarized in this chapter.

Although the empirical findings summarized in this chapter are consistent with a causal relationship between education and entrepreneurial outcomes, not all possibly confounding artifacts can be ruled out. That is why more research needs to be done on this relationship. Of particular interest is the content of the education. Here we make the argument that education contributes to general human capital and therefore the benefit arises from building general knowledge, not necessarily knowledge specific to the small business manager's tasks or the entrepreneurial task of generating new entry opportunities. What education content is of most value to small business managers in their entrepreneurial endeavors? Is more general education better because it provides the basis for a larger opportunity set? That is, are entrepreneurial outcomes more likely to come from students of history, languages and literature than from students of business? It might be that the humanities students are more likely to have knowledge useful in the discovery of opportunities and business school students more likely to have knowledge useful in the exploitation of opportunities. If this is the case, what changes in content are required to enhance business school students' ability to discover/generate opportunities? Should entrepreneurship classes be less concerned about core business class prerequisites and encourage humanities students to mix with business school students in entrepreneurship classes aimed at generating opportunities and discussing how they should be exploited? The above general rule for the positive association between education and entrepreneurial outcomes will hopefully provide an incentive to education scholars and educators to gain an even deeper understanding of this relationship.

It should also be noted that we have focused on education as a measure of general human capital (following the lead of other studies), but general human capital is broader than simply education. For example, general work and/or life experiences may be an alternate route to the building of general human capital useful in generating entrepreneurial outcomes. It might be that those young people that backpack around the world before starting their career have done much to enhance their general human capital and therefore their opportunity set. We can just imagine a Swedish or Australian backpacker sitting on a Greek island calling home and saying 'Mum, send more money, I am busy building my opportunity set'. We believe that future research that explores the impact of general experience on entrepreneurial outcomes will make an important contribution to our understanding of entrepreneurial small businesses.

General rule of thumb 3.2: *Small business managers with more start-up experience are more likely to pursue subsequent new entries than those with less start-up experience.*

This general rule focuses on specific human capital, that is, knowledge and skills that are directly applicable to the entrepreneurial outcome of new entry that have been built up through experience with starting a business. There has been considerable scholarly attention directed to the link between the knowledge gained from experience and the discovery of opportunities (Hayek, 1945; Shane, 2000; Shepherd and DeTienne, 2004). Past research from the cognitive literature suggests that increased knowledge in a particular field allows individuals to acquire important advantages. For instance, as individuals become more knowledgeable at a particular task through experience, they tend to become increasingly efficient. They learn to focus attention primarily on the key dimensions, that is, the ones that contribute most variance to the outcome of decisions (Chase and Simon, 1973; Choo and Trotman, 1991; Weber, 1980). Individuals with more knowledge also appear to think in a more intuitive way; that is, they make their decisions in a more automatic manner rather than through more conscious, step-by-step systematic processing (see Logan, 1990). This automatic processing (and decision making) is often faster. Busenitz and Barney (1997) found that entrepreneurs relied more heavily on heuristics to speed up the decision making process than did managers; without such mechanisms, windows of opportunity would often close before an opportunity could be identified.

Over and above acceleration of decision making processes, knowledgeable individuals have created categories of information based on a deep structure that involves more, stronger, and richer links between concepts (Gobbo and Chi, 1986; Chi and Koeske, 1983; Frederick, 1991; Frederick and Libby, 1986). These deeper and richer connections could enhance an individual's ability to generate new entries. For example, those individuals who are able to integrate perceived problems into a pattern are more likely to believe that the status quo may not be the most accurate description of 'reality' (Johnson et al., 1991; Gaglio and Katz, 2001) and thus have a greater chance to identify opportunities that involve the development or application of significantly new technologies and/or the creation of a previously non-existent market. For example, Cohen and Levinthal (1990: 130) in their work on absorptive capacity state, 'the prior possession of relevant knowledge and skill is what gives rise to creativity, permitting the sorts of associations and linkages that may have never been considered before'.

Start-up experience likely provides knowledge about associations and linkages that would be difficult for those without such experience to obtain. Creating a new organization provides insight into the nature of newness. For example, what makes something new, what are the attractive aspects of newness that draw customers, what are the liabilities of newness and how can these liabilities best be overcome? Through a deeper understanding of newness, the small business manager is better able to recognize which new entry possibilities offer benefits that exceed the liabilities, and is more capable of exploiting those new entries. For example, it has been argued that experience may provide entrepreneurs with benchmarks on judging the relevance of information (Cooper et al., 1995), which can speed the start-up process and enhance performance (Davidsson and Honig, 2000).

We operationalized start-up experience by whether the founder manager had started any businesses prior to 1994. A more fine-grained operationalization could capture both the number of previous start-ups and the quality of the experience gained from each. For example, the level of success of each previous start-up might impact human capital differently. Maybe entrepreneurs do learn more from their mistakes – those previous start-ups that failed. This is an empirical question and could help improve our understanding of the human capital construct.

In this chapter, we have explored only one type of specific human capital. Scholars of Austrian economics argue that people have different prior knowledge and this allows some individuals to discover certain opportunities (Hayek, 1945; Venkataraman, 1997). 'Austrian entrepreneurship stems from the discovery of the existence of profitable discrepancies, gaps, and mismatches in knowledge and information' (Cheah, 1990: 343). Prior knowledge, which refers to an individual's distinctive information about a particular subject matter, may be the result of work experience (Evans and Leighton, 1989; Cooper et al., 1994), education (Gimeno et al., 1997) or other means (Shane, 2000). It may be accumulated through experiential learning – intentional or unintentional knowledge that comes from direct experience and vicarious learning – and/or acquiring knowledge through second-hand experience (Huber, 1991). Future research that investigates different types of human capital of the small business manager specific to the management of small businesses and entrepreneurship, will make an important contribution to our knowledge. For example, start-up experience may provide knowledge of more benefit to the exploitation of an opportunity than to the discovery of an opportunity; whereas, experience as a R&D scientist in the field of biotechnology, may represent human capital specific to the discovery processes rather than to exploitation. Therefore, more work needs to be done in understanding the role of different types of specific human capital and possibly in distinguishing between the discovery and exploitation components of new entry (this latter task is considerably difficult).

General rule of thumb 3.3: *Small business managers with more developed business networks are more likely to pursue subsequent new entries than those with less developed business networks.*

This general rule, and the one that follows, relate to the social capital of the small business manager. The small business manager's social capital is important because all economic behavior is rooted in inter-personal relationships. In this regard, the entrepreneurial activity of new entry is no different (and likely more important) than other forms of economic activity. Social capital refers to the inter-personal relationships the small business manager has with others (specifically business relationships for this general rule and with formal government agencies in the next rule) and this network is a source of access to resources that are beyond the personal control of the small business manager (Leff, 1979; Portes, 1998; Lin et al., 1981).

Entrepreneurial endeavors are typically resource-intensive, in that they require considerable financial resources to experiment with ideas to evaluate whether they are likely to represent an opportunity worth pursuing and financial resources to exploit the opportunity though full scale production of the new product or entry into the new market. The need for financial resources often exceeds the personal wealth of the small business manager and this highlights the importance of a social network. One could argue that you do not necessarily require a social network to access the capital you need, just an attractive opportunity which will attract investors. While an attractive opportunity obviously helps, without the social network it will likely take longer to access the financial resources required to explore and exploit the possible opportunity and also the cost of acquiring those resources is likely to be higher than if they were accessed through one's social network. That is, the social network acts as a catalyst for the acquisition of financial resources. Financial resources are not the only resource that can be accessed through a social network. For example, information is an important resource in the pursuit of new entries. Through his or her social network, a small business manager might receive early information that, when combined with other resources, represents an attractive new entry opportunity. This general rule focused on the informal business networks of small business managers and its positive association with the pursuit of a new entry opportunity. We now turn to formal actors that small businesses can access.

General rule of thumb 3.4: *Small business managers with higher relational density with government support agencies are more likely to pursue subsequent opportunities than those with lower relational density with government support agencies.*

The explanation for the previous general rule provided the basis for social capital in general and then informal business networks specifically. This general rule builds on the previous one but focuses on a specific type of social capital; relational density with government support agencies. Government support agencies represent a formal dimension of a small business manager's social network. Here we did not investigate the nature of the relationship but rather the scope of a small business manager's relationship with these government support agencies. As reflected in the general rule above and the results summarized in this chapter, the greater number of government support agencies in which the small business had contact the more likely he or she would pursue subsequent new entries. It appears that the role of government, at least in the creation of these support agencies has a positive association with entrepreneurial outcomes.

The precise role that government should play in entrepreneurship is both a philosophical question and one that is difficult to determine empirically, at least with the data to which we have access. But it is interesting to speculate upon the results we have here and offer some prescriptions for both small business managers and government support agencies. These speculations and prescriptions are offered in the next section (after the rules of thumb).

It is important to note that we measured relational density, which captures the scope of contacts rather than the quality of any one type of contact. It appears that contact with more government support agencies provides the small business manager with more legitimacy which can help in the acquisition of other resources that enhance entrepreneurial activity. But it might also suggest the importance of different types of information, advice, and resources that may be complementary in nature (Aldrich, 1999; Johannisson, 2000). Therefore, entrepreneurs may benefit more from a diverse network of support agencies rather then closer ties with single agents.

A Qualification for General Rules 3.1–3.4 Above

It is important to note that in the four general rules above, we have been interested in who acts and who does not, and have not been interested in the performance implications of their action or non-action. It could be that those who are more highly educated, have greater start-up experience, and have a more extensive social network are more confident in their ability to exploit an opportunity and therefore do so, even if that confidence does not reflect their actual exploitation abilities. That is, those with more human and social capital are more overconfident than those with less human and social capital. When the purpose is to explain why someone acts, the distinction between perceived and actual abilities is not important. But overconfidence is unlikely to be driving the findings summarized in this chapter anyway, because, as reported in the appendix, a post-hoc analysis revealed that of those that did pursue a subsequent opportunity, there was no significant difference in the quality of the opportunity based upon the human and social capital variables.

General rule of thumb 3.5: *Of the small business managers pursuing new opportunities, those with more start-up experience are more likely to use the new independent organization mode than those with less start-up experience.*

The importance of this general rule of thumb is that resources not only help us understand which small business managers are more likely to engage in the essential act of entrepreneurship (new entry), but resources also help us understand the choice of organization mode used to exploit the discovered opportunity. Specifically, it is the start-up experience of the small business manager that distinguishes, in part, those that pursue the new entry using their existing small businesses from those that pursue the new entry by creating a new organization for its exploitation. The difference between the specific human capital of start-up experience and the general human capital of education and the social capital of informal business networks and relational density with formal government authorities, is that start-up experience can be considered an embedded resource where the others can be considered generic.

This classification of resources as embedded and generic has been used to explain why market contracting is used rather than the firm, and it appears to be beneficial in explaining the mode of organization for one's entrepreneurial activities. The finding summarized in this chapter is consistent with the notion that start-up experience is a resource embedded in the new independent organization mode. That is, start-up experience has greater value in the pursuit of new entries when those new entries are organized through the creation of a new independent organization than through one's established small business. In other words, the specific human capital of start-up experience is more specific to one mode than the other.

Although all new entries are 'new', the creation of a new independent organization offers another dimension of newness. The creation and management of a new organization offers the small business manager managerial challenges not faced, or at least not faced to the same extent, when managing an established small business. For example, compared to an established organization, a new one faces higher costs associated with learning new tasks, more employee conflicts over roles and responsibilities, less communication due to the absence of informal organizational structures (Stinchcombe, 1965; Singh et al., 1986), and a lack of legitimacy in the eyes of (potential) stakeholders (Choi and Shepherd, forthcoming).

Small business managers' knowledge on how to construct an organizational structure that specifies tasks, allocates people to those tasks, and provides avenues of authority to develop informal communication channels within the organization, and to create and foster relationships with key stakeholders, represents an important resource, one that has greater value for a small business manager of a new organization than a small business manager who decides on a new entry through his or her established organization (Shepherd, Douglas, and Shanley, 2000). That is, start-up experience is embedded in the 'new organization' mode of exploiting a new entry and is consistent with the findings summarized above: those with more start-up experience are more likely to use the new organization mode of entry than are those without start-up experience. The flipside of this argument is that those small business managers with low start-up experience must recognize that the new organization mode for new entry does offer a number of managerial challenges distinct from those of pursuing a new entry using their established small business.

The rest of the resources appeared to be more generic, and did not hold any more value in one mode over another. It would be very interesting to explore other types of resources believed to be embedded in one of the organizational mode. For example, the pursuit of a new entry using one's established small business could generate conflict between the previous status quo and the new product and/or market being pursued. Experience in change management, the integration of acquisitions into the parent corporation, and/or in innovative multiple product companies (such as Proctor and Gamble) might be an important source of knowledge that is highly valuable if new entry is pursued through the existing small business but less so if new entry occurs through the creation of a new organization.

Implications for Policymakers

The previous chapter established the link between the education of the small business manager and growth. This chapter found a positive association between his or her education and entrepreneurial activities. The next chapter will show that the level of knowledge of all staff in the small business has a positive effect on small business performance. Given that these results are derived from three different samples, it is safe to conclude that education and knowledge have positive effects on several different important small business outcomes. What are the policy implications of this general finding? We have examined years of formal schooling and it is unlikely that a small business manager has the time to go to school full-time while at the same time operating his or her business. Instead, it would be valuable to offer part-time training programs that give small business managers the chance to increase their knowledge while at the same time focusing on their business. We do not know exactly what the content of these programs should be, but our findings suggest that the general knowledge obtained from schooling is valuable.

Turning to those who have not yet started their businesses, policies should be aimed to encourage highly educated individuals to pursue an entrepreneurial career because these small business managers perform better in several ways, so long as they are sufficiently motivated. Above we have argued that the opportunity cost associated with starting a business may be higher for educated individuals because they likely give up a higher income from their current job should they switch to self-employment. One way to increase the attractiveness for highly educated people to operate their own firm would be to increase the payoffs to successful entrepreneurship (for example with tax incentives) and reduce the financial punishment in case of failure (by reforming bankruptcy laws and increasing unemployment benefits to those previously self-employed).

We also found that to small business managers, it appears that government support agencies do provide access to some resources useful in the generation and/or pursuit of entrepreneurship (see also Robson and Bennett, 2000). What exactly those resources are, should be the topic of future research. For example, do these government agencies provide small business managers resources in the form of cheaper access to financial capital (debt or equity), other financial incentives (tax incentives), valuable information (leading to the discovery or evaluation of opportunities or for gearing up for full scale production), or simply that being associated with the government agencies provides small businesses legitimacy which improves its status among other stakeholders providing access to more resources at a lower cost? It is likely that some agencies provide certain types of resources (such as financial resources or training) while others provide information. Determining the impact of providing a relevant resource on the entrepreneurial activity of small business managers will act as a guide to the government on the most appropriate allocation of its budget, that is, that a certain level of tax money is used in a way that helps entrepreneurial small business managers the most: 'more bang for the buck'. We were unable to address this question but we hope future researchers will do so.

This should not be taken as an argument for extending support services to small businesses, because there is a cost associated with operating such agencies. Rather, our findings show that they are of some value. We do not know if the value is greater than the cost. As these quotes from Australian small business managers suggest, government agencies may not have a positive image among other small business managers (Cameron, 2003).

- 'I find that they pay a lot of lip service. It's all political, and I don't think they really give a toss about small business.'
- 'A lot of advisory services are provided by people that don't have any small business experience. Or they're failures.'
- 'I'm not sure that Government agencies are staffed with anyone that knows anything about running a small business, and therefore they're not in a position to offer advice to those of us that do.'
- 'Anything I've been to from the Government – particularly local council – is that it's like being reminded that you're only a 2 year old child because all they do is speak down to you.'
- 'If you've got a small business – any sort, it doesn't matter what it is – I'm not convinced that any Government running any sort of a seminar or information session or whatever – is going to give you the silver bullet or panacea to make it a success. Not because I'm anti-Government or anti-public service – but if you've never run one, how can you counsel business owners on how to run one?'
- 'I didn't think there was a Government help agency to provide information to small businesses.'

Implications for Scholars

Having conceptually separated the act of entrepreneurship (new entry) from how it is undertaken (mode), this chapter clears the way for a deeper understanding of some of the key concepts of entrepreneurship. First, rather than operationalize habitual entrepreneurs by how an entrepreneurial activity takes place (that is, as a new entry using the new independent organization mode), we propose that future operationalizations could be based on the act of entrepreneurship (new entry) regardless of the mode. Over 40 per cent of the entrepreneurs in our sample were involved in the pursuit of subsequent new entries, but less than half of these chose the new independent organization mode. This suggests that habitual entrepreneurship is a widespread phenomenon, but much of it remains hidden unless the internal venture mode is considered. This new lens for habitual entrepreneurship research is likely to open up new ground for scholars. Second, we found that internal venturing does occur in small young organizations and there is the possibility of learning more about this type of internal venturing from the 'external entrepreneurship' literature. Third, we found that some resources explain differences in the mode used for subsequent new entries. We believe that a deeper understanding of the mode used for new entry likely resides in the embeddedness of resources which in turn requires uncovering the orchestrating themes and integrative mechanisms that ensure complementarity among a firm's various aspects (Black and Boal, 1994; Inkpen and Choudhury, 1995; Miller, 1996). We hope that scholars focus more attention on new entry across modes of organizing and investigate why a particular mode is used for entrepreneurial endeavors.

CONCLUSION

This chapter takes an important step towards an increased understanding of the role that the human and social resources of the small business manager play in the entrepreneurial activity of entry into new products and/or new markets and whether they choose to pursue this new entry using their existing small business or through a newly created organization. Specifically, small business managers' human capital (education and start-up experience), and social capital (business network and relational density) are important resources in explaining whether small business managers engage in subsequent new entries or not. Small business managers with the embedded resource of start-up experience are more likely to create a new organization for the pursuit of their new entry than are those without such experience. In the next chapter we further explore the role of resources but focus on the resources of the small business.

APPENDIX: MEASURES AND ADDITIONAL ANALYSES

Measures

Dependent variable: subsequent new entry

In operationalizing subsequent entrepreneurial activity we drew on Lumpkin and Dess (1996) who argue that the essential act of entrepreneurship is new entry, which involves engaging in new, potentially income generating, activities including entering a new or established market with a new or existing product, that is, launching a new venture either by a new start-up firm or by an existing firm. Two questions were used to capture whether the founder manager had pursued subsequent new entries. In 1998, respondents were asked: 'Have you started any other firms since 1994?' The question was repeated in 2000, probing start-ups since the previous round. In 2000, respondents were also asked: 'Have you, after the start of this company in 1994, started any new ventures within the company? We are interested in new business initiatives in your company, which has lead or could lead to new income-generating activities'.[3] Those who were involved in one or both of these new entry activities were dummy coded one, those who were not, were coded zero. Approximately 40 per cent of the founder managers in the sample were involved in subsequent new entries ($n = 908$).

Dependent variable: mode used for new entry[4]

Among founder managers who pursued subsequent new entries ($n = 908$), we singled out those who indicated they had chosen to use a new independent organization for a new entry since 1994. Those who used a new independent organization mode were dummy coded one; those who did not were coded zero. Approximately 41 per cent of the founder managers that pursued subsequent new entries did so using a new independent organization as their mode of entry ($n = 371$).

General human capital: education

The general human capital of an entrepreneur is typically operationalized by years of schooling (Rauch and Frese, 2000). We followed this lead and asked respondents in 1995 for their highest level of completed education on a scale containing the most common Swedish alternatives ranging from primary to postgraduate school. This scale was supplemented with an open-ended alternative. Only 2 per cent of the respondents chose the open-ended alternative, suggesting that the fixed alternatives indeed captured most founder managers' level of education. The responses were then recoded into years of education.

Specific human capital: start-up experience
Start-up experience refers to experience with the creation and management of a new independent organization. To operationalize prior start-up experience, respondents were asked in 1995 if they had started any other business prior to the start-up of the current firm in 1994. The responses were coded zero for no and one for yes.

Social capital: development of business network
Business networks were defined to respondents as regular cooperation with other firms, which is not based upon formal agreements. Respondents were first asked whether they participate in a business network. If they answered yes to this question, they were asked to respond to four questions using five-point scales ranging from very infrequently to very frequently. The four questions detailed below were summed to an index with a Cronbach's Alpha value of 0.76:

1. How often do you get information on new business opportunities through the network?
2. To what extent do you get access to new or more resources, including competence, through the network?
3. To what extent are your products or services delivered through the network?
4. How important has the network been for the development of new ventures?

Social capital: relational density
Relational density captures the number of relationships with formal institutions such as government agencies. Following Baum and Oliver (1996), we measured relational density in terms of the number of links to government and community organizations supporting new ventures, entrepreneurship and business development. A total of nine public support agencies were listed, and respondents were asked to mark if they had ever been in contact with each of the agencies. The listed agencies and the support they provide are detailed in the Swedish subsection of Table 3.1.

Control variables
Respondents were asked to what extent limited access to loans was an obstacle to firm growth and to what extent limited access to external

equity capital was an obstacle to firm growth. These variables were measured on four-point scales ranging from a very small obstacle to a very large obstacle. They were reverse coded to indicate access to debt and equity capital. Respondents were asked to report on the organization's profitability on a four-point scale ranging from 'very poor' to 'very good', which measures performance. Size in terms of first year's sales and number of employees was tapped during the first survey round, 1995. Respondents were asked to state their gender. The variable was coded one for females and zero for males. Legal form was taken from the sampling frame, and a dummy variable, coded one for incorporated companies, was included. Following Swedish practice (see Davidsson et al., 1996), we used six different categories of industry based on ISIC codes: high-tech manufacturing, manufacturing, professional services, private services, retail, and other. Dummy variables were used for the first five categories.

Analyses

Several of the founder managers in the sample closed their business during the six-year period studied and others did not complete all survey rounds. Because the variables that have an effect on subsequent new entries probably also impact closure, attrition is not random but instead systematic in a fashion similar to self-selection (Heckman, 1979). Therefore, unless the results are corrected for attrition, results may have a survivor bias. We therefore used the Heckman-type correction models (see Heckman, 1979).[5]

Heckman-type correction models use a two-step process. First, based on theory a model is developed for the probability of survival, which can predict this probability for each individual. To develop the model for survival (selection model), we used research findings on resource factors contributing to new venture survival and high performance (Cooper et al., 1994; Dahlqvist et al., 2000), specifically, first year's sales, immigrant status, start-up experience and incorporation (the latter two variables also appearing in the models for predicting the dependent variables). Second, a correction is made for self-selection (survival) by incorporating these predicted individual probabilities into the estimation model. A significant Rho suggests that if a correction had not been made then self-selection would have likely biased the results.

Post-hoc Analysis

It is possible that those new entries that were more related to the existing activities of the organization were pursued using the internal mode whereas those unrelated in nature were pursued using a new independent organization. If human and social capital were also correlated to the 'relatedness' of the new entry, this would lead to spurious results in our prediction of mode of entry. To minimize such concerns we conducted a post-hoc analysis.

In 2000, additional data were collected for a subset of the sample. The subsample was selected based on an affirmative answer to the following question from the original survey of 2000: 'Do you have a business initiative in progress now, which you yourself or others in the company have devoted time and possibly other resources to develop, but where the new activity does not yet create a steady income?' The 477 respondents who answered yes to this question were contacted again for a telephone interview and 437 agreed to participate. After some initial screening questions, approximately 250 respondents qualified for the full interview. To measure 'relatedness' we asked if the new activity's product/service was (1) entirely new compared to what the company has offered previously, (2) if it was a substantial improvement or change to the existing product/services, or (3) if it was the same to what the company has offered previously. Similar questions were asked for the means of distribution and customers served. The answers to these questions were summed to a relatedness index. For the prediction of mode of organizing to be spurious, an external variable would have an effect on both independent and dependent variables. If relatedness is such a variable, we would expect to find a significant relationship between the relatedness index and variables affecting mode of organizing. A regression analysis showed that none of the human or social capital variables included in our study had an association with the relatedness index. Therefore, it is unlikely that the relatedness of the new entry to the existing activities of the firm leads to spurious results.

NOTES

1. This chapter is based on a working paper: Wiklund and Shepherd (2004), 'Entrepreneurs' human and social resources, new entry, and mode of organizing'.
2. In-between modes of organizing can also be conceived (e.g. joint ventures). However, such modes are not clearly linked to particular streams of research and will therefore not be considered in this chapter.
3. They were instructed not to consider mergers or acquisitions.
4. To operationalize this distinction between modes, we use the subjective assessment of the founder manager who is in the best position to assess the issues of control – they report whether they perceive the new entry to be internal to the existing organization or involves the creation of a new independent organization.
5. Heckman correction models may still lead to biased results should the error terms of the selection equation and the dependent variables be identical (Sartori, forthcoming). We therefore chose to complement Heckman selection probit models using the full sample

with probit and logit models using only the cases that provided complete data. The magnitude of the coefficients varied across the analyses but the direction of the effects as well as the rank order of the effect sizes were the same for the statistically significant predictor variables across all analyses. This suggests that our results are robust. In the results section, we report the analyses using the Heckman selection probit models.

4. The small business's entrepreneurial orientation and knowledge-based resources[1]

INTRODUCTION

In the previous chapter we discussed the resources of the small business manager as a basis for explaining why some engaged in entrepreneurial activities and why some chose one organizational mode for the exploitation of that opportunity rather than using an alternative organization mode. The basis for such an explanation came from the human and social capital of the small business manager. Given that entrepreneurship exists at the nexus of the individual and the opportunity, the previous chapter's investigation of opportunity discovery and exploitation was of critical importance for increasing our understanding of entrepreneurial small businesses.

Although human capital can be thought of as reflecting the knowledge-based resources of the small business manager, they do not necessarily reflect the knowledge-based resources of the small business. To gain a deeper understanding of the relationship between knowledge-based resources and small business performance, we need to change gear slightly and focus on the resources of the small business rather than of its manager. To achieve this focus we take a more strategic management perspective. In fact, the resource-based view (RBV) used in the previous chapter has traditionally focused on the resources of the business and how characteristics of those resources can be the basis for a sustainable competitive advantage.

Specifically, businesses with valuable, rare and inimitable resources (and resource bundles) have the potential of achieving superior performance (for example, Barney, 1991; Wernerfelt, 1984).[2] A bundle of resources is (1) *valuable* when it enables the small business to pursue opportunities, neutralize threats, and offer products and services to the market that are valued by customers, (2) *rare* when it is possessed by few, if any, (potential) competitors, and (3) *inimitable* when it is difficult and or costly for (potential) competitors to replicate this combination of resources (Hitt et al., 1999). Knowledge-based resources often meet these criteria. Knowledge-based resources are the ways in which firms combine and transform their tangible resources (Galunic and Rodan, 1998; Teece et al., 1997), where tangible resources (also known as property-based resources) can be thought of as those inputs to production that a person can touch, such as plant and equipment, cash, a prime retail location, etc. Although tangible resources can lead to a sustainable competitive advantage, there has been considerable interest in knowledge-based resources because these resources are required to make best use of the tangible resources and are themselves a source of sustainable competitive advantage. As we will explain later in the chapter, knowledge-based resources are often valuable, rare and inimitable.

But is that enough? Are those small businesses that have knowledge-based resources that are valuable, rare, and inimitable the ones that have superior performance and those small businesses with inferior quality resources likely to be at a competitive disadvantage and suffer poor performance? Developing the so-called VRIO framework, Barney (1991, 1995) notes that a firm's resources should not only be *valuable*, *rare*, and *inimitable* to facilitate superior performance, but the firm must also have an appropriate *organization* in place to take advantage of these resources. For example, Xerox was unable to maintain superior performance despite having the knowledge and other resources for developing the first menu-based operating system, because it lacked an organization that promoted entrepreneurial initiatives. Thus, it was unable to turn its valuable, rare and inimitable resources into a competitive advantage, because the organization failed to utilize its resources effectively (Barney, 1995). In a similar vein, Eisenhardt and Martin (2000), drawing on the concept of dynamic capabilities, argue that in addition to the resources themselves, the organizational and strategic processes of firms are important because they facilitate the manipulation of resources into value-creating strategies.

On the one hand, resource-based empirical studies have mainly focused on the direct link between individual strands or configurations of resources and performance, while less attention has been devoted to how small business managers can utilize these resources more effectively (Helfat, 2000). That is, using the VRIO terminology, there has been little consideration of the inter-relationship between a firm's organization ('O') and its resources ('VRI') in explaining performance. Scholars of the resource-based view have focused on the 'VRI' and relatively ignored the 'O'. The limited evidence that exists, however, suggests that this inter-relationship is important: management can respond to new opportunities and environmental changes by taking actions that affect the small business's resource-base and how those resources are utilized (Cockburn, et al., 2000).

On the other hand, entrepreneurship scholars have attempted to explain performance by investigating a firm's entrepreneurial orientation (EO). EO refers to a firm's strategic orientation, capturing specific entrepreneurial aspects of decision making styles, methods, and practices (Lumpkin and Dess, 1996). Given the importance of entrepreneurship to firm performance (McGrath et al., 1996), EO could be an important measure of the way a firm is organized, one that enhances the performance benefit of a firm's knowledge-based resources by focusing attention on the utilization of these resources to discover and exploit opportunities. Thereby, EO can explain, in part, the managerial processes that allow some small businesses to be ahead of the competition because EO facilitates firm action based upon early signals from its internal and external environments (see Cockburn et al., 2000; Lumpkin and Dess, 1996).

Although we have considerable understanding of the independent effect of EO on performance (for example, Wiklund, 1999; Zahra and Covin, 1995) and its contingent relationship with the external environment (Covin and Slevin, 1989; Namen and Slevin, 1993; Zahra, 1993b) (which is addressed in the next chapter), we are only now starting to gain a deeper understanding of how characteristics internal to the small business impact on the relationship between EO and performance. It appears, therefore, that EO scholars have focused on how the firm is organized ('O') to undertake entrepreneurial endeavors, leaving resources internal to the firm ('VRI') aside.

By bringing the resource-based and EO perspectives together, this chapter provides a deeper understanding of how a bundle of knowledge-based resources applicable to the discovery and exploitation of opportunities improves small business performance. As we will demonstrate below, a small business's EO enhances the positive performance benefits of knowledge-based resources. In this chapter, we apply a resource-based perspective to gain a deeper understanding of the inter-relationship between knowledge-based resources and EO in explaining small business performance. First, we present the resource-based perspective and highlight the importance of knowledge in explaining performance, introduce the notion of strategic orientation and the importance of EO in explaining performance, both of which lead to proposed relationships concerning how knowledge-based resources and EO interact in explaining small business performance. Second, we introduce the sample and the results of our empirical test of these proposed relationships. Finally, we discuss the results and implications of this chapter for both scholars and practitioners.

KNOWLEDGE-BASED RESOURCES AND PERFORMANCE

Organizational knowledge is an important bundle of intangible resources that can be the source of a sustainable competitive advantage (Hitt et al., 1999).

In fact, it has been argued that knowledge has the greatest ability of all resources to serve as a source of differentiation from one's competitors over an extended period of time. Following Gupta and Govindarajan (2000), we focus on procedural knowledge as opposed to declarative knowledge (Lesgold, 1988). Procedural knowledge refers to knowing the procedures for how to do things, such as knowing how to build a prototype of a new machine, and typically arises from previous experience with similar situations (Lesgold, 1988). Whereas, declarative knowledge refers to explicit or codified knowledge such as financial results and operational data. Unlike declarative knowledge, procedural knowledge is difficult to formalize and articulate (Nonaka and Takeuchi, 1995) and difficult to transfer from one organizational context to another. Therefore, procedural knowledge meets the resource-based view's requirements of being rare and inimitable. If procedural knowledge is also valuable and organized, it can be the source of a sustainable competitive advantage.

A small business's knowledge about markets and technology represent two strands of procedural knowledge that potentially have strong performance implications (Cohen and Levinthal, 1990), because, we argue, they increase the ability of a firm to discover and exploit opportunities. Market knowledge refers to knowledge of distribution channels, product applications, and customer preferences, expectations, needs and wants (Von Hippel, 1994). Important prior knowledge about markets might include information about supplier relationships, sales techniques, or capital equipment requirements that differ across markets (Von Hippel, 1988). This type of knowledge can increase a small business's ability to discover and exploit opportunities because the locus of innovation often lies with the user of a new technology; users cannot easily articulate their needs for not-yet-developed solutions to problems, and therefore the organization must share some of the same tacit knowledge as its users (Cohen and Levinthal, 1990; Shane, 2000; Von Hippel, 1994). In support of this, Shane (2000) found that prior knowledge of customer problems and ways to serve the market influenced the discovery of solutions to customer problems. Those who lack customer familiarity (Shane, 2000; Von Hippel, 1988) and knowledge of ways to serve the market (Shane, 2000) will find it difficult to recognize solutions to customer needs and to formulate an effective marketing strategy to introduce and sell the new product/service. For example, one small business manager made the following observation:

> For us it's been identifying a major weakness in some of our marketing areas and improving it to a point where we've virtually taken over the market. We had a weakness in a certain area and we've really attacked that area by offering better services, and we've literally captured the market, because no-one else was willing to look at the market and take it on. I guess that we just listened to our customers

and thought a lot about it – it wasn't as though we had a grand plan to do what we've done, it's just that there was obviously a market there. It's not one we would have expected to find either. (Cameron, 2003)

Technological knowledge can also enhance the discovery and exploitation of opportunities. Sometimes knowledge can lead to a technological break-through that represents an opportunity despite its market applicability not being readily apparent. (Abernathy and Utterback, 1978; Rosenberg, 1982; Clark, 1985). The following quotation from Afuah (2003) demonstrate technologies without an obvious market:

- 'This "telephone" has too many shortcomings to be seriously considered as a means of communication. The device is inherently of no value to us' (Western Union internal memo, 1876).
- 'I think there is a world market of maybe five computers' (Thomas Watson, Chairman of IBM, 1943).
- 'The concept is interesting and well-formed, but in order to earn better than a "C," the idea must be feasible' (A Yale University management professor in response to Fred Smith's paper proposing a reliable overnight delivery service, that is, the Federal Express).
- 'I personally didn't see anything useful in it [the personal computer], so we never gave it a second thought' (A recollection of former Intel Chairman Gordon Moore (of Moore's law fame)).

Technological knowledge can also enhance a firm's ability to exploit an opportunity effectively by, for example, determining the product's optimal design to optimize functionality, cost, and reliability (Dixon and Duffey, 1990; Rosenberg, 1994) and ultimately the economic impact of exploiting the opportunity (Kline and Rosenberg, 1986; McEvily and Chakravarthy, 2002). Therefore, technological knowledge provides a firm with the ability to rapidly exploit opportunities, or to be able to respond quickly when competitors make technological advancements (Cohen and Levinthal, 1990). From the above, it appears that market and technological knowledge, taken together, represent important knowledge-based resources applicable to a small business's ability to discover and exploit opportunities. Such an ability can help businesses survive and prosper (Hamel and Prahalad, 1989; McGrath et al., 1996). Thus:

Proposed relationship 4.1: *A bundle of knowledge-based resources applicable to the discovery and exploitation of opportunities is positively related to small business performance.*

ENTREPRENEURIAL ORIENTATION AND PERFORMANCE

Several researchers have agreed that EO is a combination of three dimensions: innovativeness, proactiveness and risk-taking (for example, Covin and Slevin, 1989, 1990, 1991; Miller, 1983; Namen and Slevin, 1993; Wiklund, 1999; Zahra and Covin, 1995; Zahra, 1993b). The innovativeness dimension of EO reflects a tendency to support new ideas, novelty, experimentation and creative processes, thereby departing from established practices and technologies (Lumpkin and Dess, 1996). Innovative companies, creating and introducing new products and technologies, can generate extraordinary economic performance and have even been described as the engines of economic growth (Brown and Eisenhardt, 1995; Schumpeter, 1934).

The proactiveness dimension of EO reflects a posture of anticipating and acting on future wants and needs in the marketplace (Lumpkin and Dess, 1996). Proactive companies can create first-mover advantages, target premium market segments, charge high prices and 'skim' the market ahead of competitors (Zahra and Covin, 1995). They can use their first mover advantages to control the market by dominating distribution channels and establishing brand recognition (Shepherd and Shanley, 1998).

Risk-taking is associated with a willingness to commit large amounts of resources to projects where the cost of failure may be high (Miller and Friesen, 1978). It also implies committing resources to projects where the outcomes are unknown. It largely reflects the organization's willingness to break away from the tried-and-true and venture into the unknown. While tried-and-true strategies may lead to high mean performance, risky strategies leading to performance variation may be more profitable in the long run (March, 1991; McGrath, 2001).

The above suggests that businesses that have an EO are more prone to focus attention and effort towards opportunities. There is reason to believe that EO has positive performance implications for the small business. A general tendency in today's business environment is the shortening of product and business model lifecycles (Hamel, 2000). Consequently, the future profit streams from existing operations are uncertain and businesses need constantly to seek out new opportunities. An EO can assist companies in such a process. Previous empirical results provide support for a positive relationship between EO and performance (Wiklund, 1999; Zahra and Covin, 1995). Thus:

Proposed relationship 4.2: *EO is positively related to small business performance.*

KNOWLEDGE-BASED RESOURCES, ENTREPRENEURIAL ORIENTATION AND PERFORMANCE

As discussed above, EO refers to a firm's strategic orientation, capturing specific entrepreneurial aspects of decision making styles, methods, and practices. As such, it reflects how a firm operates rather than what it does (Lumpkin and Dess, 1996). Applied to the VRIO framework, EO represents how the numerous components of a small business are organized in order to discover and exploit opportunities: the higher the EO, the better prepared a small business is for the discovery and exploitation of opportunities. From resource-based theory, the way that a small business is organized, when combined with firm resources, can enhance the positive relationship between resources and firm performance (Barney, 1995). Therefore we argue that EO captures a small business's organization toward entrepreneurship and can enhance other firm resources.

In the first section of this chapter, we proposed a positive relationship between knowledge-based resources applicable to the discovery and exploitation of opportunities and small business performance. We propose that a small business well endowed with these resources will perform even better if it has an EO, that is, the methods, practices, and managers with a decisionmaking style that promote a willingness to capitalize on its knowledge-based resources by engaging in entrepreneurial activities. Small businesses with considerable knowledge-based resources know where to look for opportunities (Cohen and Levinthal, 1990), can more accurately assess the value of potential opportunities (Venkataraman, 1997; Shane, 2000), and have the ability to extract value from these opportunities (Cohen and Levinthal, 1990; Kogut and Zander, 1992; Teece et al., 1997), but unless the small business is willing to grasp and enthusiastically pursue these opportunities, then the knowledge-based resources are likely to be underutilized.[3] Thus:

Proposed relationship 4.3: *Entrepreneurial orientation enhances the positive relationship that a bundle of knowledge-based resources has with small business performance.*

In sum, the relationships stated above propose that knowledge-based resources have a positive relationship with small business performance but this relationship is further enhanced if the small business has a high EO. Although there is theoretical support for these relationships and some empirical support, it is important to conduct a thorough empirical analysis of these relationships. In the next section we will summarize our sample and report the results of our study. We realize that some readers will be less interested in this academic side of the book, and to them we suggest that they skip the next section. Other readers might be interested in more details about the research method; we refer these readers to the appendix of this chapter, which contains a description of the variables and their measures. A more technical description of the sample and results can be found in Wiklund and Shepherd (2003b).

SAMPLE AND RESULTS

Sample

We use a sample of Swedish small and medium sized businesses. The sample was stratified using the following criteria: (1) industrial sector divided into three groups based on ISIC codes (manufacturing, wholesale/retail and services); (2) employment size class, divided into two groups (10–49, 50–249, following the European Union's cutoff for small and medium sized enterprises, respectively); and (3) corporate governance, divided into three groups (independent firms, members of company groups with fewer that 250 employees, and members of company groups with 250 employees or more). The sampling population consisted of 2455 firms whose names and addresses were obtained from Statistics Sweden (the Bureau of Census). The target respondent was the CEO.

In 1997, data for the study's independent and control variables were collected. Three years later (2000), data for the dependent variables were collected. To collect these data, the small business managers were contacted by telephone in 1997, and there were 2034 responses. Shortly thereafter, all small business managers interviewed were sent a mail survey, generating 1278 responses. In 2000, businesses that responded to the 1997 telephone interview were contacted again for another telephone interview and a mail questionnaire. By then, 240 businesses had ceased to exist. Of those 1794 still in business, 1647 responded to the telephone interview and 827 also completed the mail questionnaire. Due to mergers and acquisitions and other ownership changes, we disqualified 218 small businesses because the nature of the firm could not be considered 'the same' as it was in 1997. Furthermore, 225 individuals who responded to the mail questionnaire in 2000 did not respond to the 1997 mail questionnaire. Because the research variables mainly appear in the two mail questionnaires, the responses from these individuals were incomplete and could not be used, leaving a sample size of 384.

Analysis and Results

The proposed relationships from above were tested using hierarchical regression analysis and the results are displayed in Table 4.1. The control variables were first entered as a base model reported in column two. This model explains a statistically significant share of the variance in small business performance. In the next step, the independent (main) effects of the bundle of knowledge-based resources and EO were entered. The results are reported in column three of the table. The main effects model makes a significant contribution over and above the base model in explaining small

Table 4.1   *Independent and contingency models of knowledge, EO and small business performance*

	Base model		Independent model		Contingency model	
	Coefficient	*t*-statistic	Coefficient	*t*-statistic	Coefficient	*t*-statistic
Control variables						
Heterogeneity	03	0.55				
Munificence	13*	2.44				
Firm age	01	0.25				
Firm size	04	−1.55				
Past per- formance	22***	4.36				
Manu- facturing	−10	−1.55				
Service	−11	−1.61				
Main effect variables						
EO			20***	3.72		
Knowledge			28***	5.45		
Interaction						
Knowledge × EO					94**	3.33
Model						
R^2	0.09		0.21		0.23	
Adj. R^2	0.07***		0.19***		0.21***	
F-statistic		5.11		11.04		11.31
Change in R^2			12***		02**	
Change in *F*				29.10		11.08

Notes:
Standardized regression coefficients are displayed in the Table.
* = $p < 0.05$; ** = $p < 0.01$; *** = $p < 0.001$; $n = 384$.

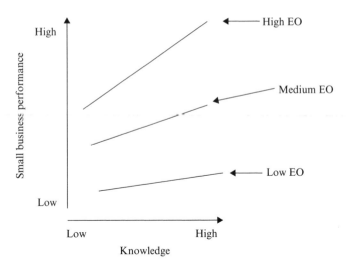

Figure 4.1   Interaction of knowledge and EO on small business
*   performance*

business performance. There is a positive and statistically significant coefficient for both knowledge-based resources and for EO. The first finding provides support for proposed relationship 4.1, namely, *A bundle of knowledge-based resources applicable to the discovery and exploitation of opportunities is positively related to small business performance.* The second finding provides support for relationship 4.2, namely, *EO is positively related to small business performance.*

As displayed in column four of the table, the addition of the interaction term for knowledge-based resources and EO makes a significant contribution over and above that of the main-effects-only model. Based on the regression coefficients provided by the analysis, we plotted the effect of the bundle of knowledge-based resources on small business performance for values of EO set at the mean and at one standard deviation above and below the mean, as suggested by Cohen and Cohen (1983). As illustrated in Figure 4.1, the nature of this interaction provides support for proposed relationship 4.3: *Entrepreneurial orientation enhances the positive relationship that a bundle of knowledge-based resources has with small business performance.*

A Summary of Key Findings

This chapter's proposed relationships and those that were found in our study are reported in Table 4.2. While we can say that those small businesses with

Table 4.2   A summary of proposed relationships and levels of support

Proposed relationship	Support?
4.1: A bundle of knowledge-based resources applicable to the discovery and exploitation of opportunities is positively related to small business performance.	Yes
4.2: Entrepreneurial orientation is positively related to small business performance.	Yes
4.3: Entrepreneurial orientation enhances the positive relationship that a bundle of knowledge-based resources has with small business performance.	Yes

more knowledge-based resources applicable to the discovery and exploitation of opportunities perform better than those with less knowledge-based resources, this general statement appears a little too simplistic. Similarly, while we can say that those small businesses that are more entrepreneurial in their orientation the better they perform, this general statement also appears too simplistic. A deeper understanding of small business performance arises from the concomitant consideration of this bundle of knowledge-based resources and EO. That is, EO enhances (magnifies) the positive relationship between knowledge-based resources applicable to the discovery and exploitation of opportunities and small business performance.

IMPLICATIONS OF THE ROLE OF THE MANAGER'S MOTIVATION ON SMALL BUSINESS GROWTH

Practical Implications

This chapter's reported findings can be thought of as rules for explaining the relationship(s) between knowledge, EO and small business performance.

General rule of thumb 4.1: *A bundle of knowledge-based resources applicable to the discovery and exploitation of opportunities is positively related to small business performance.*

This general rule of the thumb is consistent with the resource-based view of strategy. In fact, given the importance of knowledge as a resource in explaining performance, scholars have offered a knowledge-based view of strategy. In this chapter we have taken that perspective but focused on those dimensions of knowledge that we believe to be the most relevant in understanding the performance of small businesses, that is, organizational knowledge relevant to the discovery and exploitation of opportunities. This bundle of knowledge-based resources does indeed have a positive relationship with small business performance: small businesses with a greater stock of organizational knowledge relevant to the discovery and exploitation of opportunities performed better than those with less such knowledge.

General rule of thumb 4.2: *Entrepreneurial orientation is positively related to small business performance.*

This general rule conforms to common managerial wisdom, and that is those small businesses oriented towards entrepreneurship perform better than those small businesses that are less entrepreneurial. The extent to which a firm was oriented toward entrepreneurship was captured by the EO construct, which is made up of three dimensions. That is, small businesses that are more willing to innovate in order to rejuvenate market offerings, take risks in order to try out new and uncertain products, services and markets, and to be more proactive than competitors towards new marketplace opportunities are likely to perform better than those less entrepreneurially oriented. As is common practice we aggregated the three dimensions to obtain one measure of entrepreneurial orientation. But future research could investigate the independent and inter-dependent relationship between these EO dimensions in explaining small business performance.

Qualifying rule 4.1: *Entrepreneurial orientation enhances the positive relationship that a bundle of knowledge-based resources has with small business performance.*

Although the general rules of thumb 4.1 and 4.2 are generally applicable, they are simplistic in their explanation of small business performance. This is where this qualifying rule comes in: it recognizes more of the complexity in the relationship. More can be understood about small business performance when EO and knowledge-based resources are considered concomitantly. That is, the positive relationship between knowledge-based resources and small business performance is enhanced when the small business has a high EO. Although a relatively simply qualification to the two general rules above, this relationship has implications for resource-based research as well as scholars studying the EO construct (which are discussed in greater detail in the 'implications for scholars' section below).

For those utilizing resource-based theory, our finding that EO enhances the positive relationship between knowledge-based resources and performance is consistent with EO capturing a firm's organization and enhancing the relationship between a firm's resources and performance. Thus, our empirical results are consistent with hitherto largely untested arguments that, over and above a firm's stock of resources, it is how management utilizes those resources that is important in explaining firm performance. More specifically, our results complement Cockburn et al. (2000) and suggest that EO can help explain the managerial processes that provide some firms the ability to utilize their resources to identify and respond to environmental cues earlier than competitors. Similarly, our findings provide empirical support for the VRIO framework in that a firm's resources ('VRI') and organization ('O') considered conjointly provide a more complete explanation of firm performance than these variables considered independently.

For small business managers, having a small business with considerable knowledge-based resources is likely to help improve firm performance but these resources will be underutilized unless the small business also has an entrepreneurial orientation. The flipside of the same argument applies, that is, an EO is likely to improve the performance of a small business but the full potential of that orientation will not be reached unless the small business also has considerable knowledge-based resources. Managers wishing to improve the performance of their small businesses might consider building up their knowledge-based resources, particularly those pertaining to the market and technology, and also consider undertaking a more entrepreneurial orientation (more innovative, proactive and risk-taking). Building one at the expense of the other is likely to be suboptimal; both must be built because they act in concert to improve small business performance.

Categorizing Small Business Performance Outcomes by the Business's EO and Knowledge-Based Resources

We conclude that attempts to explain performance in a way that does not take into consideration both the small business's orientation and knowledge-based resources are likely to have little success. That is, without considering the EO of the small business, we are likely to underestimate the performance of those small businesses that have considerable knowledge-based resources applicable to the discovery and exploitation of opportunities and overestimate the performance of those small businesses with inferior knowledge-based resources.

Based on the information in this chapter, we present a categorization of small business performance outcomes based upon the small business's

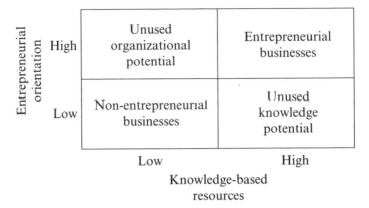

*Figure 4.2   Four classes of small businesses in terms of EO and
            knowledge-based resources*

level of knowledge-based resources and its entrepreneurial orientation.
Specifically, Figure 4.2 categorizes small businesses along two dimensions;
knowledge-based resources (applicable to the discovery and exploitation of
opportunities) represents one dimension, and EO the other. This 2×2
matrix represents a simplification of the findings presented in this chapter
but illustrates well many of the implications. Depending on their position
along these two dimensions, four classes of small businesses are identified:

1. Starting with the small businesses in the upper right quadrant, which
    both possess the knowledge-based resources to discover and exploit
    opportunities, *and* the organization necessary to pursue these entre-
    preneurial activities, we propose that these small businesses are the ones
    mostly likely to engage in *entrepreneurial activities*. These small busi-
    nesses have a good 'fit' between their resources and their orientation for
    utilizing resources. This is not to say that they will always achieve supe-
    rior performance: in fact the next chapter highlights the importance of
    also having a good 'fit' with the external environment.
2. In the upper left quadrant are the small businesses which have an
    unused organizational potential since they have the decision making
    style, methods and practices oriented toward entrepreneurship but do
    not have the key knowledge-based resources to discover and exploit
    opportunities. That is, the architecture is there for entrepreneurship
    but they are lacking some of the key input resources. To these small
    businesses we suggest that they can move to the upper right quad-
    rant if they can be 'entrepreneurial' in their acquisition of knowledge-
    based resources. This could involve hiring key personnel with a deep

knowledge of the market and with a tacit understanding of technology and to provide the organizations systems and processes to retain and build on this knowledge.

3. In the lower right quadrant are the small businesses which have an *unused knowledge potential* since these small businesses which have the knowledge-based resources for the discovery and exploitation of opportunities but lack the EO to organize them. To these small business managers, we suggest that they move out of this quadrant by changing strategic orientation to become more entrepreneurial and thus make better use of their knowledge-based resources. This means that the small business needs to become more focused on innovation, be more proactive in its approach and be more willing to take risks. Such a change might require a change in the small business's CEO. Alternatively, this small business could sell its valuable knowledge-based resources applicable to the discovery and exploitation of opportunities and acquire other knowledge-based resources more applicable to its strategic orientation.

4. Small businesses in the fourth category, are located in the lower left quadrant and have neither the knowledge-based resources nor the orientation toward entrepreneurial activities, and are classified as *non-entrepreneurial*. These small businesses may or may not have a 'fit' between their knowledge-based resources and their strategic orientation but most strategic assets erode over time as they are imitated by competitors (Shepherd and Shanley, 1998) and without entrepreneurial activities to offer new sources of advantage, long run performance is likely to suffer. These small businesses could acquire both the knowledge-based resources of discovery and exploitation of opportunities and an EO, but without one to spur the acquisition of the other such a change is likely to be difficult. We speculate that a change in EO should occur first and will likely require a change in CEO. With a more entrepreneurial CEO the reorientation of the small business can begin, followed by attempts to acquire and build the organizational knowledge necessary for entrepreneurial activities.

Implications for Policymakers

The practical implications of this chapter for policymakers are numerous. Returning to Figure 4.2, we are able to develop policy implications for each of the four groups identified in the figure. It should be noted that the policy recommendations tend to differ depending on which quadrant a small business is classified. Therefore, it is important for policy makers to understand which categories small businesses belong to and to tailor public policies for each category.

1. In terms of knowledge-based resources and an entrepreneurial strategic orientation, the upper right quadrant (*entrepreneurial businesses*) appears ideal. The important thing for policymakers is to ensure that more firms are able to reach this quadrant through suitable paths of development.

2. Firms with *unused organizational potential*, in the upper left quadrant, should be open to policy measures. The fact that these firms score high on EO indicates that they generally possess a willingness to pursue change. Thus, if they only realize that their deficits in knowledge-based resources may hamper their development, it should be possible to convince them of necessary changes. These changes mainly concern upgrading their knowledge base, which could be achieved by training existing staff or hiring new staff with the requisite knowledge. Small businesses are often reluctant to invest in training, so government sponsored training programs geared at marketing and technology have an important role in upgrading the knowledge bases of these businesses.

3. The *unused knowledge potential* category leads our thoughts to knowledge-intensive businesses located in close proximity to universities. Substantial resources are currently spent on providing the scientists of these businesses with training in the different functional areas of management. Our results suggest that knowing how to manage a business may be insufficient. Training programs should focus not only on managerial aspects but also on entrepreneurship. Alternatively, these businesses may be better off replacing scientifically oriented CEOs with those who are more entrepreneurial.

4. Small businesses in the *non-entrepreneurial* category may operate in environments where customer demands and the offerings of competitors are stable, thus requiring little innovation or specific knowledge of customers and technology. However, due to increased internationalization, shortened product life-cycles, and increased knowledge content across products and services, this situation is not likely to remain for much longer. An important role for public policy is to make these businesses aware of how the world is changing and the consequences of such changes for them.

Implications for Scholars

Our finding of a positive main-effects-only relationship between a firm's knowledge-based resources and performance is not necessarily surprising. However, our focus on, and operationalization of, knowledge-based resources applicable to the discovery and exploitation of opportunities is of particular relevance to small businesses. Despite the importance of knowledge to the entrepreneurial process (Hayek, 1945; Shane and Venkataraman, 2000) and the acknowledgement of firm-level entrepreneurship (Brown et al., 2001; Covin and Slevin, 1991; Miller, 1983), few studies have attempted to measure a firm's knowledge applicable to the discovery and exploitation of opportunities. We used a measure of knowledge-based resources that captured aspects of the type of knowledge previously found to enhance an individual's ability to produce entrepreneurial outcomes (Shane, 2000), namely, dimensions of market and technology knowledge.

We used a single construct of knowledge-based resources because our research question focused on the inter-relationship between a bundle of resources and an organization's orientation (we also found from a factor analysis that the items loaded on one common factor). However, given that measuring knowledge is of central importance to entrepreneurship research, there is a need for more scholarly attention to the development of valid measures of different types of knowledge-based resources applicable to entrepreneurship, such as separate measures of knowledge applicable to the discovery and to the exploitation of opportunities. We expect such work to draw heavily on entrepreneurship research at the individual level of analysis (for example, Shane, 2000) and organizational research on knowledge.

We have found that the level of a small business's knowledge-based resources can help explain its performance. This provides an indication that these knowledge-based resources are indeed valuable and possibly rare, but in order to determine whether they are also inimitable requires further investigation that considers the long run performance implications of these knowledge-based resources. We have focused on declarative knowledge which is believed to be more intangible, more difficult to communicate and therefore likely to be difficult for competitors to imitate. Specifically, we looked at the organizational knowledge of the market and of technology as there has been found to be a positive relationship between these aspects of knowledge and the discovery and exploitation of opportunities. But at what point does this knowledge become either less valuable, less rare, or cease to be inimitable? For example, over time the market and/or the technology frontier can change and the stock of knowledge based on the previous status quo is now less valuable; others might develop similar organizational knowledge and it is no longer rare, and over time this procedural knowledge becomes so well known that it becomes declarative in nature and therefore easily imitated.

These issues relate to how we investigate knowledge. Our understanding of entrepreneurial small businesses has increased substantially from investigating a firm's stock of knowledge. Important advancements can be made if we complement this understanding with investigations of the flows of information and how this impacts the stock of knowledge as well as the nature of the information contained in that stock of knowledge. DeCarolis and Deeds (1999: 954) use a bathtub analogy to describe the nature of knowledge:

> the 'bathtub' metaphor (Dierickx and Cool, 1989) illustrates the differences and connections between asset stocks and flows. At any point in time, the stock of water in a bathtub is indicated by the level of water in the tub. This stock of water is the cumulative result of flows. . . into the tub (through the tap) and out of the tub (through a leak). With respect to R&D capabilities, the amount of water in the tub may represent the stock of know-how at a particular point in time; current R&D spending is represented by the water flowing into the tub and the water leaking out illustrates knowledge depreciation over time. Flows like water coming and leaking out the tub may be adjusted; stocks cannot.

A model that captures both the stock and flow of a resource is likely to have greater explanatory ability (Dierckx and Cool, 1989; DeCarolis and Deeds, 1999). Therefore, we need to increase our understanding of the flow of resources (particularly knowledge-based resources) and the inter-relationship between the stock and flow. We encourage further research along these lines.

Our primary finding was that EO enhances the positive relationship that a bundle of knowledge-based resources has with small business performance. An implication of this finding for resource-based strategy scholars is that investigations of the relationship between firms' resources and performance should also consider its organization. We argue that the considerable body of research on a firm's strategic orientation (its EO) provides a construct and operationalization that allows for greater exploration of the way that a firm is organized for the discovery and exploitation of opportunities and when combined with the body of empirical work on firm resources, provides considerable scope for future research.

For EO scholars, our findings suggest that there is a contingent relationship between EO and characteristics internal to the firm. This finding provides support for Lumpkin and Dess's (1996) assertion that the relationship between EO and performance is likely more complex than a simple main-effects-only, and scholars benefit from considering the moderating effects of characteristics internal to the firm. Our finding of a contingent relationship between EO and knowledge-based resources complements those studies that have found a contingent relationship between EO and the external environment (see Covin and Slevin, 1989; Namen and Slevin, 1993; Zahra and Covin, 1995; Zahra, 1993b). Thus, an important implication for scholars of EO is the need to consider the contingent role of resources internal to the firm, specifically knowledge-based resources.

CONCLUSION

This chapter took an important step towards an increased understanding of the VRIO framework applied to the entrepreneurial context. That is, small businesses that have considerable knowledge-based resources applicable to the discovery and exploitation of opportunities are likely to perform better than those with fewer such resources but the positive performance implications of these knowledge-based resources is enhanced if the small business is also oriented toward their effective use, that is, it is entrepreneurial in its decision style, methods, and practices. Therefore, this chapter highlights the importance of a fit between a small business's EO and its internal resources. In the next chapter we further explore the interdependent relationship between EO and internal resources to explain small business performance but use a configuration approach to also include the external environment in the determination of 'fit'.

APPENDIX: VARIABLES AND MEASURES

In the text of this chapter we have summarized the sample and the results of the study. The section below details the variables and measures of the study and is directly from our paper published in the *Strategic Management Journal* (Wiklund and Shepherd, 2003b). This published paper provides some more details on the sample and results that are not included in the text of the chapter or in this appendix.

Variables and Measures

Performance
We ascribe to the view that performance is multidimensional (Cameron, 1978; Lumpkin and Dess, 1996) and that performance comparisons with competitors reveal important information (Birley and Westhead, 1990). Therefore, respondents were asked to compare the development of their own firm over the past three years relative their two most important competitors for ten different dimensions of performance (see appendix, $\alpha = 0.82$; item-to-total correlations 0.42 to 0.58). We used five-point scales ranging from 'much lower' to 'much higher'.

Our reliance on self-report data from single informants introduces the potential of common method variance. Therefore, we correlated this performance index from the mail survey with another performance measure collected during the telephone interview (see Robinson, et al., 1991). The items used in the telephone interview were identical to those for measuring past performance (see below for details) and the Cronbach's Alpha value was 0.82. The correlation between the two indices (performance measured by the mail survey and a different measure of performance from the telephone interview) was 0.53 ($p < 0.01$), suggesting that the correlation between the two underlying theoretical constructs, corrected for measurement error, is 0.65 (Cohen and Cohen, 1983), indicating that common method bias is not a major problem.

Knowledge
Following Gupta and Govindarajan (2000), CEOs evaluated the firm's knowledge position on seven-point scales in order to measure procedural knowledge. The scales measure the firm's knowledge position vis-à-vis competitors. We constructed an instrument containing eleven items pertaining to market and technological knowledge (see appendix; $\alpha = 0.84$; item-to-total correlations 0.46 to 0.62).

Entrepreneurial orientation
We used Covin and Slevin's (1989) version of the instrument, consisting of nine items ($\alpha = 0.75$; item-to-total correlations 0.33 to 0.50).

Control variables
The environment may affect a firm's performance regardless of its strategic orientation (Lumpkin and Dess, 1996) or its knowledge-based resources. We therefore control for environmental munificence and heterogeneity. The scale for measuring *munificence* was adapted from Brown (1996) and Dess and Beard (1984). It consisted of four items ($\alpha = 0.85$; item-to-total correlations 0.36 to 0.69). The scale for measuring *heterogeneity* was taken from Miller and Friesen (1982) and consisted of three items (one of their original items was dropped due to space limitations; $\alpha = 0.85$; item-to-total correlations 0.70 to 0.75). *Past performance* was measured by an index consisting of four items, comparing the respondent's company to its competitors. The items were net profit, sales growth, cash flow, and growth of net worth. The items had 5-point scales ranging from 'much worse than competitors' to 'much better than competitors' ($\alpha = 0.76$; item-to-total correlations 0.41 to 0.58). We also controlled for *firm age*. During the first telephone interview, respondents were asked what year their firms were founded, which was used to calculate firm age.[4] During the same interview,

respondents were also asked to state last year's sales figure, which was used as an indicator of *firm size*. *Industry* effects were captured by using dummy variables for the firms' main line of business (manufacturing, retail or service).

Performance

Rate your company's performance compared to your two major competitors concerning:

- Sales growth
- Revenue growth
- Growth in the number of employees
- Net profit margin
- Product/service innovation
- Process innovation
- Adoption of new technology
- Product/service quality
- Product/service variety
- Customer satisfaction

Knowledge

- Does your company have a weak or strong position in terms of staff with a positive commitment to the company's development compared to other companies in your industry?
- Does your company have a weak or strong position in terms of technical expertise compared to other companies in your industry?
- Does your company have a weak or strong position in terms of expertise regarding development of products or services compared to other companies in your industry?
- Does your company have a weak or strong position in terms of highly productive staff compared to other companies in your industry?
- Does your company have a weak or strong position in terms of expertise in marketing compared to other companies in your industry?
- Does your company have a weak or strong position in terms of special expertise regarding customer service compared to other companies in your industry?
- Does your company have a weak or strong position in terms of special expertise regarding management compared to other companies in your industry?

- Does your company have a weak or strong position in terms of innovative markets compared to other companies in your industry?
- Does your company have a weak or strong position in terms of staff educated in giving superior customer service compared to other companies in your industry?
- Does your company have a weak or strong position in terms of staff who like to contribute with ideas for new products/services compared to other companies in your industry?
- Does your company have a weak or strong position in terms of staff capable of marketing your products/services well compared to other companies in your industry?

NOTES

1. This chapter is based on: Wiklund, J. and Shepherd, D.A. (2003b).
2. Non-substitutability is a specialized type of inimitability (Barney, 1995).
3. Furthermore, the idea that the pursuit of opportunities is universally beneficial may be overly simplistic. For example, Miller (1990) argues that entrepreneurial type strategies are likely to be more successful when addressing customers that put a premium on innovation and unique services (for empirical support see Zahra (1993b) and Miller (1988)). Knowledge-based resources likely inform the appropriateness of whether or not to pursue a discovered opportunity, and in doing so, enhance performance.
4. It is worth noting that because our sample has a mean firm age of 32 years and a high standard deviation (28 years), there is sufficient variation that we can effectively control for the influence of firm age. That is, we can control for aspects of newness such as the liabilities of newness (Stinchcombe, 1965; Singh et al., 1986).

5. The small business's entrepreneurial orientation, financial capital and the environment[1]

INTRODUCTION

The previous chapter established the benefit to a small business from adopting an 'entrepreneurial strategic orientation' (EO). We found that more knowledge-based resources were associated with higher performance but that the relationship was particularly strong if the firm also had an entrepreneurial orientation. In this chapter we further explore under which conditions that an EO is particularly valuable. We do so on the basis of some conflicting findings in previous research (see Smart and Conant; 1994; Hart, 1992) and recent insights into why these inconsistencies may have appeared (Lumpkin and Dess, 1996). Our argument is that EO may sometimes, but not always, contribute to improved performance.

Conceptualizing the relationship between EO and performance, Lumpkin and Dess (1996) note the complexity of this relationship, suggesting that the performance implications of EO are context specific. That is, the strength of the relationship between EO and performance depends on the characteristics of the external environment as well as internal organizational characteristics. Therefore, it appears that the relationship between EO and performance may be more complex than a simple main-effects-only relationship. In the previous chapter we explored an aspect of the internal organizational characteristics when we found that the positive relationship between knowledge-based resources and performance was enhanced by an EO. As we will detail below, the relationship between EO, the external environment and performance has also been investigated. These studies have investigated some of the complexity in the EO–performance relationship but have they gone far enough?

The dominant approach to date has been to assume that EO is universally beneficial, or to rely on contingency models that capture the two-way interaction between EO and a characteristic of the external environment, or between EO and an internal organizational characteristic. For example, EO seems to have a larger positive effect on performance in hostile than in benign environments (Covin and Slevin, 1989; Zahra and Covin, 1995). Concerning internal characteristics, access to financial capital provides the resource slack necessary to encourage experimentation within the firm allowing it to pursue new opportunities (March and Simon, 1963; Bourgeois, 1981; Zahra, 1991).

Conversely, resource constraints may be associated with internal control and attempts to conserve the limited resources at hand, stifling entrepreneurial initiatives. Hence, resources appear to be relevant for enacting an EO. These examinations have started to generate knowledge about the situations in which an EO has a greater or smaller effect on performance. However, as argued by Lumpkin and Dess (1996), additional insights may be gained by concurrently assessing the joint performance implications of EO and *both* these sets of variables, in short by utilizing a configuration approach (in this case a three-way interaction) to investigate EO, aspects of the external environment and resources internal to the business. Configurational models thus represent alternatives to the universal effect and contingency models used to date. More specifically, in this chapter we explore the environmental conditions and resource endowments in which EO is most beneficial to small businesses.

The configuration approach argues that in firms, certain elements of strategy, structure, process and environment tend to cluster together to form configurations (Meyer et al., 1993). For example, firms with innovative strategies are likely to have organizational structures that are organic as opposed to bureaucratic and reside in dynamic as opposed to stable environments. Thus, in a large sample of firms, a relatively small number of configurations will arise where key variables are aligned. Performance results from both the consistency of structural and strategic factors (internal to the small business) and the congruence of the structural and strategic factors with contextual factors external to the small business. This implies that in order to be maximally effective, firms must have configurations that are internally consistent and that fit with the environment (Doty et al., 1993; Ketchen et al., 1993; Miller, 1990, 1996).

The above suggests that a configuration approach might provide an opportunity to gain a deeper understanding of the link between EO and firm performance. Following the recommendations by Lumpkin and Dess (1996), this article investigates the relevance of the configuration approach by comparing a configuration model of EO and performance to contingency models and a universal (direct effect) model.

The chapter proceeds as follows. First, we hypothesize a universal effect model to explain EO's relationship with small business performance, but then acknowledge that the EO–performance relationship is likely more complex than a universal effect model. We therefore test a contingency model (two-way interaction) and then move on to propose the benefits of a configuration approach over and above a contingency model and the universal effect model. Second, we introduce the sample and the results of our empirical test of these propositions. Finally, we discuss the results and implications of this chapter for both scholars and practitioners.

ENTREPRENEURIAL ORIENTATION AND PERFORMANCE

As introduced in the previous chapter, entrepreneurial orientation (EO) refers to a firm's strategic orientation, capturing specific entrepreneurial aspects of decision-making styles, methods, and practices. Miller summarizes the characteristics of an entrepreneurial firm as: 'An entrepreneurial firm is one that engages in product-market innovation, undertakes somewhat risky ventures, and is first to come up with "proactive" innovations, beating competitors to the punch' (Miller, 1983: 771). Based on this, several researchers have agreed that EO is a combination of the three dimensions: innovativeness, proactiveness and risk-taking. Thus, EO involves a willingness to innovate in order to rejuvenate market offerings, take risks in order to try out new and uncertain products, services and markets, and to be more proactive than competitors towards new marketplace opportunities (for example, Covin and Slevin, 1989, 1990, 1991; Knight, 1997; Miller, 1983; Namen and Slevin, 1993; Wiklund, 1999; Zahra and Covin, 1995; Zahra, 1993b).

Although previous research suggests that each dimension of EO can have a universal positive influence on performance, there is reason to believe that EO as an overarching construct can have universal positive performance implications.[2] A general tendency in today's business environment is the shortening of product and business model lifecycles (Hamel, 2000). Consequently, the future profit streams from existing operations are uncertain and businesses need to constantly seek out new opportunities. An EO can assist companies in such a process. Several empirical studies find support for EO's positive impact on performance (Wiklund, 1999; Wiklund and Shepherd, 2003b; Zahra, 1991; Zahra and Covin, 1995). It was also the results we obtained in the previous chapter when we analysed a different sample. Thus:

Proposed relationship 5.1: *EO has a universal positive effect on small business performance.*

However, this idea of EO being universally beneficial may be overly simplistic. For example, an empirical study found that EO was associated with performance among small firms operating in hostile environments but not among those operating in benign environments (Covin and Slevin, 1989). Lumpkin and Dess (1996) suggest that the performance implications of EO are context specific, so that the relationship between EO and performance depends on the characteristics of the external environment as well as internal organizational characteristics. Therefore, increased understanding of the association between EO and performance can be achieved through a configuration approach (Lumpkin and Dess, 1996; Dess et al., 1997). Empirical research supports the proposition that the effect of EO on performance varies across different types of external environments (Covin and Slevin, 1989; Namen and Slevin, 1993; Zahra and Covin, 1995; Zahra, 1993b) and resources internal to the firm (Brush et al., 2001; Wiklund and Shepherd, 2003b, described in the previous chapter). The subsections that follow argue for the value of the configuration approach and develop hypotheses concerning interactions of EO, the environment and access to resources.

A Configuration Approach to the EO–Performance Relationship

Configuration scholars argue that increased understanding of organizational phenomena, such as performance, can be better achieved by identifying commonality among distinct, internally consistent sets of firms than by seeking to uncover relationships that hold across all firms (Ketchen et al., 1993; Miller, 1996). Consequently, a deeper understanding of performance likely resides in uncovering the orchestrating themes and integrative mechanisms that ensure complementarity among a firm's various aspects (Black and Boal, 1994; Inkpen and Choudhury, 1995; Miller, 1996). Like an orchestra or a sports team, an investigation of the talents of the individual members might reveal some information about performance, but greater insight is likely to be gained by observing the individual members operating together and in a specific venue. The orchestra might be made up of very talented musicians but there is little 'chemistry' between them and/or with the venue (symphony hall or an open-air auditorium) and as a result the symphony does not live up to expectations.

The logic of the configuration approach rests on the premise that small businesses that are able to align certain firm attributes with the characteristics of the environment outperform other businesses (Ketchen et al., 1993). Those small businesses that fail to achieve such alignment will eventually be competed out (that is, they will go bankrupt or be forced to use some other form of exit). Thus, a limited number of configurations of firm and environmental attributes can be used to describe large proportions of high-performing firms (Miller, 1986, 1990, 1996). A failure to align these elements, however, will be detrimental to performance: a small business with a simple structure is likely to benefit from a niche strategy, but not from a cost leadership strategy (Miller, 1986).

Zajac et al., (2000) note that previous configuration research has tended to emphasize environment–structure–strategy relationships at the expense of examining how firms can use their strategy to align organizational resources with the opportunities and threats of the environment. This may be a shortcoming because matching internal resources with the environment is a fundamental issue in strategic management (Zajac et al., 2000). Because small businesses tend to be resource constrained (Storey, 1994) and vulnerable to environmental influences (Chandler and Hanks, 1994) it is likely particularly important for small businesses to succeed in matching their scarce resources with the environment. Therefore, we agree with Zajac et al. (2000) and assess configurations of EO, environment and resources.

Empirically, configurations can be represented by the simultaneous interaction of three or more variables (Baker and Cullen, 1993; Dess et al., 1997; Miller, 1988). In other words, the configurations we are interested in can be represented as the interaction of EO and elements of resources and the environment. Building our argument hierarchically, we first partial out two-way interactions and hypothesize how environment and resources respectively moderate the relationship between EO and small business performance. We then move on to propose the three-way interaction of these constructs.

The interaction of EO and the environment
Miller (1990) argues that entrepreneurial type strategies are likely to be more successful when addressing customers that put a premium on innovation and unique services. This is consistent with a dynamic environment. Dynamic environments are associated with high unpredictability of customers and competitors, and high rates of change in market trends and industry innovation (Dess and Beard, 1984; Miller, 1986). In such dynamic environments where demand constantly shifts, opportunities become abundant and performance should be highest for those small businesses that have an orientation for pursuing new opportunities because they have a good fit between their strategic orientation and the environment. In other words, we would expect the alignment of a high EO and a dynamic environment to have positive performance implications. A small business manager noted that it comes to performance: 'it's really about keeping an open mind about where you're going, and accepting diversity if you need to. So if you have to turn a corner sharply you can – because all of a sudden

you see a glimmer of light and you think "hello, no-one's looking after this little market area here"' (Cameron, 2003).

Small businesses more content with existing operations, however, are less likely to benefit from a dynamic environment, because market demand might shift away from the small business's products negatively impacting performance.

Empirical observations support this notion. Zahra (1993b) found that there was a strong positive relationship between EO and performance among firms in dynamic environments, whereas these relationships were largely negative among the firms present in static and impoverished environments. Similarly, Miller (1988) found that innovative strategies in uncertain (unpredictable and dynamic) environments were associated with higher performance. Thus:

Proposed relationship 5.2: *The positive relationship between EO and small business performance is enhanced when small businesses reside in dynamic environments.*

The interaction of EO and financial resources

The pursuit of entrepreneurial strategies requires resources. The strategic options open to a firm are broader, should more resources be available (Romanelli, 1987; Tushman and Anderson, 1986), and EO is a resource consuming strategic orientation (Covin and Slevin, 1991; Romanelli, 1987). Thus, an EO is fueled by access to more resources. Financial capital is the most generic type of resource and can relatively easily be converted into other types of resources (Dollinger, 1999). For example, access to financial capital makes it is possible to buy valuable equipment or pay high salaries to attract talent. Therefore, resource constraints in other areas can to some extent be mitigated by access to financial resources. Further, small businesses often face difficulties obtaining equity and debt financing (the subject of Chapters 6 and 7 respectively), putting severe restrictions on their development (Stanworth and Grey, 1991; Storey, 1994; Winborg and Landström, 2000), but small businesses involved in innovation and striving for high performance will have 'a very great need for financial resources' (Greene and Brown, 1997: 170). This is reflected in the venture capital industry that provides large sums of money to individual businesses, but typically only to innovative firms with the potential of achieving extraordinary performance (Zacharakis and Meyer, 2000).

As mentioned before, there are three dimensions to EO: innovativeness, risk taking and proactiveness. We now examine how access to financial capital should interact with each of these dimensions of EO in explaining performance. Financial capital provides firms with the slack to experiment with new strategies and innovative projects that might not be approved in a more resource-constrained environment (Cyert and March, 1963; Levinthal and March, 1981; Cooper et al., 1994). Financial slack fosters a culture of experimentation because it offers some protection for small businesses from the uncertain outcomes of those projects, facilitating experimentation with new strategies and practices (Bourgeois, 1981) including product innovation (Zahra, 1991). Thus, financial capital should stimulate a small business's innovativeness.

Risk taking involves making large and risky resource commitments, investing in untried technologies or bringing new products to the market, in the interest of potentially obtaining high returns by seizing opportunities in the marketplace (Baird and Thomas, 1985; Lumpkin and Dess, 1996; Miller and Friesen, 1978). Greater access to financial capital can mitigate the chance of risky projects becoming fatal, which has the effect of stimulating risk taking. Proactiveness involves withdrawing resources from operations and products in mature stages of the lifecycle and investing resources in new products and processes (Venkatraman, 1989b). Such a process requires reinvestments and should be considerably easier if the small business has greater access to financial capital. In summary, the successful implementation of an EO as a strategic orientation appears to require access to considerable resources (Covin and Slevin, 1991). Thus:

Proposed relationship 5.3: *The positive relationship between EO and small business performance is enhanced by greater access to financial capital.*

The configuration of EO, resources and the environment
Proposed relationship 5.2 above suggests a moderating role for the external environment, whereas proposed relationship 5.3 addresses the moderating role of access to financial resources. However, configuration research argues that firms which are configured on many dimensions perform better than those that manage to align on only two of those dimensions. To investigate this configuration perspective, we concomitantly consider the interaction of all three constructs: EO, environmental dynamism, and access to financial resources.

There is empirical research to suggest that in addition to the alignment of EO with resources and environment respectively, firms may benefit from aligning their resources with the environment. The value of different resources varies across environmental contexts (Miller and Shamsie, 1996). In dynamic and unpredictable environments, the value of physical and technological resources becomes uncertain. Rapid change in customer preferences or competitors' product innovation may render such resources obsolete. Therefore, in this environment, it may harm performance to commit large amounts of resources to long-term 'sticky' investments. Financial resources, however, are liquid and flexible, and can rapidly be directed towards new initiatives, should new opportunities arise. Thus, a configuration of EO, access to financial resources and environmental dynamism appears to be associated with higher small business performance.

Less effective configurations of EO are also conceivable. An EO in a dynamic environment may be detrimental to performance if the small business has only limited access to capital. Abundant opportunities, such as those that arise in a dynamic environment, are likely to be pursued by those small businesses with a high EO. But we know that this entrepreneurial behavior is resource intensive. What are the performance implications of acting entrepreneurially when the small business has insufficient access to financial capital to explore the viability of an opportunity effectively and/or insufficient access to financial capital to exploit the opportunity efficiently? We expect that performance will suffer. Similarly, the configuration of small businesses with access to financial capital and an EO towards utilizing those financial resources for entrepreneurial endeavors might pursue marginal opportunities when opportunities are not abundant in the environment, such as in stable environments. This would appear to be an unrewarding allocation of time, energy and financial resources that could adversely impact performance.

In summary, a configuration approach argues that small businesses can benefit the most from an EO when it is active in a dynamic environment and has substantial access to financial resources. That is, EO has the strongest positive effect on performance among small businesses in dynamic environments with substantial access to financial capital and the strongest negative effect on performance among small businesses in stable environments with little access to capital. This suggests the following configurational hypothesis:

Proposed relationship 5.4: *Small business performance is explained by configurations of EO, access to capital, and environmental dynamism.*

In sum, the relationships stated above propose that a deeper understanding of the relationship between EO and small business performance likely resides in configurations that consider the dynamism of the external environment and the small business's access to financial resources. Although there is theoretical and some empirical support for these relationships, it is important to conduct a thorough empirical analysis of these relationships. In the next section we will summarize our sample and report the results of our study. We realize that some readers will be less interested in this academic side of the book, and to them we suggest that they skip the next section. Other readers might be interested in more details about the research method; we refer these readers to the appendix of this chapter, which contains a description of the variables and their measures. A more technical description of the sample and results can be found in Wiklund and Shepherd (2005).

SAMPLE AND RESULTS

Sample

In testing these relationships we return to the sample used in Chapter 2. The exact number of small businesses in the sample may differ somewhat due to differences in internal non-responses. Briefly, the sampling frame was taken from the CD-ROM database UC-Select including all incorporated Swedish companies. We randomly sampled independent firms from four sectors: knowledge intensive manufacturing, labor-intensive manufacturing, professional services and retail. A total of 808 small business managers from the sampling frame were contacted of which 465 first responded to a telephone interview and then to a mail questionnaire. Half of the sample had between 10 and 19 employees and half between 20 and 49 employees, as stated in their latest annual report. These business sizes correspond to the European Union definition of a small business.[3] Data was collected on the independent and control variables. One year later, these 465 small business managers were again asked to complete a telephone interview, this time concerning only the dependent variable. Eighteen failed to do so, of which five had gone out of business. Thirty-four managing directors had been replaced during the period and were therefore excluded from the analyses. The final sample, therefore, consists of 413 small business managers (overall response rate of 51 per cent).

Analysis and Results

Hierarchical linear regression analysis was used to test whether the universal, contingency or configuration models best explain variance in small business performance. The results are reported in Table 5.1. We first added the control variables (results reported in column 2), then the independent variables (main-effects-only model in column 3), then the two-way interaction terms (contingency models in column 4), and finally the three-way interaction term (configuration model in column 5). The control variables

Table 5.1   Small business performance: universal, contingency and configurational

	Control variables		Universal model, control variables		Contingency model		Configuration model	
	Beta	Std Error	Beta	Std Error	Beta	Std Error	Beta	Std Error
Firm size	0.21***	0.02	0.16**	0.02	0.17**	2.44	0.17**	0.02
Firm age	−0.16**	0.01	−0.14***	0.01	−0.13*	−1.78	−0.13*	0.01
Manufacturing	−0.27***	0.73	−0.16*	0.67	−0.17*	−1.87	−0.20**	0.66
Service	−0.29***	0.80	−0.24***	0.73	−0.24***	−2.66	−0.28***	0.72
Entrepreneurial orientation			0.18**	0.04	0.45	1.56	1.03***	0.20
Environmental dynamism			0.12*	0.10	0.29	1.08	0.41	0.35
Access to financial capital			0.36***	0.14	0.64**	2.37	0.89***	0.54
EO × dynamism					−0.25	−0.60	−1.00**	0.02
EO × capital					−0.18	−0.62	−1.33***	0.04
Capital × dynamism					−0.17	−1.54	−0.16	0.01
EO × dynamism × capital							1.03***	0.002
R^2	0.11***		0.29***		0.31***		0.35***	
Adj. R^2	0.09***		0.26***		0.26***		0.30***	
ΔR^2	0.11***		0.18***		0.02		0.04***	

Note: Standardized regression coefficients are displayed in the table.
a = in the presence of higher-order interactions, the coefficients for the lower-order terms of the higher-order terms convey no meaningful, but possibly misleading information (Cohen and Cohen, 1983).
$* = p < 0.10; ** = p < 0.05; *** = p < 0.01; n = 413.$

of business size, business age, manufacturing, and service explain a significant amount of the variance in small business performance. The next step of the analysis shows that the universal influence of EO, access to capital, and environmental dynamism together offer an additional explanation of small business performance over and above the base model. EO and access to financial capital both have a statistically significant positive relationship with small business performance, that is, higher small business performance is associated with a greater EO and greater access to financial capital. The positive and significant coefficient for EO provides support for proposed relationship 5.1: *EO has a universal positive effect on small business performance.* A marginally statistically significant contribution was noted for environmental dynamism.

The contingency model does not significantly increase the amount of explained variance over the universal model, and none of the two-way interactions are statistically significant. Thus, the findings do not provide support for the proposed contingent relationship 5.2 (for EO, environmental dynamism, and small business performance) nor for proposed contingent relationship 5.3 (for EO, access to financial capital, and small business performance). However, the inclusion of the three-way interaction term, displayed in column five, does significantly increase explained variance over and above both the universal mode and the contingent models. This suggests a configuration of EO, environmental dynamism and access to financial capital, supporting proposed relationship 5.4, namely, *Small business performance is explained by configurations of EO, access to capital, and environmental dynamism.*

Based on the regression coefficients given by our analysis, we plotted the effect of EO on performance (considering the three main effects, the two two-way interactions and the three-way interaction term) for given values of environmental dynamism and access to financial capital. Values of dynamism and capital were set at one standard deviation above and below the mean, and we entered a range of values for EO, as suggested by Cohen and Cohen (1983). This gives us a total of four plots, as shown in Figure 5.1.

The nature of the interaction indicates that at low levels of EO, small businesses with a dynamic environment and considerable access to financial capital are relatively high performers. Those in a stable environment with little access to financial capital are the worst performers. All lines slope upwards, indicating that regardless of financial and environmental conditions, performance increases with increased EO. This provides additional support for proposed relationship 5.1, and validates the findings from previous research on the universal positive influence of EO. It is interesting to note, however, that while performance increases with increasing EO for all

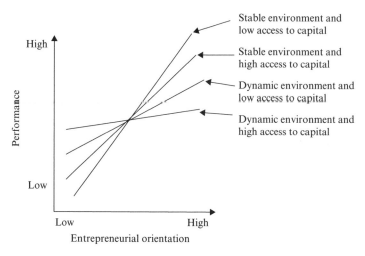

High

Performance

Low

Low   High

Entrepreneurial orientation

Stable environment and
low access to capital

Stable environment and
high access to capital

Dynamic environment and
low access to capital

Dynamic environment and
high access to capital

Figure 5.1   EO × environmental dynamism × access to capital

configurations, it increases at a faster rate for those in a stable environment and little access to financial capital than for all other combinations of access to financial capital and environmental dynamism. Performance increases with increasing EO at the slowest rate for those in a dynamic environment and high access to capital. These rates of increase differ so much that the highest performing configuration is high EO, low environmental dynamism and low access to financial capital.

A Summary of Key Findings

This chapter's proposed relationships and those that were found in our study are reported in Table 5.2. In this chapter we set out to explore empirically the explanatory ability of three models of small business performance: (1) a universal model which relies on the main effect of EO to explain small business performance, (2) two contingency models which rely on the two-way interactions of EO with both environmental dynamism and access to capital to provide additional explanation of small business performance, and (3) a configurational model which relies on the three-way interaction of EO, environmental dynamism and access to capital to provide additional explanation of small business performance. We found that the universal model provided some insight into small business performance, and the contingency models did not, but it was the configurational model that provided the best explanation of small business performance. We now discuss these findings in greater detail.

Table 5.2   A summary of proposed relationships and levels of support

Proposed relationship	Support?
5.1: EO has a universal positive effect on small business performance.	Yes
5.2: The relationship between EO and small business performance is moderated by environmental dynamism. The positive relationship between EO and small business performance is enhanced when in dynamic environments.	No
5.3: The relationship between EO and small business performance is moderated by access to financial capital. The positive relationship between EO and small business performance is enhanced by greater access to financial capital.	No
5.4: Small business performance is explained by configurations of EO access to capital, and environmental dynamism.	Yes

DISCUSSION

Practical Implications

General rule of thumb 5.1: *EO has a universal positive effect on small business performance.*

This general rule of thumb is the same as general rule of thumb 4.1 in the previous chapter. It is consistent with the widely held belief that an orientation towards entrepreneurship is of benefit to small businesses. For further implications of this finding we refer the reader to the discussion detailed in the previous chapter.

General rule of thumb 5.2: *Small business performance is explained by configurations of EO, access to capital, and environmental dynamism.*

The findings of this chapter suggest that an EO, that is, proactiveness, innovativeness and risk-taking, positively influences small business performance. Small business performance is also positively influenced by access to financial capital. However, relying on these main effect relationships provides an incomplete understanding of small business performance. A greater understanding can be gained by the concomitant consideration of EO, access to capital and environmental dynamism. While a contingency approach (two-way interactions) does not provide additional information over and above a main-effects-only model, a configuration of these three factors (three-way interaction) does. For example, an interesting finding is that when either a main-effects-only or contingency model is used, the role of environmental dynamism appears insignificant which is inconsistent with those that find dynamic environments can improve performance (Chandler and Hanks, 1994; Covin and Slevin, 1991; Zahra, 1993b). However, it is only when we use a configuration approach that we find the relationship between environmental dynamism and small business performance depends on the business's EO and its access to financial capital.

The results of the study summarized in this chapter are consistent with the finding of Dess et al. (1997) that a configurational model was more relevant than contingency models for studying the relationship between entrepreneurial strategy making and performance. The factors configured with EO here are different from previous studies and include constructs that we have argued to be important in explaining small business performance. Specifically, the results suggest that businesses facing severe constraints in terms of limited access to finance and a stable environment benefit the most from adopting an EO. In other words, an EO is not the luxury of firms in high growth industries with abundant financial capital, rather EO can be used to overcome environmental and resource constraints. In fact, firms in these situations can be superior performers if they have a high EO.

At first this finding is surprising because we would expect that the configuration of high EO, high access to capital and a dynamic environment would be associated with superior small business performance. However, this expectation is based on the 'traditional' view of configuration and strategic fit (Zajac et al., 2000). The emphasis in this literature has been on isomorphism, that is, on the notion that firms in similar environments exhibit similar configurations (Zajac et al., 2000). Firms that fail to adopt these configurations will be competed out and eventually disappear (for example, Meyer et al., 1993; Miller, 1990). Resource-based theory instead emphasizes differentiation, and suggests that differences in organizations' resources endowments explain differences in performance via competitive advantage (see Barney, 1991). Therefore, while our finding that EO in combination with minimal financial resources and a non-dynamic environment leads to higher relative performance may be inconsistent with the expectations of the 'traditionalist' view, it appears that instead it is consistent with resource-based logic. That is, EO may, under resource constraints and stable market conditions, provide more of a differentiation mechanism than it does in situations of resource abundance and market dynamism.

So while our findings are surprising from a traditional view of configurations and isomorphism among firms in similar environments, they can be explained from a perspective focusing on differentiation. Schumpeter (1934) argues that entrepreneurship is about creating new products, processes, sources of supply and so on that create disequilibrium in the market. It is the creation of a disequilibrium that allows these firms to be successful. It appears to be a high performance strategy to shake up an industry that is in equilibrium, that is, an industry that has a stable environment and businesses within it having only limited access to financial capital. EO provides businesses with the ability to find and/or discover new opportunities that can differentiate them from other firms and create a competitive advantage. Relevant to our results, Covin et al. (1990) found that EO had a stronger association with performance in low-tech industries than in high-tech industries. Similar to us, they hold that EO may provide more of a differentiation mechanism for firms operating under less favorable conditions. While an orientation is different from an organizational culture, Burt et al.'s (1994) finding that a strong culture is important in tough environments but is less so in attractive environments, and this provides some support for our possible explanation offered above.

What about businesses facing disequilibrium? When the environment is dynamic and investors want to supply capital, it appears that opportunities and resources abound. Under such conditions, we speculate the ability to find and/or discover new opportunities may be of little help. Rather than having an orientation of innovation, risk taking and proactiveness (a high EO), small business performance might be improved by a more inwardly focused orientation that better capitalizes on these abundant opportunities by focusing on efficient exploitation. The development of e-commerce may serve as an illustration. During the recent shake-out in e-commerce, the development of efficient logistics systems appeared to be more important than development of new innovative products and services or involvement in new risky projects.

Categorizing Small Business Performance Outcomes by Entrepreneurial Orientation, Environmental Dynamism, and Access to Financial Capital

In this chapter we carefully examine under which internal and external conditions an entrepreneurial strategic orientation (EO) appears most beneficial. We can conclude that regardless of how much financial capital a business can access, or how static or dynamic is the environment it operates within, businesses with a higher EO perform better. In a previous chapter (Chapter 4) we also found that EO had a positive impact on performance for businesses with high and low levels of knowledge alike. Thus, it makes sense for small businesses to invest in being entrepreneurial irrespective of other conditions. This being said, it should be kept in mind that EO appears particularly valuable under certain environmental conditions and levels of capital. For those small businesses that are in stable environments and have limited access to financial capital, EO not only compensates for that lack of these resources (opportunities and financial resources, respectively), but, in fact, can lead to a competitive advantage. It appears that EO fuels performance particularly in stable environments in which it is somewhat less dependent upon access to financial capital.

To give an overview of our relatively complex findings, we provide a figure. Specifically, Figure 5.2 categorizes small business growth along three dimensions. The first dimension is EO and is represented on the x axis by high and low. There is a box for low EO and a box for high EO. Both boxes are constructed using environmental dynamism as one dimension and access to the capital as the other. The y axis captures performance, only to the extent that the high EO box outperforms the low EO box, but does not capture the performance of the different categories represented by a cell within a box. We now list each cell in decreasing order of performance.

1. *Differentiators.* Small businesses that have a configuration of high EO but are in static environments and have limited access to capital are the top performers in our sample. We have labeled this group the 'differentiators' but could equally well have called them the 'disequilibriators'. It appears that EO is of most value when resources such as financial capital and opportunities are not abundant because the

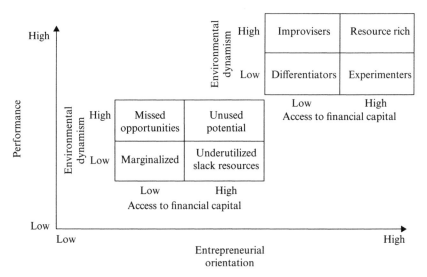

Figure 5.2   Configuration of EO, environmental dynamism, access to financial capital and small business performance

resulting entrepreneurial outcomes, such as new products and/or entry into new markets, provide excitement to an otherwise 'dreary' environment providing the business with a competitive advantage. This group of small businesses epitomizes the saying that 'necessity is the mother of invention' and it appears that in these circumstances the resulting innovations can have a considerable positive impact on performance. In a way, it is where we least expect entrepreneurship that it has the highest payoffs. EO can be used as a mechanism to overcome constraints imposed by limited access to financial capital and an environment where new opportunities rarely appear. It is under these conditions that managers really can benefit from being innovative, proactive and from pursuing risky new initiatives, thus differentiating their business from competitors. We must note here that our sample captures the survivors, and it might be that this configuration also has the greatest number of businesses that have failed: that is, high levels of EO under these conditions could constitute a high stakes configuration.

2. *Experimenters*. Small businesses that have a configuration of high EO, considerable access to financial capital and are in static environments experience high performance. Similar to the configuration above, this group of small businesses is able to use their high EO to differentiate themselves from competitors in a static environment but this group likely uses its access to financial capital to fund experimentation that generates entrepreneurial activities that are the source of their competitive advantages. Interestingly though, in these stable environments, greater access to financial capital does not provide an advantage to entrepreneurial firms. It could be that the extra money is used for projects that are unnecessarily extensive and tie up other resources within the firm.

3. *Improvisers*. Small businesses that have a configuration of high EO, limited access to financial capital and are in dynamic environments experience moderately high performance. Despite the fact that these businesses have limited access to financial capital to fund experimentation and exploitation of opportunities, this group of small businesses improvises with the resources that it does have access to and pursues opportunities: opportunities which abound in this dynamic environment. Limited access to financial capital might provide an important performance related function for entrepreneurially oriented businesses in dynamic environments, restricting the number of opportunities that can be pursued. Limited access to financial capital may force the small business to be more selective about the opportunities it pursues such that only those that show the greatest potential are pursued.

4. *Resource rich*. Small businesses that have a configuration of high EO, considerable access to financial capital and are in dynamic environments experience moderately high performance. These small businesses appear to have everything going for them: an orientation toward pursuing opportunities, the resources to pursue opportunities, and an environment in which there are a greater number of opportunities from which to choose; and while they perform well they are not the top performers. It appears that a stable environment and limited access to capital provide some important constraints on EO that direct the small business's orientation toward more profitable pursuits or where EO provides greater 'bang for your buck'. Stated differently, EO seems to have the smallest influence on performance for this category of firms. Given that an EO requires resources, these businesses may be better off turning their attention to matters other than being entrepreneurial. The development of e-commerce may serve as an illustration of a highly dynamic environment where access to financial capital abounded. As detailed in General Rule 5.2 above, the early stages of e-commerce development provides a rich example of a highly dynamic environment where there is considerable access to financial capital. Although with shake-out in this industry, importance shifted from the development of new innovative products and services to the development of efficient logistics systems. Small businesses in the resource rich category may need to institute some controls on EO. Because of their rich access to money and opportunities in the environment there are few restrictions on their possibility to be entrepreneurial and substantial entrepreneurial activities may lead them to become unfocused.

5. *Unused potential*. Small businesses that have a configuration of low EO, considerable access to financial capital and are in dynamic environments experience moderately low performance. Consistent with the findings of Chapter 4, it appears that having access to resources (internal and external to the business) enhance performance but are underutilized if the small business does not have a willingness to use these resource for entrepreneurial purposes. These small business managers currently benefit from their resource rich environment but over time one or both of these dimensions will likely change and these small businesses will move to one of the categories that follow.

6. *Missed opportunities*. Small businesses that have a configuration of low EO, limited access to financial capital and are in dynamic environments experience moderately low performance. Despite the fact that the environment presents opportunities to improve performance the small business is unable to take advantage of them: they lack the orientation to 'see' and/or 'pursue' these opportunities and this mind set is reinforced

as they have limited resources to be invested in experimentation. These small businesses are likely to be inward looking and their strategies inconsistent with their external environment.

7. *Underutilized slack resources.* Small businesses that have a configuration of low EO, considerable access to financial capital and are in stable environments, experience low performance. These small businesses have access to financial capital but do not have the orientation toward utilizing those resources for experimentation to 'shake up' the environment and differentiate themselves from their competitors. In this case, access to financial capital insulates the small business from environmental pressures and demotes experimentation. This means that the small business has little incentive or urgency to do something about their competitive position and likely blame the environment for their low performance, when in fact, we suggest that it is their strategic orientation that places a ceiling on their performance potential.

8. *Marginalized.* Small businesses that have a configuration of low EO, limited access to financial capital, and are in stable environments experience low performance. These businesses have little going for them: they lack internal resources, external resources, and the orientation to do something about it. We refer to them as *marginalized.* Of most interest here is that, while these small businesses are the worst performers of our sample, those small businesses with the same resource constraints (low access to financial capital and static environments) but an EO were the top performers. This highlights the importance of an entrepreneurial orientation, regardless of the resources at one's disposal. In fact, Stevenson and Jarillo (1990), defined entrepreneurship as the pursuit of opportunities regardless of resources controlled. Consistent with our findings, they argued that abundant resources in fact may limit the willingness and ability of the business to pursue new opportunities.

Implications for Policymakers

Our finding that small businesses with scarce access to finance operating in stable environments benefit the most from an EO and, given that they have an EO, achieve the highest performance of all types of businesses included in the study, has some interesting policy implications. First, it shows the importance of instilling an entrepreneurial spirit in society. Entrepreneurial spirit is often associated with the propensity of people starting businesses, but our results suggest that greater entrepreneurship has substantial value among existing small businesses. For some types of small businesses, more entrepreneurial attitudes and a willingness to innovate and take risks can have profound performance implications. Second, our results show that many businesses that operate in stable environments and not in new dynamic markets (and that therefore may appear less exciting) in fact may unleash a great unused potential should they be more entrepreneurial.

Therefore, it appears relevant to develop public policy programs focusing on assisting this type of small businesses in becoming more entrepreneurial. Building on the insights from research conducted on entrepreneurial orientation, this likely involves ensuring that the organization structure is decentralized, thus promoting that entrepreneurial initiatives are taken among the small business staff; that the market and technology knowledge of top management and other key employees is sufficient for discovering new opportunities; and most importantly, that the strategic orientation is focused on innovation, proactiveness and risk taking rather than conservatively focusing on existing activities. Of course, such a strategic orientation must be matched with an approach to resource allocation that does not risk the livelihood of the small business should new initiatives fail. Several authors (such as Stevenson, 1984) suggest that a gradual commitment of resources to new initiatives, where 'probes' are sent out into the market at early development stages, provides valuable information that can be used for making 'go/no go' decisions early on. That way, it is possible to try new initiatives in the market place without risking the whole business should the new initiative fail.

Sweden, where the data for this study were collected, provides an interesting case showing the relevance of an entrepreneurial orientation of 'traditional' firms. Only two Swedish businesses started since the Second World War have made it to the list of Sweden's largest firms. These are IKEA and H&M. Both these are retail businesses and both were built without any external funding. These businesses entered stable environments and relied on retained earnings only for their expansion. Nevertheless they were able to shake up and reformulate otherwise stable industries. It is thanks to their extraordinary entrepreneurial approach that they have become what they are today.

Another important implication from these findings is that for entrepreneurial small businesses, limited access to financial capital does not seem to be a major problem, while greater access to money appears important to less entrepreneurial businesses. Additionally, entrepreneurial businesses achieved higher performance than non-entrepreneurial businesses. Most countries have small business loan schemes or similar programs that assist small businesses. These schemes appear to be of particular value if they are linked to making non-entrepreneurial businesses more entrepreneurial. By becoming more entrepreneurial, these small businesses can achieve higher performance and expand more, which is valuable to society at large as well as to the small businesses themselves. The schemes are likely to be of less value if they are directed towards supporting those businesses that already have a high level of EO: such businesses can turn to market sources of funds to pursue growth opportunities.

Implications for Scholars

The findings of this chapter make a number of contributions to the entre-preneurship literature. While moderators to the EO–performance relation-ship have been investigated, access to capital and environmental dynamism has not previously been investigated together in a configurational model of small firm performance. Further, single indicators have typically oper-ationalized small firm performance. We operationalize small business per-formance as an index of seven commonly used performance measures pertaining to financial performance and growth. Moreover, most studies of EO and performance use cross-sectional designs. We use longitudinal data to empirically test whether an EO actually leads to better performance.

This chapter's finding of support for a configurational approach to small business performance suggests that scholars may need to pay greater atten-tion to both the joint and interdependent affects of performance predictors rather than a reliance solely on main effects or two-way interactions. We have statistically analysed three-way interactions to gain a deeper under-standing of this configurational approach but maybe it would be useful to go beyond three-way interactions and '[B]egin to identify some central themes that orchestrate the alignment among a great many variables' (Miller, 1996: 505). Several alternative methods to study multi-variate con-figurations have been suggested, such as cluster analysis of key variables (Miller and Friesen, 1984).

Our empirical results of the effect of configurations of EO, access to capital, and environmental dynamism on performance run counter to what was hypothesized. While we expected EO to have the strongest effect on performance in dynamic environments with substantial access to finan-cial capital, the effect was strongest in stable environments with less access to capital. This reinforces the notion of EO being a differentiator. Configuration scholars have noted that certain alignments among variables are more common (for example, Meyer et al., 1993; Miller, 1990, 1996; Miller and Friesen, 1984), but it may be that certain deviations from such patterns have positive performance implications.

CONCLUSION

In this chapter we find that while an EO positively influences small busi-ness performance, relying solely on this main effect relationship provides an incomplete understanding of small business performance. A greater understanding is gained by the concomitant consideration of EO, access to capital and environmental dynamism (three-way interaction). The nature of the configurations suggests that businesses that face performance constraints, in terms of a stable environment and limited access to capital, can be superior performers if they have a high EO. This finding is consistent with the saying that 'necessity is the mother of invention'. It appears that a high EO provides businesses with the ability to find and/or discover new opportunities that can differentiate them from other firms and create a competitive advantage. When the environment is dynamic and the firm has considerable access to capital, it appears that small business performance might be improved by a more inwardly focused orientation that better capitalizes on these abundant opportunities by focusing on efficient exploitation. The small business manager must simultaneously consider EO, environmental dynamism and access to capital. In the next two chapters we explore further the important issue of access to financial capital by first exploring the decision policies of venture capitalists (Chapter 6) and then by exploring the decision policies of loan officers (Chapter 7).

APPENDIX: VARIABLES AND MEASURES

Small Business Performance

In previous studies, growth is used as a proxy for business performance (Brush and Vander Werf, 1992; Chandler and Hanks, 1993; Fombrun and Wally, 1989; Tsai et al., 1991). Growth as a measure of performance may be more accurate and accessible than accounting measures of financial performance. However, a firm could, for example, choose to trade off long-term growth for short-term profitability (Zahra, 1991). We subscribe to the view that performance is multidimensional in nature, and it is therefore advantageous to integrate different dimensions of performance in empirical studies. To capture different aspects of small business performance, we combined measures of financial performance and growth.

For financial performance we used self-reported measures of gross margin, and of profitability and cash flow relative to competitors. Respondents were asked to state the previous year's profits and sales, and gross margin was calculated as the ratio of gross profits to sales. For the other financial performance measures, respondents were asked to estimate profits and cash flow compared to competitors on five-point scales ranging from 'much worse than our competitors' to 'much better than our competitors'. For growth we used four indicators. At each of the survey rounds, respondents were asked to state the previous year's sales and current number of full-time equivalents. Sales and employee growth were calculated as the ratio of the change in size between surveys (a one-year period) and the size at the time of the first survey. Five-point scales were used for the measures of sales and employee growth relative to competitors, anchored by 'much less than our competitors' and 'much more than our competitors'. The financial performance and growth measures were standardized and then combined (the Cronbach's Alpha for this global performance index is 0.70).

Entrepreneurial Orientation

Miller's original scale for EO consisting of eight items was used. These items are of the forced choice type, with pairs of opposite statements. A seven-point scale divides the two statements. In order to avoid response set contamination, the questions were arranged so that the entrepreneurial and non-entrepreneurial statements appeared on both the right and left sides. In the present study, the scale reports acceptable reliability (with a Cronbach's Alpha value of 0.64).

Access to Financial Capital

Financial capital is an important resource (Cooper et al., 1994) and it is not so much the ownership of the financial resources that is important but access to it (Stevenson and Jarillo, 1990). Previous research has argued that in order to be successful, new opportunities pursued should be in line with the existing resource base of the firm (Hamel, 2000; Hamel and Prahalad, 1990; Wiklund, 1998). Thus, if there are sufficient resources for the development of the small business then the manager will likely be satisfied with his/her access to this important resource but if there are insufficient resources for firm development, then the small business manager is likely to be dissatisfied with his/her access to financial capital. In this study we use a subjective measure of the small business manager's level of satisfaction with his/her access to financial capital. This measure is original and on a seven-point scale with the opposite statements 'insufficient and a great impediment for our development' and 'fully satisfactory for the firm's development'.

In order to establish the convergent and discriminant validity of this single-item measure, we followed the recommendations provided by Robinson et al. (1991). In the same questionnaire, respondents were asked to estimate the average profits over the previous three years, measured on a five-point scale ranging from large losses to large profits. Also, in a follow-up study conducted three years later, respondents were again asked to state their level of satisfaction with access to financial capital, utilizing the same instrument. The correlations between our access to financial capital variable and the two measures were 0.50 and 0.53 respectively ($p < 0.001$). Because small firms can have access to other sources of financing than retained earnings, and because access to capital may change over time, these measures do not tap the exact same variable, and much higher correlations could not be expected. Also, common method bias should be small because the items did not appear consecutively in the questionnaire and the format for asking the questions varied (see Lindell and Whitney, 2001). Therefore, we argue that these results indicate convergent validity. To ensure discriminant validity, we also correlated the variable with ten different variables of strategy and decision making that appeared on the same page of the questionnaire, utilizing the same type of opposite statements on seven-point scales. These correlations range from -0.07 to 0.07 ($p > 0.1$), which suggests discriminant validity.

Environmental Dynamism

Environmental dynamism was operationalized using items from Miller (1987). These four items are of the forced choice type, with pairs of opposite statements. A seven-point scale divides the two statements. In order to avoid response-set contamination, the questions were arranged so that the dynamic and non-dynamic statements appeared on both the right and left sides. The Cronbach's Alpha value of the scale is 0.69.

Control Variables

Businesses of different size and age may exhibit different organizational and environmental characteristics, which in turn may influence performance. The same is true for firms in different industries. Therefore, these variables were included as controls. To determine the industry, respondents were asked if the firm's main line of business was manufacturing, service or retailing. Respondents were then asked what year their firms were founded, which was used to calculate firm age. The respondents were finally asked how many individuals worked in the firm at the present time, including working owners and part-timers and to estimate the corresponding full-time equivalent number of employees. This variable was used to control for firm size.

NOTES

1. This chapter is based on Wiklund, J. and Shepherd, D.A. (2005).
2. Arguments have been raised that the dimensions of EO may, in fact, vary independently (see Lumpkin and Dess, 1996). However, the aforementioned studies all find that empirically, a single construct comprising the three dimensions can be constructed. Thus, we treat it as one joint construct. Further, it appears logical that the three dimensions should be closely related. For instance, a new company that comes up with a radically new product based on a technological innovation typically takes a risk, as the demand for the new product is unknown. Given that other firms do not introduce the same new product at the same time, it is also proactive in relation to competitors.
3. According to the European Union definition, firms smaller than 10 employees are considered microenterprises and those larger than 50 employees medium enterprises.

6. Venture capitalists' investment decision policies and maintaining a good relationship[1]

With Andrew Zacharakis

INTRODUCTION

From time to time it may be necessary for a small firm to turn to outside actors in order to receive equity or debt capital. It may be because a major new investment is needed and the business fails to generate sufficient cash flow. The preceding chapter (Chapter 5) highlighted how easy or difficult it is for a small business to access financial capital will affect its performance. This chapter deals with equity capital provided by venture capitalists (VCs), while the next chapter concerns debt capital from banks.

Obtaining equity capital from a venture capitalist is not easy because venture capitalists are selective in their investments and only choose to invest in those companies that they believe have the potential to generate very high returns. Venture capitalists have developed decision models that help them decide on which companies to invest in and which not to. Understanding these decision policies is important for small businesses because it can assist them in knowing whether they are attractive to venture capital investments, what potential changes they need to make in order to become attractive, and what information VCs evaluate in their investment decisions. In this chapter we first look specifically into what importance VCs place on leadership experience as well as some other characteristics of the potential portfolio company and how these affect their decision whether to invest in a small business. We then move on to examine the relationship between the VC and the portfolio company post investment. That is, we examine how trust can be increased in the relationship between the VC and portfolio company in order to facilitate good cooperation.

The resource-based view suggests that some businesses possess specific resource endowments that may lead to superior performance (Amit and Schoemaker, 1993; Barney, 1991). In short, firm resources can provide the basis for competitive advantage that enables firms to earn rents. As such, VCs can evaluate a business's potential by examining its resource assets. Fundamental to the resource-based perspective is the belief that those resources and capabilities that are valuable, rare, and costly to imitate (including non-substitutable) become core competencies and serve as a source of the business's competitive advantage over its rivals (Barney, 1991).

For a theoretical framework, we return to our elaboration on the resource-based view in Chapter 4 where we found that firms with valuable, rare and costly to imitate resources performed even better if they were also able to pursue a strategic orientation that was suitable for these resources. Here we argue that the strategic leadership of the top management team (the ability to anticipate, envision, maintain flexibility and empower others to create strategic change) is important to maneuver the business's resources, and thus achieve above average returns (Ireland and Hitt, 1999). For example, an experienced team may be able to utilize proprietary technology to establish a longer lead-time over potential entrants thereby earning higher rents (Shepherd and Shanley, 1998). Or, the team that has greater market experience should be able to best position the company to take advantage of an opportunity. Thus, we ask to what extent strategic leadership is critical to VCs' investment assessments and whether it is of equal importance in all situations or is affected by the resource endowments of the potential portfolio company. In doing so, we shed light on the managerial decision of a VC to invest in potential portfolio companies. First, we describe the importance of strategic leadership, and other decision criteria likely to be of importance in assessing firm performance, and hypothesize the moderating roles that leadership experience has on these other decision criteria. We test these relationships and offer a number of general and qualifying rules of thumb. Second, we move from understanding how VCs choose the portfolio companies in which they want to invest to gaining a deeper understanding of the nature of the relationship between small business managers (post investment) and VCs and how that relationship can be enhanced.

THE IMPORTANCE OF STRATEGIC LEADERSHIP

VCs appreciate that the resources of the potential portfolio firm can lead to superior performance, and the strategic leadership ability of the management team is a resource that can give the small business a competitive advantage. But how do people acquire strategic leadership abilities? While the process is complicated, we do know that the amount of experience people have affects the strategic choices they make and the models they use to make those decisions (Hitt and Tyler, 1991). The cognitive science literature suggests that experience is a good proxy for expertise (Choo and Trotman, 1991; Simon, 1985), meaning that experienced decision makers in a given task may indeed employ better decision processes than do less experienced ones (Nosofsky, 1987). Simon (1985) argues that it takes ten years to achieve '50 000 chunks of knowledge', which often add up to superior decision performance. Furthermore, as individuals become more experienced with respect to a particular task, they learn to focus attention primarily on the key dimensions (Choo and Trotman, 1991) and create categories of information based on a deep structure that involves more, stronger, and richer links between concepts (Frederick, 1991). Therefore, leadership experience is a valid indicator or leadership ability.

Just as in Chapter 4 we argue that leadership experience is complementary to other resources of the small business. Entrepreneurs bring together resources in unique combinations based upon their interpretation of the environment. The bundle is durable to the extent that it is a function of the firm's unique resource pool and to the extent that the market continues to value the bundle. We assert that leadership experience is more beneficial to the small business in the presence of these resources; that is, leadership experience is *complementary* because the value of leadership experience is greater in the presence of these resources than alone. Just as complementary resources increase total value, resources that are *substitutable* for each other decrease total value (Amit and Schoemaker, 1993). An example of complementary resources from sports could be size and speed. An ice-hockey player who is big has certain advantages, while a fast player has other advantages. But a player who is both fast and big is virtually unstoppable. Thus, if one player possesses both the size and speed resources, they are complementary.

The VC decision-making literature suggests that valuable small business resources include leadership experience, proprietary technology, market familiarity and previous start-up experience (MacMillan et al., 1985; Muzyka et al., 1996), but does not consider whether these resources are complementary or substitutable. Most of the previous VC decision-making literature views the criteria independently, as main effects (for example, MacMillan et al., 1985; Muzyka et al., 1996; Zacharakis and Meyer, 2000). It appears that environmental conditions also significantly influence the effectiveness of leadership (Pettigrew, 1987); but again the VC decision-making literature does not sufficiently consider whether environmental conditions provide the context for leadership and may serve as a moderator of the effects of experience on decisions. Therefore, in the following we develop an argument concerning the complementarity of leadership experience and other resources.

Proprietary Technology and Leadership Experience

The resource-based model proposes that proprietary technology can lead to a competitive advantage when it helps a business neutralize threats and/or exploit opportunities (is valuable); is not possessed by others (is rare); is difficult and costly to imitate; and has no strategic equivalents (is non-substitutable) (Mata et al., 1995). But ownership of proprietary technology is not sufficient. It is often difficult to protect a product's proprietary nature as competitors can hire away key individuals, reverse engineer the technology and so forth. Leaders must enable their organizations to exploit the technology in the market (Ireland and Hitt, 1999; Mata et al., 1995). The opportunity to exploit proprietary technology increases the firm's options, or strategic degrees of freedom. It is when strategic degrees of freedom are high that choosing the 'best' course of action has the greatest impact on business success (Porter, 1980; Quinn, 1980). Thus, strong leadership and proprietary technology are complementary resources.

Proposed relationship 6.1: *VCs value leadership experience more when the business's technology is more proprietary.*

Market Familiarity and Leadership Experience

As we showed in Chapter 4, intangible resources such as knowledge are valuable and a potential source of competitive advantage. We found that market knowledge was important for the ability to discover and exploit new business opportunities and affected performance. Market familiarity provides a good indication of the small business manager's ability to cope with changing market circumstances (Roure and Maidique, 1986). The more deeply entrepreneurs understand the market, the better they are at anticipating converging trends and opportunities, as well as competitor moves and threats. Combining market familiarity with leadership experience enables the small business to develop and execute an effective strategy. Leadership experience and market familiarity are complementary; together they increase the value of the resource bundle by making it rarer and more difficult to imitate (Amit and Schoemaker, 1993).

Proposed relationship 6.2: *VCs value leadership experience more when the business's market familiarity is high.*

Start-up Experience and Leadership Experience

We have also found, in Chapters 2 and 3 that start-up experience was important for small business outcomes and previous research suggests that VCs value such experience (MacMillan et al., 1985). Serial entrepreneurs better understand how to organize start-ups (Wright et al., 1997). By their nature, new organizations experience conflict and confusion in recognizing the tasks that need to be performed and allocating people to those tasks. Entrepreneurs with start-up experience understand these issues and have likely developed strategies to resolve them. Wright et al. (1997) found that 75 per cent of 55 British VCs preferred to invest in serial entrepreneurs because of their wider management experience, demonstrated motivation and proven track record. However, these authors call into question the value of start-up experience. They found that VCs did not report serial entrepreneurs as performing any better than first-time entrepreneurs did. Why this apparent discrepancy between studies?

There are a number of possible explanations. First, experienced entrepreneurs may attempt to repeat actions that were successful in an earlier business in new circumstances that are quite different (Westhead and Wright, 1998). Second, an entrepreneur's motivation to succeed may lessen, particularly if their previous business was successful (Starr and Bygrave, 1992). Third, serial entrepreneurs may not recognize their own limitations (Wright et al., 1997). Thus, it may be too simplistic to assume that there is a direct effect of start-up experience on business performance, such as growth. As we found in Chapter 2, experience had an impact on growth only in interaction with other variables (growth motivation). Based on this finding, we argue that leadership experience may enhance the power of previous start-up experience making it scarcer, more durable and more difficult to imitate than either factor separately so that start-up experience complements leadership experience.

> **Proposed relationship 6.3:** *VCs value leadership experience more when the team also has previous start-up experience.*

Environmental Conditions and Leadership Experience

An environment that can support sustained growth by a particular organization is described as 'munificent' (Castrogiovanni, 1991; Goll and Rasheed, 1997). Castrogiovanni (1991) distinguishes among three kinds of munificence: (1) capacity, or market size; (2) rate of market growth; and (3) opportunity, or resource availability in excess of industry usage. Highly competitive environments indicate low levels of resource availability beyond industry usage and therefore low munificence. The VC decision-making literature has found that VCs view munificence in terms of market size, growth, and competition as key attributes to consider in making their investment decision (MacMillan et al., 1985; Muzyka et al., 1996).

In a situation where munificence is low and, consequently, competitive forces are high, the firm is highly dependent upon the environment, and therefore a leader's strategic choices are severely limited (Hrebiniak and Joyce 1985; Lawless and Finch, 1989). However, where munificence is high and competitive forces are low, there are multiple means of achieving desired outcomes (Hrebiniak and Joyce 1985), and therefore a strong leader has more opportunity to influence a company's ultimate success (Goll and Rasheed, 1997). In essence, this suggests that leadership ability has a stronger effect on performance outcomes in munificent than in impoverished environments. As a consequence, to the extent that VCs are aware of this, we would expect that they place greater importance on leadership experience in environments that are more munificent.

We propose that the environment is more munificent when the target market is large and its projected growth rate is high. Large markets likely have a longer operating history. Hence, the problems ventures are likely to face are understood and easier to identify. In such a market, strong entrepreneurial leaders can use this information to make decisions that lead to superior performance. Less accomplished leaders may not interpret the industry as effectively. Growing markets, on the other hand, are forgiving. One or two bad decisions can be learning points. Thus, effective leaders can have a greater impact in munificent environments. If a small business can capture 5 per cent of a large market, it can derive significant sales often without incurring the ire of other market participants. And if the market is growing, new entrants typically go after new customers rather than those of their competitors. In a small market, venture growth is constrained not only by market size but also by competitor awareness. Thus, a leader's decision effectiveness is similarly constrained.[2] Thus,

Proposed relationship 6.4: *VCs value leadership experience more for markets that are (a) larger, and (b) faster growing.*

Proposed relationship 6.5: *VCs value leadership experience more when competitors are (a) fewer and (b) relatively weaker.*

Summary

We propose that interactions between leadership experience and other internal resources, and between leadership experience and environmental munificence, impact venture capitalists' decision-making. We propose that while venture capitalists always prefer greater general experience in leadership, they value it more highly for technology that is more proprietary, management teams with greater market familiarity and start-up experience, markets that are larger and faster growing, and when competitors are fewer and relatively weaker. Although there is theoretical and some empirical support for these relationships, it is important to conduct a thorough empirical analysis of these relationships. In the next section we will summarize our sample and report the results of our study. We realize that some readers will be less interested in this academic side of the book, and to them we suggest that they skip the next section of the chapter. Other readers might be interested in more details about the research method or a more detailed description of the results; we refer these readers to the appendix which contains the relevant information on research method as described in Zacharakis and Shepherd (2005).

SAMPLE AND RESULTS

Sample

This study uses policy capturing. It is an experimental research design that is similar to conjoint analysis presented in the next chapter. For more details see Chapter 7. As with conjoint analysis, policy capturing requires respondents to make a series of judgments based on a set of attributes from which the underlying structure of their decisions can be decomposed by means of hierarchical linear modeling. In other words, it is possible to determine which factors influence the VC's decision whether to invest in a potential portfolio company. The sample for this experiment was 41 practicing VCs from three entrepreneurial 'hotbeds', the Colorado Front Range (primarily the Denver/Boulder metro area), the Silicon Valley in California and Boston, all in the USA. The typical VC in the sample was male (90 per cent), 42 years old (range 29 to 72; s.d. = 11.7), had a master's degree (most likely in business), and had been a VC for 9 years (s.d. = 6.6). The typical firm for which the VC worked had $215 million under management (range $2 million to $5 billion; s.d. = $323 million), employed 14 investment professionals (range 1 to 65; s.d. = 16.6), focused primarily on early stage ventures, had been in business for 13.3 years (range 1 to 32; s.d. = 7.8), and invested $4.1 million per venture (s.d. = 3.9). This sample is relatively representative of the VC community in this US as a whole, although slightly biased towards the more successful, well-known firms. For example, seven of the ten top VC firms that invest in early stage deals, as rated on 10 metrics, are represented in the sample (Aragon, 2001) and the sample firms tend to be larger – $215 million versus $155 million for population (*Venture Economics*, 2000a, 2000b).

Results

Hierarchical linear modeling (HLM) was used to analyse the VCs' decisions. We generated both a main effects only model and a full model (one that includes proposed two-way interactions), the results of which are displayed in Table 6.1.[3] Presented in the top section of Table 6.1 are the

Table 6.1   VCs' assessment policies

	Coefficient[a]	Standard Error	*t*-ratio
Main effects only model			
Market size	0.20	0.06	3.413***
Market growth	0.23	0.04	5.39***
Proprietary technology	0.02	0.04	5.26***
Market familiarity	0.22	0.04	5.01***
Leadership experience	0.20	0.04	4.95***
Startup experience	0.02	0.04	0.521
Number of competitors	−0.34	0.04	−8.66***
Strength of competition	−0.30	0.06	−4.52***
Intercept	3.96	0.09	46.51***
Full Model			
Market size	−0.03	0.08	−0.416
Market growth	0.30	0.11	2.82***
Proprietary technology	0.17	0.05	3.08***
Market familiarity	0.29	0.06	4.69***
Leadership experience	0.41	0.12	3.48***
Startup experience	0.20	0.08	2.47**
Number of competitors	−0.49	0.07	−6.79***
Strength of competition	−0.10	0.09	−1.03
Leadership × size	0.27	0.07	3.88***
Leadership × growth	−0.10	0.12	−0.83
Leadership × prop. tech.	0.01	0.08	0.112
Leadership × familiarity	−0.13	0.09	−1.56
Leadership × start-up exp.	−0.22	0.07	−3.01***
Leadership × competitors	0.24	0.09	2.58**
Leadership × strength	−0.30	0.10	−3.05***
Intercept	3.96	0.09	46.51***

Notes:
a = All variables were standardized and group-centered.
** = $p < 0.05$; *** = $p < 0.01$; $n = 1900$.

coefficients (from HLM of standardized values), and corresponding standard error, *t*-ratio and levels of significance for the main-effects-only model. This indicates that VCs' prediction of success is higher for those ventures with more leadership experience, more proprietary technology, greater market familiarity, faster market growth, a larger market, and fewer as well as weaker competitors. From this main-effects-only analysis it appears that VCs do not use start-up experience in their assessments of business success.

The coefficients, and corresponding standard error, *t*-ratio and levels of significance for the full model are presented in the lower section of Table 6.1. In the full model, the significant variables are leadership experience, proprietary technology, market familiarity, market growth, and number of competitors, and some interactions were also significant. For internal resources, the interaction between leadership and start-up experience was significant. Start-up experience moderates the relationship between leadership experience and the VC's assessment of success. The form of this interaction is plotted in Figure 6.1 and indicates that while VCs always prefer more leadership experience, that preference is greater when start-up experience is low. It appears that start-up experience is a substitute for leadership experience rather than a complement as expected in proposed relationship 6.3.

Leadership experience interacts with market size, number of competitors, and competitor strength. The nature of the interactions is plotted in Figures 6.2 to 6.4. In all cases, VCs prefer greater leadership experience. VCs value leadership experience more when the market size is larger (Figure 6.2) and when the relative competitor strength is lower (Figure 6.4). These findings provide support for proposed relationship 6.4a and 6.5b respectively. For the leadership × number of competitors interaction, we proposed that leadership experience be valued more by VCs when the number of competitors is low. As shown in Figure 6.3 we found the opposite and therefore did not provide support for proposed relationship 6.5a. Leadership's interaction with proprietary technology, market familiarity and market growth were not significant and therefore did not support proposed relationships, 6.1, 6.2, and 6.4b, respectively.

A Summary of Key Findings

This chapter's proposed relationships and those that were found in our study are reported in Table 6.2 and summarized in Table 6.3. In this chapter we used theory from the resource-based view (RBV) of strategy to investigate VCs' decision policies when making their investment decision. A policy capturing experiment finds that VCs do indeed use a contingency decision policy, that is, they use two-way interactions. Specifically, we find

Figure 6.1   Start-up experience × leadership

Figure 6.2   Market size × leadership

that interactions between leadership experience and other internal resources, and between leadership experience and environmental attributes, impact venture capitalists' decision-making. Although venture capitalists always prefer greater general experience in leadership, they value it more highly in large markets, when there are many competitors, and when the competitors are relatively weak. Previous start-up experience of the venture's management team may substitute for leadership experience. We now discuss these findings in greater detail.

Figure 6.3   Competitors × leadership

Figure 6.4   Competition strength × leadership

DISCUSSION

Practical Implications

This chapter's proposed relationships and those that were found in our study (reported in Table 6.2) can be thought of as rules for explaining the relationship that leadership experience has with other attributes of the small business in the way that VCs assess the likelihood of business success. There are seen the following general rules of thumb.

General rule of thumb 6.1: *VCs value more highly those businesses with highly proprietary technology.*

*Table 6.2   A summary of proposed relationships, levels of support, and
the relationships found*

Proposed relationship	Support?	Relationship found
6.1: VCs value leadership experience more when the technology is more proprietary.	No	VCs value technology more when it is more proprietary and this value does not appear to depend on the level of leadership experience.
6.2: VCs value leadership experience more when the team's market familiarity is high.	No	VCs value market familiarity and this value does not appear to depend on the level of leadership experience.
6.3: VCs value leadership experience *more* when the team also has previous start-up experience.	No	VCs value leadership experience *less* when the team also has previous start-up experience.
6.4a: VCs value leadership experience more for markets that are larger.	Yes	VCs value leadership experience more for markets that are larger.
6.4b: VCs value leadership experience more for markets that are faster growing.	No	VCs value faster growing markets and this value does not appear to depend on the level of leadership experience.
6.5a: VCs value leadership experience more when competitors are fewer.	No	VCs value leadership experience more when competitors are many.
6.5b: VCs value leadership experience more when competitors are relatively weaker.	Yes	VCs value leadership experience more when competitors are relatively weaker.

General rule of thumb 6.2: *VCs value more highly those businesses with considerable market familiarity.*

General rule of thumb 6.3: *VCs value more highly those businesses in fast growing markets.*

These general rules of thumb reflect main-effects-only relationships; that is, the relationship that the level of proprietary technology, market familiarity and market growth have with VCs' assessments of success are

Table 6.3   The role of leadership experience on VCs' assessment of likely business success

Enhances benefits of:	Compensates for:	Independent effect of:
Large market size	Low start-up experience	High market growth
Low number of competitors		Highly proprietary technology
Low strength of competitors		High market familiarity

not influenced by leadership experience. VCs appear to value proprietary technology because it means that any advantage arising from the technology is rare and hopefully has intellectual property protection to make it more difficult for (potential) competitors to imitate this source of advantage. Beyond the technology, VCs also look at the management team and favor those businesses whose management team has familiarity with the market. As discussed in Chapter three of this book, market knowledge is an important resource that increases one's ability to discover and exploit opportunities. VCs also look to the business's environmental conditions to make their assessment of likely business performance, in this case, the market's rate of growth, which is an important dimension of environmental munificence. VCs prefer markets that are growing rapidly, as rapid growth indicates that customers find the products and services provided in the particular market niche attractive. Furthermore, there is typically less competition in a growing market because industry participants can increase sales from market growth rather than taking market share from a competitor. So a company can get more pie without increasing the width of the slice because the pie is growing. These general rules of thumb cover the characteristics of the product (technology), the management team and the environment. VCs also consider other factors in their assessments of likely business performance, but the impact of these business attributes on the VCs' decision policies is not a simple main-effects-only relationship as those in general rules of thumb 6.1–6.3 above.

General rule of thumb 6.4: *VCs value leadership experience more for those businesses in large markets.*

General rule of thumb 6.5: *VCs value leadership experience more for those businesses that face many competitors.*

General rule of thumb 6.6: *VCs value leadership experience more for those businesses that face weak competitors.*

We find that VCs use contingent decision policies: the more munificent the environment in terms of weak competitors, the more importance the VC attaches to leadership experience. It appears that weaker competitors allow those businesses with greater leadership experience to position their businesses to exploit these weaknesses. Although this aspect of the competitive environment influenced VCs' decision policies in a way that we expected, the nature of the competitive environment in terms of the number of competitors produced an initially surprising result. VCs place greater emphasis on leadership experience in environments that have a greater number of competitors. Although we maintain that a more munificent environment provides greater scope for leaders to impact on performance, a possible explanation is that an increasing number of competitors (holding other attributes of environmental munificence constant) increases the VC's reliance on a leader to act and react to the many possible, and a priori unforeseeable, competitive interactions, that is, they rely on the leader's tactical ability. Moreover, VCs may like to see other competitors as it validates the opportunity's existence, that is, to see others enter an emerging industry provides that industry legitimacy in the eyes of VCs. If one looks at the past VC boom in e-commerce, optical networking and other internet-related investments, VCs were competitive amongst themselves in backing similar companies. Each VC believed that there was something unique about her/his own investments that would allow them to survive and excel in spite of the many competitors in an emerging market.

General rule of thumb 6.7: *VCs value leadership experience less for those businesses with a management team that has start-up experience.*

Somewhat surprisingly, it appears that start-up experience is a *substitute* for leadership experience. The greater the entrepreneur's previous start-up experience, the less important is his/her leadership experience. Considering that start-up experience is not significant in the main-effects-only model, it is possible that VCs look at leadership experience first; if it is weak, they may consider start-up experience as compensating for weaker leadership experience. The finding that start-up experience substitutes for leadership experience adds to our understanding of VCs' decision policies over and above those studies that find for the main-effects-only use of these attributes and may explain the contradictory findings in previous studies. That is, the reason why some studies find start-up experience is important and others that it is not, is that it depends on the level of leadership experience.

The above general rules of thumb provide business managers with insight into the decision policies of VCs, which in turn can help the manager provide the information (and possibly position it in a way) that helps VCs more favorably assess the business and thereby increase the chance of receiving funding.

Categorizing Small Businesses' Likelihood of Receiving Venture Capital by Leadership Experience and Environmental Characteristics

We conclude that VCs value leadership experience more under certain environmental contingencies. Based on these contingencies it is possible to identify four types of small businesses depending on the leadership experience of their managers and the environmental conditions in which they operate. These four types of small firms are depicted in Figure 6.5 where leadership experience provides one dimension and environmental conditions the other.

1. We label the small businesses in the upper right hand corner *high fliers*. These are the ones most likely to receive VC funding. They reside in environments that can be viewed as munificent because competitors are few and/or weak and the potential market is large. At the same time, these small businesses possess substantial leadership experience. Thanks to this experience, VCs expect that they are able to take advantage of their relatively strong position in the market.
2. In the upper left hand corner, we find the *potentials*. These small businesses are less likely to receive VC funding than the previous category. However, their chances of receiving such funding would increase considerably should they make changes to their management team. By hiring individuals with previous leadership experience, VCs are likely to view them much more favorably. However, taking on new team members is a delicate matter. Existing team members develop some shared expectations for how the business should operate. New members can arrive with very different perspectives and agendas. They require time to learn the cultural norms established by existing team members. As a result, individuals added to the team can be disruptive to existing practices. Therefore, care must be taken in integrating new team members that have the requisite leadership experience.
3. The bottom right corner contains the *misplaced*. We argue that they are misplaced because the management team possesses the requisite experience, but these small businesses operate in environments that are viewed as less munificent, and therefore offer less potential. As a result, VCs are less likely to provide funding to these businesses. In order to make the environmental conditions more favorable, these businesses likely need to change their product market. In other words, by developing new products or extending their products to new customer groups, these businesses can ensure that there are fewer or weaker competitors

and that their total market size is larger. Thereby, they would be viewed more positively by VCs.

4.   In the bottom left corner we find the small businesses that lack leadership experience and operate in less munificent markets that are small and where competitors are many and/or strong. This category is the least likely to receive VC funding and we label them *unattractive*. This is not to say that they are unattractive as workplaces, but merely indicates that they are likely to be of limited interest to VCs. Venture capital is only available to a select few businesses. As the next chapter will discuss, for small businesses that are unable or unwilling to attract venture capital there are other options, such as bank loans. The 'unattractive' small businesses are probably better off not spending time and energy on trying to attract equity capital from VCs because substantial changes are needed in order to make them more attractive to this type of investor. Instead, they may seek out other options to obtain the financial resources they need.

Implications for Policy Makers

In several countries there are agencies that assist entrepreneurs and companies in receiving venture capital. One example of such an organization is Connect that operates in several countries in Europe and North America. The findings obtained above provide some important implications for this type of organization. The positive direct influence of proprietary technology and market knowledge, operating in fast growing markets, is not surprising. This largely represents conventional wisdom. However, the fact that these variables did not interact with leadership experience suggests that VCs value these factors independently of leadership experience. In other words, if these aspects of the environment, the technology, and the team are in place, small businesses that lack leadership (and start-up) experience still have a chance of receiving venture capital.

The interaction effect of leadership experience suggests that it can serve to mitigate deficiencies (such as lack of start-up experience) as well as to enhance strengths of the business (such as operating in markets with weak competitors). Therefore, the importance of leadership experience varies depending on the environment in which the small business operates.

Based on the 2×2 matrix presented in Figure 6.5, we are able to develop policy implications for each of the four categories of small businesses.

1.   The '*high fliers*' in the upper right-hand corner, that have substantial leadership experience and reside in environments characterized by weak and/or few competitors and/or large markets are the ones most

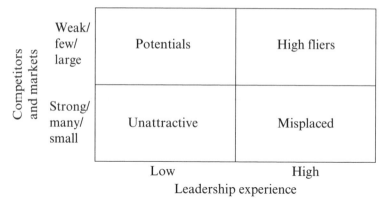

Figure 6.5   VC evaluation of small businesses in terms of leadership experience and market characteristics

likely to receive venture capital funding. It would be easy to believe that these businesses receive the venture capital they need. However, it appears that in many countries, VCs tend to cluster together in major cities, and businesses outside of these locations may face problems establishing the necessary relationships with VCs. It is often the case that the only way for an entrepreneur to gain access to VCs is through an introduction by a third party who already knows the VC. Public agencies, such as Connect, can have an important role here acting as mediators or brokers between venture capital firms and those high fliers operating in locations outside of the major cities.

2. The *'potentials'* operate in attractive environments but are less appealing to VCs because they lack some leadership experience among their teams. As mentioned above, integrating new team members could be a difficult task. For this category of business, public policy could focus on assisting these businesses in finding suitable new team members and supporting them in their integration into the team. Consequently, in order to support this category of business, it is important that support agencies, such as Connect, develop large networks of contacts with people who can contribute to management teams.

3. *'Misplaced'* businesses in the lower right-hand corner are characterized by having sufficient leadership experience on their management teams, but operate in environments that do not have the growth potential that VCs desire. Given that these businesses intend to enter product markets that VCs consider being small and competitive may suggest that these businesses lack market information. Support agencies could assist these businesses by providing such information.

4.   For the '*unattractive*' category, that lacks relevant leadership experience on their management teams and operate in environments that appear less attractive, the best policy of support agencies may be to inform them on what is needed to qualify as an attractive investment for a VC and point these small businesses to the other more appropriate funding alternatives, such as business angels with interest in specific types of businesses or debt capital from banks or other financial institutions.

BUILDING AND NURTURING A RELATIONSHIP WITH A VENTURE CAPITALIST

The Importance of Cooperation with VCs

We now turn to the second part of this chapter which concerns the relationship between the VC and the portfolio company post investment. Once a small business has received equity capital from a VC, the VC owns part of the company and it is essential that the relationship between the owners runs smoothly for the small business to be able to perform well and possibly to receive more funding from the same VC. Here we develop a number of propositions but we do not test them empirically. We hope that we or other scholars have the chance to test if these propositions are supported by empirical findings.

Cooperative relationships between venture capitalists (VCs) and entrepreneurs are necessary for the success of VC-backed small businesses (Sapienza and Korsgard, 1996; Steier and Greenwood, 1995; Cable and Shane, 1997). Timmons and Bygrave (1986) propose that the cooperative relationship between a VC and entrepreneur are more important to the success of the business than the capital itself. While it appears that cooperation provides significant benefits it does not characterize all VC–entrepreneur relationships (Sahlman, 1990). Sapienza and Korsgard (1996) propose that entrepreneurs have an incentive to be uncooperative with the VC by withholding information such as technical details that makes it difficult for the VC fully to evaluate the business for future funding (Bowden, 1994). There is also an incentive for entrepreneurs to put a positive 'spin' on (overstate) the performance of the business and/or underplay the importance of detrimental information when communicating with the VC (Bowden, 1994). To a certain extent VCs are dependent upon the entrepreneur for information and the entrepreneur has the opportunity to act as a gatekeeper actively managing this information boundary to their own self-interest.

Apart from having the potential to manage the information opportunistically, the entrepreneur also has an incentive to be opportunistic in their use of resources. While entrepreneurs prefer their ventures to be successful there is a wide variability between entrepreneurs' consciousness and devotion to the venture (Amit et al., 1990). For example, promises originally made in earnest may become more onerous and the entrepreneur might start focusing on other activities (Cable and Shane, 1997) or using funds to conduct those activities that provide them the greatest pleasure. In other words, the funds being used by the entrepreneurs are more costly to the VC than they are to the entrepreneur (Sahlman, 1990). Therefore there is an incentive for entrepreneurs to be uncooperative.[4]

There is also an incentive for VCs to pursue opportunistic behavior at the expense of cooperation, and thereby at the expense of the entrepreneur. VCs typically do not receive a return on their investment until after the limited partners (those that invested in the VC fund) have received their return. Such an arrangement may tempt VCs to harvest a business and obtain their profits rather than reinvest in the business's future products and development (Sahlman, 1990). They may pressure the entrepreneur to seek short-term profits (Gomez-Mejia et al., 1990) even to the detriment of long-term profitability and/or the VCs may under-invest in the business (Cable and Shane, 1997; Gorman and Sahlman, 1989; Bygrave and Timmons, 1991). The VC who is diversified among a number of portfolio companies can benefit from the above strategy to the detriment of the entrepreneur who typically has his/her financial returns dependent upon the success of this single business.

The above suggests that while cooperation between the entrepreneur and VC is important there are incentives for both parties to be opportunistically uncooperative. Currently, little is known about what makes the relationship between a VC and a small business work (Sapienza and Korsgard, 1996; Cable and Shane, 1997; Bowden, 1994). Therefore it is important to understand the processes that generate confidence that the partner will behave in a cooperative manner. 'Confidence in partner cooperation' refers to the perceived level of certainty that a partner will pursue mutually compatible interests in the relationship, rather than act opportunistically (adapted from Das and Teng, 1998). Confidence in partner cooperation has been of recent interest to scholars such as those utilizing an agency perspective (Amit et al., 1990), and a prisoner's dilemma perspective (Cable and Shane, 1997).

We argue, however, that there is more to establishing a functional relationship between an entrepreneur and a VC than obtaining control through various mechanisms. Based on research from a number of literatures, we propose that trust is also an important consideration in attempting to gain a greater insight into the VC–entrepreneur relationship. This raises a number of questions not sufficiently addressed by previous research. For

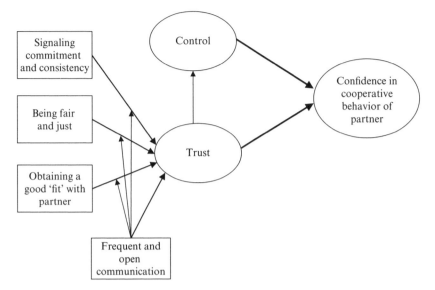

Figure 6.6   A model of confidence in partner cooperation

example, is control a substitute for trust in order to increase confidence in partner cooperation so that if there is little trust between the VC and portfolio firm the parties will develop mechanisms to control the behavior of the other party? Or can the relationship between control and trust be complementary so that one enhances the other?

We argue that in order to gain a deeper understanding of confidence in partner cooperation both control and trust need to be considered simultaneously. What is the nature of such a relationship? To address these questions we offer an integrated model of cooperative behavior taking into consideration both mechanisms: to gain control and to generate trust (see Figure 6.6).

Control and Confidence in Partner Cooperation

The majority of studies that have investigated the development of cooperation in the VC–entrepreneur relationship have proposed mechanisms for the VC to increase their control over the entrepreneur and in doing so 'forcing' cooperative behavior. For example, the VC could introduce penalties for not complying with the agreement in order to increase the likelihood that the small business will cooperate. Such penalties include a dilution of the entrepreneur's equity in the venture (Sahlman, 1990); replacement of the entrepreneur with professional management

(Barney et al., 1996; Hoffman and Blakey, 1987); and compensation structures (Sahlman, 1990), should the small business fail to comply with the agreement. These control mechanisms increase confidence in partner cooperation. Such an approach underlies the agency and prisoner's dilemma perspectives, which are now reviewed.

Agency Theory and Prisoner's Dilemma Perspectives of the VC–Entrepreneur Relationship

Agency risk is the degree of uncertainty that either the entrepreneur or the VC will pursue his or her own self interest rather than comply with the requirements of the contract for venture capital (Fiet, 1995). The literature using this perspective emphasizes the importance of the contract between the VC and the small business and of monitoring as mechanisms for control. This perspective offers a description of the risks associated with the principal (the VC) and the agent (the entrepreneur) and actions that the VC can take to 'force' the entrepreneur to cooperate. In sum, this literature suggests that VCs should implement control mechanisms to ensure that the entrepreneur does not act opportunistically to their detriment.

Cable and Shane (1997) question the appropriateness of agency theory suggesting that it is not always the case that the parties have unequal power where a principle seeks control of an agent's behavior. As discussed above, both parties may act opportunistically. For example, VCs can also choose defection strategies (Sahlman, 1990) but the agency perspective describes the relationship in only one direction; it focuses on VC control over entrepreneur's opportunistic behavior while ignoring the entrepreneur's concern that the VC may act opportunistically.

Underlying the prisoner's dilemma perspective is an assumption that each individual actor has an incentive to act according to competitive, narrow self-interest even though all actors are collectively better off (that is, they receive higher rewards) if they cooperate. The payoffs for each actor are dictated by the strategy adapted by the other actor. For the party that does not know the other party's strategy, their own optimal strategy is to defect even though cooperation is collectively optimal for both parties (Komorita et al., 1991). In this way the prisoner's dilemma framework incorporates much of what agency theory has to offer (issues of uncertainty and goal conflict). This discussion from the agency and prisoner's dilemma perspective leads to the following proposed relationship:

Proposed relationship 6.6: *The greater control the VC has over the entrepreneur the greater confidence the VC has that the entrepreneur will be cooperative. The same holds for the control an entrepreneur has over a VC.*

Trust and Confidence in Partner Cooperation

Cable and Shane (1997) propose that control mechanisms (penalties for defection) are required to increase the likelihood of cooperation when trust is absent. Sapienza and Korsgaard (1996) emphasize the importance of the entrepreneur engendering investor trust. They argue that the entrepreneur can build trust by encouraging investors to believe that the procedures used by the entrepreneur are fair and include consideration of the investor's interests. As Sweeting (1991: 619) puts it: 'VCs . . . were seeking to establish whether or not they could simply "get along with" team members and trust them. The benefits of this mutual understanding and trust were evident even before the deal was made.'

But if trust is so important, what is it? While most people have a vague idea of what the term means, a clear definition is needed in order to research its importance. Rousseau et al. (1998) propose that trust is a psychological state comprising the intention to accept vulnerability upon positive expectations of the intention or behavior of another. This formal definition means that by trusting someone I realize that the person has the potential to hurt me but I am willing to take that risk because I believe that the chance that this will happen is low while the chance that something positive will occur is high. From this definition it is important to note that trust is not a behavior or a choice, but a psychological state. Implicit in the concept of trust is some form of risk (perceived probability of loss) and interdependence (the attainment of one party's interests cannot be achieved without reliance on another party) (Rousseau et al., 1998). An important distinction between trust and control is that trust (a perception) does not directly influence others' behavior whereas control (control mechanisms) does (Leifer and Mills, 1996; Das and Teng, 1998). From this definition of trust, the following proposition applied to the relationship between a VC and an entrepreneur emerges:

> **Proposed relationship 6.7:** *As a VC's trust in the entrepreneur increases his/her confidence that the entrepreneur will cooperate also increases. The same holds for an entrepreneur's trust in the VC.*

If the above proposed relationship is accepted, then the question becomes how both parties build the level of trust in order to gain the mutual benefits of cooperation. We propose that trust can be built by both parties in the relationship by (1) signaling commitment and consistency, (2) being fair and just, (3) obtaining a good 'fit' with the partner, and (4) frequent and open communications. We now explore how each of these dimensions influences cooperation between the two parties.

Signaling commitment and consistency

When one party 'trusts' the other it means that it makes itself vulnerable to the partner's opportunistic behavior thereby taking a risk. But this vulnerability will encourage the other party to be trustworthy and cooperate because reciprocity is an important element to building trust (Johnson et al., 1997; Larson, 1992; McAllister, 1995; Creed and Miles, 1996). This gradual and incremental process of signaling commitment and building greater levels of trust represents a trial and error approach (in an environment of uncertainty) to relationship building. This accumulation of experiences can contribute to increasing trust between the parties but is conditioned on the behavior being consistent. If behavior is inconsistent and erratic, little trust will develop (Butler, 1991; Gabarro, 1978; Jennings, 1971; Johnson-George and Swap, 1982; Robinson and Rousseau, 1994). This leads to the following proposition:

> **Proposed relationship 6.8:** *An initial signal of commitment by the entrepreneur sent to the VC will initially increase the VC's confidence that the entrepreneur will cooperate so long as the VC perceives behavioral consistency. The same holds for signals of commitment by the VC.*

Perceived as fair and just

As the word indicates, it is easier to put trust in someone who is trustworthy. By telling the truth and keeping promises, other parties can be confident that a small business is honest, fair and trustworthy. This provides a first piece of evidence that other parties can put trust in the small business and is likely to lead to increased trust in a relationship. In addition to being a trustworthy business, the procedures and processes by which the small business and the VC interact in their relationship must be perceived as fair and just in order for trust to develop. The perception of fair and just procedures largely stems from the perception of the other party being trustworthy, so these two areas are closely related. One important part of a fair and just behavior in a relationship lies in the allocation of rewards, that is, the party contributing the most to the relationship (by building the most value) should receive more of the rewards generated by the partnership (Korsgaard, Schweiger and Sapienza, 1995; Sheppard and Tuchinsky, 1996). Sometimes the need for equality (fairness in the distribution of outcomes) becomes more important than the efficiency of obtaining that outcome (Ring and Van de Ven, 1994) because fairness and justice may be more important than maximizing profits. The above discussion leads to the following relationship:

> **Proposed relationship 6.9:** *An entrepreneur instituting a procedure that is 'fair' will increase the VC's confidence that the entrepreneur will cooperate*

(so long as the VC perceives 'fairness'). The same holds for the VC instituting 'fair' procedures.

Obtain a 'fit' with the other party

Making adjustments to accommodate the needs of the partner increases the fit between the two parties and thereby increases trust in the relationship (Heide and John, 1992; Madhok, 1995). Of course those parties that are similar (or at least perceive that they are similar) to each other are likely to need less adjustment to obtain a fit. Therefore trust is often developed quicker by parties that are attracted to each other and perceive that they have similar characteristics (Creed and Miles, 1996; McAllister, 1995; Zucker, 1986). Sheppard and Sherman (1998) propose that over time parties can develop highly similar internalized views, beliefs and values. Thus,

> **Proposed relationship 6.10:** *By the entrepreneur selecting a VC with whom they have a good fit and by making adjustments to obtain a better fit will initially increase the VC's confidence that the entrepreneur will cooperate. The same holds for the VC selecting an entrepreneur.*

Frequent and open communication

Trust in a relationship can increase when adequate explanations and timely feedback are offered (Folger and Konovsky, 1989; Konovosky and Cropanzano, 1991; Thomas and Trevino, 1993; Whitener et al., 1998; Das and Teng, 1998; Larson, 1992). It appears that communication speeds up the process by which the parties can assess the other's 'trustworthiness' (Creed and Miles, 1996). For example, co-location and electronic communication linkages have been found to increase communication and trust (Womack et al., 1990). Thus,

> **Proposed relationship 6.11:** *Open and frequent communications from the entrepreneur to the VC will initially increase the VC's confidence that the entrepreneur will cooperate. The same holds for open and frequent communications from the VC.*

The Moderating Relationship of 'Frequent and Open Communication'

Communication is also a catalyst for the other means of trust-building proposed above. For example, the unsolicited communication of information (especially if that information is sensitive) can provide a clear and strong signal of commitment to the relationship (Das and Teng, 1998) encouraging reciprocity. Communication may also act as the vehicle to exchange information about adjustments/accommodations made as well as feedback, thus increasing trust in the relationship (Thomas and Trevino, 1993). Communication also helps bring the parties closer together, without explicitly comprising adjustments of one party, by helping the partners further develop common values and togetherness (Leifer and Mills, 1996; Madhok, 1995). Sheppard and Sherman (1998) refer to it as active discovery through communication and research. Communication through the use of timely feedback, is perceived by the other party as behavior that is fair and just (there is procedural justice) and therefore influences another trust building dimension (see Sapienza and Korsgard, 1996). Thus,

Proposed relationship 6.12: *The level of open and frequent communication moderates the relationship between the generation of trust and (a) signaling commitment and consistency, (b) enhancing perceived fairness and justice, and (c) obtaining a better fit. In the presence of open and frequent communication the other mechanisms of trust generation are more effective.*

We propose that in order to understand the relationship between the mechanisms of building trust and the level of trust, we must also consider the moderating role of communication. Similarly, we propose for the necessity of a contingency approach to understanding the relationship between control, trust and confidence in partner cooperation. This contingency approach is now explored.

Control, Trust and Confidence in Cooperation

There is inconsistency in the literature over the relationship between trust and control. There are some scholars who suggest trust is a type of control mechanism (similar to the argument made by agency theorists). Others suggest that trust and control are substitutes (that is, control is required when trust is absent: Cable and Shane, 1997; Sitkin and Roth, 1993). We propose that there is some optimal level of control that will allow trust in the relationship to develop and thereby generate the maximum level of confidence in partner cooperation and the level of trust influences the choice of control. Such an explanation may reconcile what currently appears to be conflicting perspectives in the literature, i.e. reconcile those who argue that the introduction of control mechanisms implies one party does not trust the other and therefore inhibits trust generation (Argyris, 1952) with those who argue control mechanisms allow trust to develop (Goold and Campbell, 1987; Sitkin, 1995). We suggest that both are right but are not always applicable. It depends on the amount of control.

We propose that there is a curvilinear relationship such that at low levels of control there will be low levels of trust. We argue that the perceived risk from being vulnerable is 'too high' to encourage trust by one or both parties. Such an argument is consistent with previous research (Argyris, 1952). At the other extreme, where control is high there is less need for trust as the partner is already coerced into the desired behavior. In fact, the act of one partner implementing (or requiring) such high levels of control might send a signal that they see the other party as untrustworthy. Such a perception might erode any trust that exists and might even build distrust.[5] Somewhere between these two extreme levels of control (minimal control and maximal control) is an optimal level that allows and encourages trust in the relationship to be developed. We propose that an assessment of one's current level of trust is likely to influence directly the choice and magnitude of the control mechanisms implemented. In this way the assessment of trust can act as a feedback mechanism informing the control decision in order to fine tune the combination of trust and control towards an optimal level of confidence in partner cooperation. Thus,

Proposed relationship 6.13: *The relationship between a VC's control mechanisms and the generation of trust in the entrepreneur is curvilinear in nature: an inverted U shape. The same holds for an entrepreneur's control mechanisms.*

Proposed relationship 6.14: *A VC's assessment of his/her level of trust in the entrepreneur influences the choice of control. The same holds for an entrepreneur's assessment of his/her level of trust.*

The above implies that there is an optimal level of both control and trust that maximizes partner cooperation. A parabola in three-dimensional space with control, trust, and confidence in partner cooperation as the axis, indicates the optimal combination of control and trust that maximizes partner cooperation. The actual optimal combination becomes an empirical question, of course, and while it is likely to vary from relationship to relationship we propose that this concept of an optimal combination of trust and control is useful in appreciating how different classes of parties may interact. This issue is explored further in the section below.

Optimal levels of control and trust

The optimal level of trust likely differs from one entrepreneur/VC relationship to the other. Greater variance, however, probably exists between different classes of equity investors/entrepreneur dyads. The entrepreneurial

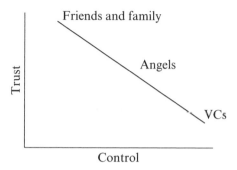

Figure 6.7   Typical level of trust by investor

financing process can be roughly thought of as a progression from one source of equity capital to another based upon venture type, stage, etc. After self-investing, most entrepreneurs progress through family, friends, business contacts, and maybe business angels (high net worth individuals). Only those businesses that have high potential, are relatively established, and need large cash infusions ever capture the VC's attention. We propose that the typical combination of trust and control differs based upon the type of investor and that these points can be plotted on a three dimensional graph with confidence in partner cooperation, control and trust as the axis (see Figure 6.7).

The three dimensional figure suggests that each type of investor can achieve high confidence in partner cooperation but only through a unique combination of trust and control. We argue that family and friends achieve high confidence in entrepreneur cooperation through low control and high trust, business angels through a moderate level of both control and trust, and venture capitalists through a high level of control and low trust.

Examining investor type along the proposed dimensions of trust indicates why the tradeoff with control varies (see Table 6.4). For instance, signaling commitment and consistency is very high with family and friends and diminishes to low with VCs. Both parties in the family/friends–entrepreneur dyad are highly vulnerable to each other. Informal repayment schedules and terms increase family/friends' exposure. On the other side, the threat to friendships or family relationships of a failed venture increases the entrepreneur's vulnerability. Within the VC–entrepreneur dyad, on the other hand, vulnerability is limited due to the VC's extensive conditions detailed on their boilerplate term sheets. Similarly the details on the term sheet give the entrepreneur more certainty in how the relationship will unfold.

Table 6.4   Types of investors and typical levels of trust antecedents

	Friends and family	Angels	VCs
Signaling commitment and consistency	Very high	High	Low
Perceived fairness and justice	Very high	High	Low
Fit	Very high	High	Moderate
Open communication	Moderate	Very high	Moderate
Control	Very low	Moderate	Very high

Perceived fairness and justice is a function of perceived fair processes and allocation of rewards. From the entrepreneur's perspective, the allocation of rewards is best with friends/family and decreases through to VCs. The less formal the investment process, assuming that the entrepreneur does secure the investment, the greater the perception of fairness because the added flexibility of the process means that the investor paid individual attention to the entrepreneur rather than just following a formula. Fit tends to be highest with family and friends and then decreases across investor types. The entrepreneur has the longest history with family and friends. The family shaped the entrepreneur, and the entrepreneur chooses his/her friends. Thus, the fit between these groups is likely to be the highest. Fit with traditional angels (wealthy individuals) is also relatively high as angels typically invest in industries where they have operational experience. Therefore, the angel is the mentor who has been there and done that. As the investor becomes more formalized (and institutionalized), the fit likely decreases because the investor is less apt to have the same life experiences.

Communication also follows a decreasing trend across investors with one notable exception. Whereas traditional angels are likely to have a 'hands-on' approach to working with the entrepreneur (by offering expertise on operational aspects), family and friends may have considerably less involvement in the operations of the business. Communication between the entrepreneur and family/friends investors may often take place during social settings (such as family dinners) and not at the same level of depth as with traditional angels. As we progress towards VCs, the day-to-day involvement decreases as the portfolio of companies these groups manage increases. Thus, VCs have relatively less time to invest in each portfolio company than do traditional angels. Given the proposed interaction that communication has with the other trust dimensions suggests that business angels are quite capable of building considerable confidence in partner cooperation.

Implications for Scholars

VCs' decision policies
This study uses the RBV of strategy to hypothesize leadership's interaction with other venture and environmental characteristics. However, we are not proposing that the RBV is the only perspective that can provide insight into VCs' decision policies, in fact we encourage the investigation of VCs' decisions from a number of different theoretical perspectives. The industrial organization (IO) perspective of strategy, for example, could provide additional insight into the relationships between important industry characteristics (some of which are represented in this study).

This study focuses on VCs' assessment of new ventures, that is, investment proposals seeking seed to development capital. An interesting question then becomes: do VCs weight criteria differently in their assessments of businesses in different stages of development (such as mezzanine financing or leveraged buyouts)? Also, while the environmental factors in this study likely capture industry differences, there is the opportunity to create a sample of VCs that are experts in a particular industry and model their decisions based on the scenarios specific to that industry. Whether for a different stage of venture development or for specific industries, there is the opportunity to create more narrowly focused decision-aids in attempt to further improve decision accuracy.

Other implications for scholars that arise from this chapter relate to the dimensions of building a relationship between entrepreneurs and VCs: (1) signaling commitment and consistency, (2) being fair and just, (3) obtaining a fit, (4) engaging in frequent and open communication, and finally (5) explaining the nature of the relationship between control, trust and partner cooperation.

Signaling commitment and consistency
Entrepreneurs and VCs signal commitment and consistency in many ways, but perhaps the most important is by their past record of achievement. The VC mantra of preferring an 'A' team with a 'B' idea to a 'B' team with an 'A' idea implies that VCs trust those entrepreneurs who have higher qualifications, especially if those qualifications include past entrepreneurial experiences and/or evidence of trustworthiness in their relationships with investors. Thus, entrepreneurs espouse their commitment by showing what they have accomplished and what they are willing to give up in order to pursue the small business (such as a high paying, prestigious job). Sophisticated entrepreneurs also screen VCs to gauge whether the VC can add value beyond merely the funds. Thus, VCs signal their commitment and consistency via web pages that show their portfolio of companies, press

releases, testimonials from entrepreneurs of portfolio companies, qualifications and reputations of individual venture capitalists, and so on. There are likely other actions and factors that signal vulnerability and trust: the question is how, effective are these actions?

Understanding which signals are more clearly perceived might allow the maximum amount of trust building for the least amount of actual exposure (vulnerability). Future research should explore a number of issues in more detail. How much vulnerability is appropriate? What is the relationship between the amount of vulnerability and the effectiveness of this action as a risk staging (options) process? Which signals are going to lead to the most productive trial and error process: most efficiently build accumulated experiences between the VC and the entrepreneur? Along with signaling vulnerability, what is the best way to signal your behavioral consistency? For example, instead of one action that shows considerable vulnerability, is an entrepreneur (or VC) better served by consistently offering a series of actions that show lower levels of vulnerability?

Being fair and just
Perceived fairness most often focuses on valuation and equity dilution to secure funding. Valuation is often highly contentious primarily because of a lack of information. While each party clearly has a vested interest in the valuation, it is critically important for both the VC and entrepreneur to detail the procedure they used to value the business as this likely increases the perception of fairness by both parties. For the VC this might mean showing valuations of comparable companies, validating pro forma projections, and so on.

There has been little research on evoking a sense of obligation in the VC context. While some findings from other contexts likely apply to the VC–entrepreneur context others likely do not. Which actions do apply and which do not? This represents an empirical question that requires scholarly attention. Sapienza and Korsgaard (1996) investigated VCs' responses to the timeliness with which entrepreneurs shared information, and the level of influence the VC had over the strategic direction of the venture. More research needs to follow Sapienza and Korsgaard's lead.

Fit
Oftentimes, the only way for an entrepreneur to gain access to VCs is through an introduction. The very fact that someone the VC trusts is an advocate for an entrepreneur may transfer that trust to the entrepreneur and the VC can be more confident that the entrepreneur will not act in a detrimental way. Likewise, the fact that someone the entrepreneur trusts is recommending a particular VC may transfer some trust to that VC. In essence,

the entrepreneur's and VC's network signal commitment and consistency. The common network that brings an entrepreneur and VC together also suggests higher degrees of fit. The fact that both the entrepreneur and VC have common associations implies that they have some similarities. At the very least, they share the intermediary (such as accountant, friend, professor, third party entrepreneur) in common. Fit over time often increases as VCs tap their network to help fill out the entrepreneurial team.

While the general prescription to choose a partner who has similar internalized views, beliefs, and values as yourself is beneficial, it may be difficult to achieve. Which views, beliefs and values are most important in selecting a VC (or entrepreneur)? Is an initial assessment of fit accurate or are we overconfident in our ability to make such assessments? There is evidence to suggest VCs (as most people) are overconfident in their assessments of small business success (Zacharakis and Shepherd, 2001). Maybe more emphasis should be placed on making adjustments to accommodate the needs of the entrepreneur (or VC) and/or encourage them also to make adjustments towards your needs. What types of adjustments are typically required/desired? How can the VC (or entrepreneur) be encouraged to accommodate your needs? This represents a fruitful line of inquiry.

Frequent and open communication

Once a venture has been funded, the level and quality of interaction between VCs and entrepreneurs varies. Many factors influence the level and quality of interaction. For example, smaller VCs likely spend more time with each venture. Those VCs who constrain their investments to close geographic proximity also may spend more time with their portfolio companies. Stage of development also likely impacts on time and energy spent on a portfolio company. On the other hand, large VC firms have more portfolio companies, typically have broader geographic scopes, and often invest in later stage ventures. As such, they may only interact with entrepreneurs at board meetings or if the venture faces difficulty. Ginger More, a partner with Oak Ventures, noted that VCs, in general, are becoming more like money managers rather than active partners (More, 1999). As the size and style of VC firms has changed, the frequency and quality of communication has also changed. This changing nature raises a number of interesting research questions.

How important is it to choose a VC (or entrepreneur) within close geographical proximity? Are there more effective ways to communicate that are not geographically dependent? Do entrepreneurs and VCs communicate via e-mail? Do those VC–entrepreneur relationships that meet more frequently have greater confidence in partner cooperation? Does the context of such meetings (such as where the meeting is held, for example, whether in an attorney's office or in a bar over a drink) affect the openness of the communication? Are there other factors that affect the openness of a series of communications? Does communication act as a catalyst between the other trust-building mechanisms and confidence in partner cooperation as proposed in this chapter?

Trust, control and confidence in partner cooperation
While there has been some excellent work in this area (see Fiet, 1995; Sahlman, 1990; Barney et al., 1996) more scholarly attention needs to focus on the joint effect these control mechanisms have on both trust and confidence in partner cooperation. Are there some control mechanisms that in isolation increase confidence in partner cooperation (direct effect) and also foster the building of trust, which also increases confidence in partner cooperation (indirect effect)? By better understanding both the direct and indirect effect of control mechanisms the entrepreneur and VC might be able to better structure the relationship for mutual benefit. Which control mechanisms are merely a substitute for trust and which complement or even foster the building of trust? What is the optimal combination of control and trust in a specific VC–entrepreneur dyad?

CONCLUSION

This chapter explores the decision policies of venture capitalists in their assessments of the likelihood of business success and focuses on the moderating role of an entrepreneur's leadership experience. The study, summarized in this chapter, found that interactions between leadership experience and other internal resources, and between leadership experience and environmental munificence, impact on venture capitalists' decision policies. Although venture capitalists always prefer greater general experience in leadership, they value it more highly in large markets, when there are many competitors, and when the competitors are relatively weak. Previous start-up experience may substitute for leadership experience. If venture capitalists are sufficiently convinced of the business's likely success, they may invest. This investment is the start of a relationship that is important in determining the business's level of success (and that of the venture capitalist).

This chapter also acknowledges the complexity of the relationship between an entrepreneur and a VC and the importance of achieving confidence in partner cooperation. First, we proposed that the entrepreneur can build trust with the VC (and vice versa) through (1) signaling commitment and consistency, (2) being fair and just, (3) obtaining a good fit with one's partner and (4) frequent and open communication. Second, we proposed that open and frequent communications can act as a catalyst for the other trust building mechanisms. Third, we proposed that the relationships among control, trust and confidence in partner cooperation is curvilinear in nature: low levels of control foster trust and therefore confidence in partner cooperation while high levels of control does the opposite. The entrepreneur and the VC need to balance the level of control to build trust so that the optimal level of confidence in partner cooperation can be achieved.

Venture capital is not the only source of funds for all small businesses; in fact, it is only a source of funds for those that have very high potential. Another source of funds is debt capital, in other words, loans from banks. The next chapter focuses on debt capital and the decision policies of loan officers.

NOTES

1. This chapter is based on Zacharakis and Shepherd (2005); and Shepherd and Zacharakis (2001), **3** (2): 129–50.
2. A possible alternate explanation is that the room for error is less in slower growing markets and therefore leadership experience would be more valued.
3. We tested for differences in decision policies among the sample of VCs. Age and venture capital experience were a priori the demographic variables most likely to distinguish between decision policies. We included these two level 2 variables in a HLM analysis to determine if those who are older or more experienced had a significantly different decision policy than those who were younger or less experienced. We did not find any significant differences.
4. This is not to say that there is not an incentive to cooperate (as described above) but merely to say that in many cases cooperation is not always the selected strategy by entrepreneurs (Amit et al., 1990).
5. Some scholars view distrust as a concept distinct from trust (Lewicki, McAllister, and Bies, 1998).

7. Loan officers' decision policies towards small businesses[1]

With Volker Bruns

INTRODUCTION

When small business managers seek outside financing to expand their businesses it is important that they understand the logic of those supplying the funding in order to increase their chances of receiving the money they need. The previous chapter provided insight into the decision making of venture capitalists. However, venture capital is only available to a select few firms. Further, the vast majority of small businesses are unwilling to give up ownership in return for funding (Wiklund, 1998). Most small businesses prefer to rely on retained earnings only as the source for growth capital, but when that is insufficient, bank loans are the preferred external source of growth capital among most businesses. Berger and Udell (2003) report figures from the USA that indicate the importance of debt to small and new business (debt represents 50 per cent of the capital structure in small firms and of those less than two years old, 52 per cent had debt as their major source of funding) with commercial bank loans the most common source of debt funding. Even among the most prestigious venture capital backed firms that make IPOs (initial public offerings), bank financing is a major source of finance (Berger and Udell, 2003). Given this, we believe that it is time to devote more interest to the decision making of loan officers, who provide the majority of growth capital to businesses, but of whom little is known.

However, small businesses generally have difficulties obtaining bank loans because of their special characteristics (Walker 1989; Binks, et al., 1992). This has led to the so-called 'financial gap' (see Storey, 1994), which constrains the growth of many small businesses (see Hughes, 1996). In particular, small businesses publish little formal information about their operations and performance, which can lead to information asymmetry between the small business manager and the bank representative. It is simply difficult for the bank to know very much about the small business applying for a loan. This in turn makes banks less prone to lend money to small businesses.

Let us develop the three primary reasons for information asymmetry in some more detail. These are: (1) lack of legally enforced transparency, (2) informal governance of the small business necessitating few internal documents and (3) small size leading to informal management. First, publicly traded firms are scrutinized by the stock exchange, investors, and other stakeholders who require substantial and accurate information, and there is legally enforced transparency. Consequently, publicly traded firms divulge substantial and detailed information, which banks can use to make decisions on credit granting. Most small businesses are typically not public and therefore produce and divulge far less information. Second, most small businesses are owner-managed. As a result, few agency relationships arise, and there is little need for written contracts, reports and other formal documents. Instead, operations can be informally controlled. As a result, few formal documents exist within the business. Third, because these businesses are small, their operations are typically relatively simple, which means that they can be controlled without the need for formal control systems. Taken together, this suggests that while many entrepreneurs hold substantial information about all aspects of their business, this information is not easily accessible for banks.

This information advantage of the small business (that is, information asymmetry) can be used opportunistically by the small business manager at the expense of the investor (Fiet, 1995), leading to an adverse selection problem (Stiglitz and Weiss, 1981). Adverse selection means that borrowers have a strong incentive to use their own money for the projects where returns are large and certain, and attempt to borrow money for riskier and less profitable projects. Hence, adverse selection may lead entrepreneurs to ask for external funding only for their riskiest projects, but it is difficult for potential lenders to find out if this is the case because of information asymmetry.

Because of this information asymmetry, it is critical for banks properly to evaluate the credit risk of a borrower. The accuracy of credit decisions has a significant impact on the overall profitability of a bank (Ruth, 1987; Ammann, 2001). Consequently, it is essential that banks develop methods that reduce risk and uncertainty in the loans that they make. Because decisions on granting credit to small businesses are made by individual loan officers, such methods translate directly into the decision policies of loan officers.[2]

In this chapter we complement the previous chapter on venture capital for gazelles and venture capitalists' decision policies, to investigate debt capital for small businesses and loan officers' decision policies. Although we believe that the research on venture capitalists has increased our understanding of the funding of some small businesses, most small businesses looking to grow are more concerned with obtaining debt funding from banks because this source is a more attractive and more realistic possibility.

In this chapter we propose how loan officers manage the information asymmetry between themselves and small business managers and how loan officers differ in those decision policies based on their human capital. Second, we introduce the sample and the results of our empirical test of these proposed relationships. Finally, we discuss the results and implications of this chapter for both scholars and practitioners.

BANK LENDING AND INFORMATION ASYMMETRY

The information asymmetry between small business managers and bank lending officers makes it difficult for loan officers to identify and distinguish small businesses that are able and willing to repay their loans from small businesses that are not. Therefore, loan officers have developed screening criteria (Stiglitz and Weiss, 1981) examining the characteristics of the borrower in order to discriminate good customers from bad ones. (Sargent and Young 1991; Sinkey, 1992; Scherr et al., 1993). But a small business wanting to borrow money for a project that seems to carry high credit risk can affect the chance of receiving a bank loan by ensuring that the bank will receive its money back regardless of the success of the project. For example, if a small business gets involved in a risky project, providing excellent collateral should make the bank less worried about the outcome of the project. The small business could also use its own money to fund most of the project and only borrow a small amount. Thereby the bank should know that the small business believes in the project and is not using its information advantage opportunistically. Finally, if a small business has a strong financial standing, the bank knows that even if the project may fail, the borrower has enough money to repay the loan.

Therefore, screening criteria should not been seen in isolation, but the collateral, the share of investment made by the borrower, and the financial position of the borrower are likely to influence the relationship between screening criteria and the likelihood that a borrower will receive a bank loan (Stiglitz and Weiss, 1981). In the following, we detail how different screening criteria are likely to affect the probability of a small business receiving a bank loan as well as how collateral, the share of investment made by the borrower, and the financial position of the borrower affect these relationships.

Characteristics of the Borrower and Loan Officers' Assessments of Credit

The human capital of the borrower's management team is a critical factor in determining the success of expansion efforts (Dess and Picke, 1999) and it is therefore an important indication of the ability to repay the loan. However, the quality of human capital is not easily observed or measured by external parties, such as loan officers (Pettit and Singer, 1985; Keasey and McGuiness, 1990; Scherr et al., 1993). Instead, tangible aspects of human capital, such as the management team's competence with previous projects related to the proposed project, can be assessed and a more general indication of the borrower's ability to perform in the future can be gauged by their recent past performance (Brüderl and Schüssler, 1990).

The previous chapter on venture capitalists' decision making revealed that the primary criteria they use in assessing new venture proposals are managerial capabilities and other factors related to competence such as management skills and management expertise. In a similar way, loan officers attempt to assess the management team's competence, specifically as it relates to the new project requiring funding. Competence represents a business's skills that can be applied towards strategic performance, which includes financial, managerial, functional and organizational skills, and is influenced by the business's reputation and history (Andrews, 1987). When a firm's competencies and resources are scarce, valuable and difficult to imitate, they can form the basis for project success and overall sustained business profitability. By sustainable we refer to an advantage that persists despite competitive pressures and attempted imitation (Shepherd and Shanley, 1998). This is a fundamental insight of the 'resource-based view of the firm' that has been developed by strategic scholars in recent years (Barney, 1991; Peteraf, 1993) and used in Chapters 3 and 4.

Along with the management team's competence, the past financial performance of a business is an important consideration in assessing the ability of a business to repay a loan (Gibson, 1993). Past performance sends important signals about the ability of the management team to formulate and implement growth strategies. A business that has successfully completed a project that requires related competencies provides important signals to lenders that further increases the likelihood of a favorable credit decision (Sargent and Young, 1991; Scherr et al., 1993). External stakeholders, including potential resource providers, typically obtain information on past performance from the analysis of financial statements (Kam, 1990). This information can be a source for understanding the quality of the human capital of the small business applying for a loan. Based on the above discussion, we propose that information about recent successes and other indications of relevant human capital likely increases the probability that loan officers will favorably assess the business for a loan. Thus:

Proposed relationship 7.1: *The probability that lending officers will support a loan request by a small business is higher when the past financial performance of that business is high than when it is low.*

Proposed relationship 7.2: *The probability that lending officers will support a loan request by a small business is higher when the related competence of that business is high than when it is low.*

The Effect of Collateral, Share of Investment, and Financial Standing

Banks are generally risk averse and prefer to lend money to projects where the risk of the borrower defaulting is low. Therefore, the riskier the project, the less likely the bank will be to provide the loan. However, loan officers may view the situation differently if they know that the bank can retrieve its loan regardless of the outcome of the project. We expect that the relationship between project risk and loan officers' probability of offering a loan is affected by the ability of the bank retrieving its loan regardless of the outcome of the project. As mentioned above, collateral, share of investment made by the borrower, and the financial standing of the borrower can serve the purpose of making otherwise risky projects worthy of consideration by the loan officer. Therefore, we propose that such project risk mitigation is achieved when (1) the small business's financial position is strong, (2) its collateral is independent and (3) the business has a substantial investment in the project. For example, this means that a small business could receive a bank loan for a risky project if they make a substantial investment in the project themselves, or they may not receive a loan for a less risky project should they have a weak financial standing.

Above, we spoke of past performance as an indicator of competence. In the long run past performance affects the financial position of the small business, but the two should not be confused. The financial position indicates the business's ability to repay the loan regardless of the project's performance while past performance is an indicator of the chance that the project will succeed. Financial position ensures that the financial standing of the small business is solid enough to repay the loan should the project fail (Altman, 1983; Sinkey, 1992; Beaulieu, 1994, 1996). Therefore, a strong financial position can compensate, in part, for a higher level of project risk, whereas a weak financial position places greater emphasis on the level of project risk. Thus,

Proposed relationship 7.3: *The probability that lending officers will support a loan request by a small business is lower when project risk is high than when it is low but this negative relationship is diminished when the business's financial position is strong.*

Collateral represents an alternative source of repayment for the bank and is liquidated if the borrower defaults. Besides collateral in the form of the business's assets, lenders often require non-corporate assets, such as personal guarantees or collateral on the entrepreneur's personal wealth (such as his or her house). Personal collateral is equivalent to the entrepreneur investing their own equity in the business because they are placing their personal funds at risk (Thorne, 1989), exposing the borrower to personal losses in the case of failure, and can help ensure that the borrower is committed to the small business and motivated to resolve serious problems (Berger, 1997/1998). This limits the bank's risk that the small business manager will act opportunistically to the detriment of the lender (Toivanen and Cressy, 2000). The following quote from a small business manager with her experience with lending officers is consistent with the importance of collateral:

> The banks are really just bricks and mortar lenders. I mean, if you go along to a bank, they don't want to know whether you've got a good or bad business, just whether you've got adequate security – such as your own residence that will give them enough security. In my instance I can give you an example where we had confirmed orders from overseas – we had confirmed letters and orders – and I went off to the bank to get some working capital out of them – and even though it was endorsed, they said 'no, we can't lend for that, have you got bricks and mortar?' . . . They weren't interested in knowing about my business and what we're doing. They just didn't care about the business, it was all about the security. (Cameron, 2003)

We propose that the relationship between project risk and the probability that the loan officer will provide a loan to a small business is moderated by the quality of collateral offered. Thus:

Proposed relationship 7.4: *The probability that lending officers will support a loan request by a small business is lower when project risk is high than when it is low but this negative relationship is diminished when the business can offer collateral that is independent of the project.*

The willingness of the business to self-finance a greater portion of the overall resources needed by the project likely sends a positive signal to loan officers when making their lending decisions. First, a larger share of the investment being financed by the borrower or through internally generated funds can be interpreted as a sign that the entrepreneur strongly believes in the success of the project and is willing to risk either personal or internally generated funds. Thus, it serves to align the interests and the risk bearing function of the lender and borrower, decreasing chances of opportunistic behavior (Myers and Majluf, 1984; Shapiro, 1990)

Second, financing a larger share through internally generated funds, or by additional borrower investment, decreases the amount of external funding required, which decreases the credit risk of the bank due to a lower proportion of external funding. Therefore, a higher portion of the small business's share of project funding can compensate, in part, for a higher level of project risk. Thus:

Proposed relationship 7.5: *The probability that lending officers will support a loan request by a small business is lower when project risk is high than when it is low but this negative relationship is diminished when the business has a large share of the investment.*

THE HUMAN CAPITAL OF LOAN OFFICERS AND ITS IMPACT ON THEIR DECISION POLICIES

Like most studies of resource providers' decisions, we have focused on loan officers' perceptions of the important dimensions that can be used to distinguish those businesses which should receive loans and those that should not based on the impact these loans will have on bank profitability. In doing so, we have assessed loan officers as a group, so these findings are relevant to loan officers in general. But most likely, not all loan officers make identical decisions based on the same information. In this section therefore, we explore possible differences in the decision policies of loan officers. We do so on the basis of how they differ in terms of human capital, because human capital likely influences decision making. More specifically, we examine their general experiences, specific experiences, education, and age.

Previous research suggests that the level of expertise of loan officers influences how they perform at the lending task (see Andersson, 2001, for a review of the literature). Human capital theory has been used to investigate and explain the expertise of people in a range of different tasks and we have done so in exploring the relationship between motivation and small business growth (Chapter 2) and the role of human capital in the discovery and exploitation of opportunities and the organizational mode used for that exploitation (Chapter 3). Specifically, human capital theory posits that individuals with more or higher quality human capital achieve higher performance in executing relevant tasks (Becker, 1975). Importantly, human capital varies in its degree of specificity. Some aspects of human capital are very general and provide the individual with general knowledge, skills and problem-solving abilities that are transferable across many different situations. While general human capital is generalizable across contexts, specific human capital is not and refers to the education, training and experience that are valuable to specific activities, but have few applications outside of this domain (Becker, 1975).

It is possible to identify a number of such human capital aspects that may help explain differences among the decision policies of loan officers. A general aspect of human capital is age. Increased age typically translates into increased experience and, therefore, a higher level of human capital (Fisher and Govindarajan, 1992; Mincer, 1997). Hence, we would expect that the age of the lending officer could affect his or her lending decision policies. Another aspect of general human capital is education (see Becker, 1975; Fisher and Govindarajan, 1992; Chapter 3 of this book), which is also expected to affect the lending decision task.

Turning to more specific aspects of human capital, the experience of working with the actual lending task is likely to influence how the lending officers deal with this task. This study is concerned with lending to privately held small businesses. The types of information and other decision cues that loan officers consider may be different depending on whether the business is closely held and the size of the business. Therefore, the extent to which loan officers are experienced in lending to this specific category of firms is likely to influence their decision policies. Little research exists that explicitly addresses how differences in human capital should influence the degree to which various attributes of the small business and the nature of the loan are used, and the empirical findings that have been presented are inconclusive (for example, Bédard, 1991; Camerer and Johnson, 1991). Given the emergent and inconclusive nature of the literature, we explore these relationships using non-directional proposed relationships.

Proposed relationship 7.6: *Assessment policies differ among loan officers depending on their lending experience, relative experience with small businesses, age, and education.*

Summary
In sum, the relationships stated above propose that loan officers are more likely to provide a small business loan if that business's past performance had been high and/or the business's competence was related to the project for which funding was required. We also propose that the relationship between project risk and the assessment of investment likelihood is moderated by the

small business's financial standing, the independence of collateral, and the share of the project being self-financed by the small business. Although we expect some commonality across the decision policies of all loan officers we do expect some differences and those differences to be explained by the human capital of the loan officers. Although there is theoretical support for these relationships and some empirical support, it is important to conduct a thorough empirical analysis of these relationships. In the next section we will summarize our sample and report the results of our study. We realize that some readers will be less interested in this academic side of the book, and to them we suggest that they skip the next section of the book. Other readers might be interested in more details about the research method; we refer these readers to the appendix of this chapter, which contains a description of data collection using a conjoint experiment and the variables and their levels. A more technical description of the sample and results can be found in Bruns et al., 2004.

SAMPLE AND RESULTS

Sample

The sampling frame for this research is loan officers involved in assessing loan applications by businesses, including those from small and medium sized businesses. We focused on loan officers employed by one of the five commercial banks in Sweden, who work in branches within a 100-mile radius of one of our places of work. A geographical criterion for selecting the sample was necessary because we wanted the experiment to be conducted in the presence of a researcher to ensure that any of the respondents' questions could be immediately addressed, to conduct a post-experiment interview, and to enhance the response rate. A hundred miles represented a maximum commute of two hours. We also wish to point out that this region is well known for its prevalence of small businesses.

We contacted, by telephone, the district manager, division manager, or branch manager representing each branch of the banks in the region to illicit support for the current project. One hundred and fourteen loan officers were contacted and all agreed to participate in the study. These 114 lending officers represented four of the five banks and 56 branches. A sample size of 114 exceeds other conjoint or policy capturing studies, for example, in studies of the decision policies of venture capitalists, sample sizes of 73 (Muzyka et al., 1996), 66 (Shepherd, 1999) and 53 (Zacharakis and Meyer, 1998) have been used. The characteristics of the branches and the loan officers captured by the sample are detailed in Table 7.1.

Table 7.1   Descriptive statistics for loan officers in the sample

	Mean	Std deviation
Age	45.52	8.44
Experience in banking (years)	22.86	9.74
Tenure at present bank (years)	18.82	11.52
Experience as lending officer (years)	12.97	7.39
Average number of loans approved per week	5.70	15.86
Average amount per loan (SEK)	1 855 056	3 675 208
Micro businesses as proportion of total loan number (%)	54	0.29
Small businesses as proportion of total loan number (%)	35	0.23
Medium businesses as proportion of total loan number (%)	10	0.15
Micro businesses as proportion of total loan amount (%)	13	0.17
Small businesses as proportion of total loan amount (%)	34	0.28
Medium businesses as proportion of total loan amount (%)	51	0.37
Total amount lent to micro businesses (SEK)	25 770 211	39 636 918
Total amount lent to small businesses (SEK)	102 578 053	396 802 344
Total amount lent to medium-sized businesses (SEK)	196 686 134	1 026 218 503
Lending amount limit for any one loan (SEK)	12 394 505	22 111 682

The average total capital lent by a loan officer in the previous year was SEK 322 388 041 (approximately US$ 40 705 560).

ANALYSIS AND RESULTS

The results of the hierarchical linear modeling are shown in Table 7.2 and indicate that all main effects in the main-effects-only model were significantly used by loan officers in their decisions on the likelihood of providing the small business a loan. A positive coefficient for recent performance and for competence related to the project provides support for proposed relationships 7.1 and 7.2, respectively. That is, *the probability that lending officers*

Table 7.2   *Results of hierarchical linear modeling of loan officers'*
assessments of small business applications for debt capital

	Base model		Main-effects model		Full model	
	Coefficient	Std error	Coefficient	Std error	Coefficient	Std error
Intercept	5.047	0.047***	5.047	0.072***	5.047	0.071***
CEO Tenure	0.062	0.072***	0.494	0.048***	0.495	0.049***
Comprehensiveness of strategic plan	0.152	0.072*	0.029	0.045	0.030	0.046
Competence related to project			1.269	0.066***	1.268	0.066***
Past performance			1.759	0.061***	1.759	0.062***
Current financial position			1.674	0.062***	1.675	0.062***
Independence of collateral			1.180	0.066***	1.181	0.066***
Share of investment			1.122	0.059***	1.123	0.059***
Project risk			0.141	0.044**	0.140	0.045**
Project risk × financial position					−0.237	0.077**
Project risk × independence of collateral					0.242	0.082**
Project risk × share of investment					0.062	0.077
Model[a]						
R^2		0.021***		0.549***		0.550***
Change in R^2		0.021***		0.528***		0.001**

Notes:
a = These model statistics were calculated using hierarchical regression analysis.
* = $p<0.05$; ** = $p<0.01$; *** = $p<0.001$; $n = 3648$ at level 1; 112 at level 2.

will support a loan request by a small business is higher when the past financial performance of that business is high than when it is low (7.1) and *the probability that lending officers will support a loan request by a small business is higher when the related competence of that business is high than when it is low* (7.2).

We also find that the main effects for project risk, financial position, independence of collateral and share of investment are significant. This suggests that the probability that lending officers will support a loan request by a small business is higher when project risk is low, higher when the small business can offer collateral that is independent of the project and higher when the business makes a large share of the investment. However, care must be taken in generalizing the findings of main effect relationships in the presence of significant interactions.

The full model, also in Table 7.2, reports that two of the three hypothesized interaction effects were statistically significant, specifically the interactions between project risk and financial state, and between project risk and collateral. The interaction between project risk and the business's share of investment was not significant, and therefore, proposed relationship 7.5 is not supported. The nature of each significant interaction is plotted in Figures 1(a) and 1(b).

In Figure 1(a), high and low levels of financial standing are plotted on an *x*-axis of 'project risk' and a *y*-axis of 'likelihood of providing a loan'. The plot indicates that strong financial standing mitigates the negative impact of high risk on the probability of providing a loan. This finding provides support for proposed relationship 7.3, that is, the probability that lending officers will support a loan request by a small business is lower when project

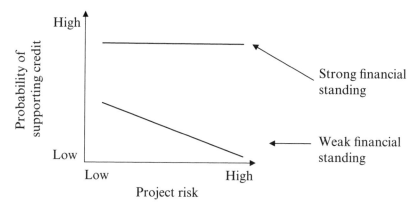

Figure 7.1a   *Interaction of project risk and current financial position on the probability of loan officer making a loan to the small business*

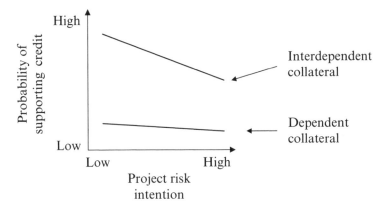

Figure 7.1b   *Interaction of project risk and independence of collateral*
                 on the probability of loan officer making a loan to the
                 small business

risk is high than when it is low but this negative relationship is diminished
when the business's financial position is strong. In Figure 1(b), high and low
levels of collateral independence are plotted on the axes, and indicate that
highly independent collateral mitigates the negative impact of high risk on
the probability of providing a loan. This finding provides support for proposed relationship 7.4, that is, *the probability that lending officers will
support a loan request by a small business is lower when project risk is high
than when it is low but this negative relationship is diminished when the business can offer collateral that is independent of the project.*

Human Capital and Differences in Decision Policies

We use hierarchical linear modeling to explain variance in loan officers'
decision policies by their human capital. HLM produces a model for each
decision criteria as represented by an intercept, age, lending experience, education, and relative loan experience with small businesses (compared to
medium and larger businesses). These models are reported in Table 7.3. The
first column lists the decision criteria. Each subsequent column represents the
results for a model that explains variance in the use of the specified decision
cue by the intercepts (columns two and three), age (columns four and five),
lending experience (columns six and seven), relative experience with small
businesses, and education.[3]

We find that the use of the 'relatedness of the firm's competence' attribute varies depending on the loan officers' level of lending experience and

Table 7.3   Results of hierarchical linear modeling of human capital variables on loan officers' decision policies

	Intercept		Age		Lending experience		Education		Relative loan exp.	
	Coefficient[a]	Std error	Coefficient[a]	Std error	Coefficient[a]	Std error	Coefficient[a]	Std error	Coefficient[a]	Std error
Intercept	5.047	0.079***	−0.017	0.013	0.024	0.015	0.123	0.164	0.547	0.249*
Competence related to project	1.271	0.072***	−0.008	0.010	0.024	0.012*	−0.293	0.149*	−0.021	0.193
Past performance	1.744	0.070***								
Current financial position	1.621	0.065***	0.003	0.012	0.017	0.012	0.007	0.014	0.072	0.176
Independence of collateral	1.238	0.074***	0.009	0.014	−0.021	0.015	0.264	0.145	−0.025	0.194
Share of investment	1.051	0.061***	0	0.010	0.001	0.012	−0.046	0.134	0.307	0.184
Project risk	0.161	0.051**	−0.008	0.007	0.010	0.008	0.061	0.097	0.003	0.162
Project risk × financial position	−0.221	0.077**	0.006	0.011	−0.016	0.016	0.376	0.177*	−0.665	0.222**
Project risk × ind. of collateral	0.339	0.090***	0.001	0.015	0.009	0.015	−0.197	0.201	0.102	0.278
Project risk × share of investment	0.103	0.084	0.007	0.014	−0.010	0.014	−0.073	0.177	−0.396	0.276

Notes:

a = These model statistics were calculated using hierarchical regression analysis.

$* = p < 0.05$; $** = p < 0.01$; $*** = p < 0.001$; $n = 3648$ at level 1; 112 at level 2.

education. The positive coefficient for lending experience suggests that those loan officers with more lending experience place *greater* emphasis on the relatedness of the business's competence to the proposed project than do those with less lending experience. The negative coefficient for education suggests that those loan officers with a higher level of education (under-graduate degree or higher) place *less* emphasis on the relatedness of the business's competence to the proposed project than do those with a lower level of education.

We find that the use of the interaction between project risk and financial position varies depending on the loan officers' education and the relative level of their experience with small businesses. The positive coefficient for education suggests that those loan officers with more education place *greater* emphasis on the interaction between project risk and financial position than do those with less education. The negative coefficient for relative experience with small business suggests that those loan officers with greater relative experience with small businesses place *less* emphasis on the interaction between project risk and financial position than do those with less relative experience with small businesses. Finally, relative experience with small businesses is significant for the intercept model, which indicates that the likelihood of a small business receiving a loan is higher with those loan officers with greater relative experience with small businesses than those with less such experience, when we hold constant the decision cues and the other human capital variables of the loan officers.

A Summary of Key Findings

This chapter's proposed relationships and those that were found in our study are reported in Table 7.4. In this chapter we investigated the decision policies of loan officers in their assessments of small businesses requesting a loan. We found that loan officers were more likely to provide a small business loan if that business's past performance had been high and/or the business's competence was related to the project for which funding was required. The findings also suggest that the relationship between project risk and the assessment of investment likelihood was moderated by other considerations. Specifically, project risk decreased the likelihood of a loan officer granting a loan for those businesses in weak financial standing but had little to no impact on those businesses in strong financial standing. Similarly, project risk decreased the likelihood of a loan officer granting a loan to those businesses with collateral dependent on the success of the project but had little to no impact for those businesses that were able to offer collateral independent of project success. We also found that loan officers differed somewhat in the emphasis they

Table 7.4 A summary of proposed relationships and levels of support

Proposed relationship	Support?
7.1: The probability that lending officers will support a loan request by a small business is higher when the past financial performance of that business is high than when it is low.	Yes
7.2: The probability that lending officers will support a loan request by a small business is higher when the related competence of that business is high than when it is low.	Yes
7.3: The probability that lending officers will support a loan request by a small business is lower when project risk is high than when it is low but this negative relationship is diminished when the business's financial position is strong.	Yes
7.4: The probability that lending officers will support a loan request by a small business is lower when project risk is high than when it is low but this negative relationship is diminished when the business can offer collateral that is independent of the project.	Yes
7.5: The probability that lending officers will support a loan request by a small business is lower when project risk is high than when it is low but this negative relationship is diminished when the business has a large share of the investment.	No
7.6: Assessment policies differ among loan officers depending on their lending experience, relative experience with small businesses, age, and education.	Yes

placed on certain attributes of the loan application. We now discuss these findings in greater detail.

DISCUSSION

Practical Implications

This chapter's proposed relationships and those that were found in our study are reported in Table 7.4. These can be thought of as rules for understanding the decision policies of loan officers in assessing the likelihood that they will give a small business a loan.

General rule of thumb 7.1: *The probability that lending officers will support a loan request by a small business is higher when the past financial performance of that business is high than when it is low.*

General rule of thumb 7.2: *The probability that lending officers will support a loan request by a small business is higher when the related competence of that business is high than when it is low.*

General rule of thumb 7.3: *The probability that lending officers will support a loan request by a small business is higher when the small business's share of risk is high than when it is low.*

These general rules of thumb are relatively straightforward and indicate that those small businesses that have performed well in the past, have related competence in the project requiring the funds and are willing to invest more of their internal funds are more likely to receive the requested funds from a loan officer. In fact, one of these relationships was simpler than we expected. We believed that for those small businesses that were not willing to make more of an investment of their own internal funds into the project that such a negative (in the eyes of loan officers) could be somewhat compensated by offering collateral independent of the project success. This was not the case. It appears that a small business manager with minimal investment in the project which requires funding will not likely have much success trying to persuade the loan officer to give him or her the loan by offering more collateral.

General rule of thumb 7.4: *The probability that lending officers will support a loan request by a small business is higher when the business's financial position is strong than when it is weak.*

General rule of thumb 7.5: *The probability that lending officers will support a loan request by a small business is higher when the independence of the collateral being offered is high than when it is low.*

General rule of thumb 7.6: *The probability that lending officers will support a loan request by a small business is higher when project risk is low than when it is high.*

These general rules are consistent with common wisdom but as the following qualifications demonstrate, these general rules are too simplistic in that they do not capture the contingent decision policies of loan officers. That is, loan officers may compensate for an undesirable attribute of the loan application if another specific attribute of the loan application is desirable. These leads to the following two qualifications to the general rules of thumb 7.4, 7.5, and 7.6.

Qualifying rule 7.1: *The negative relationship between high project risk and the probability that lending officers will support a loan request by a small business is diminished when the business's financial position is strong.*

Qualifying rule 7.2: *The negative relationship between high project risk and the probability that lending officers will support a loan request by a small business is diminished when the business can offer collateral that is independent of the project.*

The use of these contingent decision policies by loan officers is particularly interesting because if we were to rely solely on the main-effects-only models to understand the decision policies of loan officers this would lead to an overly simplified account of their actual practice and might lead to inappropriate conclusions. For example, the results of the main-effects-only model suggest that loan officers are less likely to provide a loan to businesses that are undertaking highly risky projects. While on the average (across all businesses) this might be the case, it provides a distorted picture of the way that loan officers make their decisions. This relationship is appropriate for only a subset of businesses that apply for loans; it does not appear to be the case for businesses that are in strong financial standing or those that can offer collateral that is independent of project success.

Therefore, while a financing gap might exist for small businesses, the gap is smaller for some than others: those that can demonstrate recent successes, demonstrate competence related to the project being funded, and those that can mitigate project risk through evidence of good financial standing and collateral independent of project success are more likely to secure debt capital from banks. Even for those businesses that could obtain venture capital, recognition of the conditions under which a loan is more likely might entice some entrepreneurs to choose a loan over equity funding.

How Small Businesses Can Receive Bank Loans for Risky Projects

In previous chapters we have shown that an entrepreneurial orientation (EO) can be beneficial to small firms. An EO includes being innovative and introducing new products or services, being proactive and acting before competitors, and this involves taking risks. If the small firm needs external funding for conducting its entrepreneurial activities and turns to a bank to receive this funding, it could run into problems, because banks tend to be risk averse and deny loans to risky projects. However, in this chapter we show that the negative assessment of risky projects can be mitigated. Attempts to explain loan officers' decisions on whether or not to grant a loan that do not take into account the joint impact of project risk and financial standing (Figure 7.3) as well as the joint impact of project risk and collateral (Figure 7.4) are unlikely to be successful. That is, without considering the financial standing of the small business or the independence of the collateral being offered, we are likely to overestimate the negative impact that

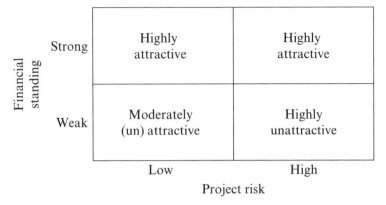

Figure 7.2   Loan attractiveness of four types of small businesses in terms of financial standing and project risk

project risk has on the likelihood that some small business will receive a loan (for those with strong financial standing and those that offer independent collateral) and underestimate the negative impact of project risk for others (those in weak financial standing and those whose collateral is dependent upon the success of the project).

Based on the information in this chapter, we present two categorizations of small businesses in terms of their attractiveness to loan officers. Specifically, Figure 7.2 categorizes small businesses along two dimensions; financial standing provides one dimension, and project risk the other. Depending on their position along these two dimensions, four types of small businesses are identified.

1.   We start with the small businesses in the upper left quadrant, which are currently in strong financial standing and are requesting a loan for a project that is considered to be low risk. Based solely on these two dimensions, loan officers find this loan application highly attractive and there is a high likelihood of their granting a loan to this small business.
2.   In the upper right quadrant are the small businesses that also have strong financial standing but are requesting a loan for a more risky project (that is, a more risky project than those of small businesses in the category above). Despite our intuition that these small businesses could be considered less attractive because the project risk is higher, project risk appears to have little impact on the loan officers' assessments of attractiveness. In the presence of strong financial standing, project risk does not appear to be a major consideration in the granting of a loan to a small business.

3. In the lower left quadrant are the small businesses that have weak financial standing but are requesting a loan for a project with little risk. Because financial standing is not strong, the loan officers consider project risk – the low financial standing is considered a negative and the low project risk a positive. These small businesses are moderately attractive/unattractive.

4. In the lower right quadrant are the small businesses that have weak financial standing and are requesting a loan for a project with considerable risk. Because financial standing is not strong, the loan officers consider project risk – the low financial standing is considered a negative and the low project risk is also considered a negative. In this case, two negatives do not make a positive, these small businesses are considered to be highly unattractive to loan officers and would stand the least chance of receiving a loan. It is interesting to point out the difference between this category of small businesses and those in the upper right quadrant. Both groups of small businesses have high project risk, but the project risk does not have much (if any) of a negative impact when financial standing is high but does have a large negative impact when financial standing is weak.

Now we present the second of our two categorizations. Figure 7.3 categorizes small businesses along two dimensions; independence of collateral represents the first dimension, and project risk, again, represents the second dimension. Depending on their position along these two dimensions, four types of small businesses are identified.

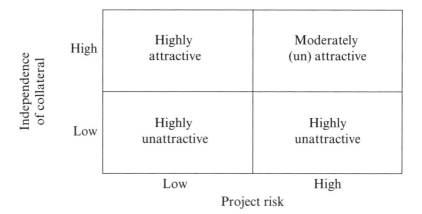

Figure 7.3   Loan attractiveness of four types of small businesses in terms
of independence of collateral and project risk

1. Small businesses in the upper left quadrant can offer the bank collateral independent of the success of the project and that project is low in risk. Based solely on these two dimensions, loan officers find this loan application highly attractive and there is a high likelihood of granting a loan to this small business.

2. In the upper right quadrant are the small businesses that can offer collateral independent of project risk but the project is high risk. Loan officers see the collateral situation as a positive and the project risk as a negative and therefore these small businesses are assessed as being moderately attractive/unattractive.

3. In the lower left quadrant are the small businesses that will not (or cannot) offer collateral independent of project success but have a project of low risk. In this case the loan officers place little emphasis on the level of project risk and focus on the negative aspect of low collateral. Small businesses in this quadrant are considered to be highly unattractive and unlikely to receive a bank loan.

4. In the lower right quadrant are the small businesses that will not (or cannot) offer collateral independent of project success and face high project risk. Negatives on both these dimensions means that loan officers find the small businesses of this quadrant to be highly unattractive and are unlikely to issue them a loan.

It is interesting to compare the two categorizations. In the first, project risk has little impact on loan officers' assessments of attractiveness when the small businesses are in strong financial standing: the small businesses of the top quadrants one are assessed to be similarly highly attractive. In the second categorization, project risk has little impact on loan officers' assessments of attractiveness when the small business will not (or cannot) offer collateral independent of project success: the small businesses of the bottom quadrants are assessed to be similarly highly unattractive.

There are two lessons for small businesses wishing to pursue risky projects in this survey. First, a strong financial standing is a sufficient condition for receiving bank loans for risky projects. If the small business has reached this position thanks to the ability to accumulate retained earnings, through large private cash infusions by the main owners, or through outside venture capital is probably irrelevant. The old saying that banks only lend money to those who already have money appears relevant for risky projects. It seems to be an unwise decision to start a business on a shoestring if the intention is to subsequently pursue risky projects with debt funding. Such businesses are not likely to receive the bank loans they wish for. The second lesson is that the quality of collateral is important. It appears that providing collateral that is independent of project success (such as bonds or private property) is a necessary but not sufficient condition for receiving a bank loan. If the collateral is dependent on project success (such as a floating charge or receivables) small businesses are unlikely to receive credits for projects irrespectively of the risk involved. Small businesses wanting to pursue risky projects definitely benefit from independent collateral, but it seems that this cannot completely mitigate the negative assessment of the loan officer.

Differences in the Decision Policies of Loan Officers

These findings on the decision policies of loan officers complements our understanding of the decision policies of venture capitalists: we now have an understanding of the decision policies of resource providers on both sides of the funding gap. While venture capitalists focus primarily on the 'upside potential' of possible portfolio companies, loan officers focus on the possibility of downside loss and are attracted to those businesses where it is low or where it is mitigated such that it is not directly transferred to the risk that the business will default on the loan.

While we have used human capital theory as a basis for explaining differences between small business managers who pursue subsequent opportunities and those who do not (Chapter 3), previous research on the decision policies of resource providers (primarily those of venture capitalists) has typically explicitly or implicitly treated these decision makers as a homogeneous group. In this study we took an exploratory perspective to investigate whether differences did exist, the nature of these differences, and, in particular, whether those with more human capital were more likely to use decision policies with contingent relationships than those with less human capital. We found that loan officers did differ in their decision policies and those differences could be explained, in part, by differences in human capital. These differences are detailed in Table 7.5.

This information is useful in understanding differences among loan officers in the relative importance of the decision criteria. Interestingly, this exploratory portion of the study revealed that aspects of human capital may not have the same effect on a loan officer's decision policies. For the decision criteria of the relatedness of the business's competence to the project being proposed, those loan officers with more lending experience placed greater emphasis on this decision criteria than those with less such experience but the reverse was the case for when comparing loan officers' with educational qualifications: those more highly educated loan officers placed less emphasis on this decision criteria than those less well educated. Similarly, aspects of human capital had differential effects on the use of the contingent relationship between project risk and financial standing. Those loan officers with higher education placed greater emphasis on this con-

Table 7.5   Differences in loan officers

Relationships found

1. Loan officers with more lending experience place *greater* emphasis on the relatedness of the business's competence to the proposed project than do those with less lending experience.

2. Loan officers with a higher level of education (undergraduate degree or higher) place *less* emphasis on the relatedness of the business's competence to the proposed project than do those with a lower level of education.

3. Loan officers with more education place *greater* emphasis on the interaction between project risk and financial position than do those with less education.

4. Loan officers with greater relative experience with small businesses place *less* emphasis on the interaction between project risk and financial position than do those with less relative experience with small businesses.

5. The likelihood of a small business receiving a loan is higher with those loan officers with greater relative experience with small businesses than those with less such experience, when we hold constant the decision cues and the other human capital variables of the loan officers.

tingent relationship than those with less education but those with more relative experience with small business placed less emphasis on this contingent relationship than those with less such experience. In this case the more highly educated loan officers had more complex decision policies than less educated loan officers and those with more relative experience with small businesses seem to rely on it less or use a simplified decision rule. These exploratory findings provide the basis for greater theorizing and more empirical work on the differential effect that human capital variables can have on the decision policies of loan officers and resource providers more generally. For those small business managers applying for a loan, there are general and qualifying rules of thumb to help them understand the loan officers' decision policies as a group, and even within this group, how loan officers' decision policies differ based on the level and type of their human capital.

Implications for Policymakers

Bank financing of small businesses and its policy implications is an area which has received considerable attention. The general finding from such studies is that there are liquidity constraints among small businesses, and that they have problems obtaining the bank loans that they need. In this chapter we have been able to provide more nuance to this statement. We find that while some small businesses are very unlikely to receive bank loans, others should have little problem. Turning to Figure 7.2, we have identified three levels of attractiveness of small businesses on the basis of their financial standing and the risk of the project that they intend to pursue.

1. The *highly attractive* small businesses in the upper half of the figure have a strong financial standing and are likely to receive back loans irrespectively of the risk that the bank associates with the project (within reasonable boundaries, of course), thus being attractive to bank lending. Economic policies are important to this category of small businesses because such policies affect interest rates. Like all businesses, they benefit from policies ensuring low and stable interest rates. That way it is possible for these small businesses to borrow the money they need knowing it is affordable.

2. Small businesses in the *highly unattractive* category are the least likely to receive bank funding. Statistics from several countries show that small businesses generally have weak financial positions, thus belonging to this category. In this study we showed that if a small business has a weak financial standing, it is unlikely to receive bank loans for pursuing risky projects. This situation may stifle the entrepreneurship and innovativeness of these small businesses, which can hurt their long-term competitiveness as well as of the economy at large. It is for these *highly unattractive* small businesses that government support programs are of particular value. Under some programs, governments offer guarantees to financiers in return for a fee to cover the risks as well as administrative and processing costs. These schemes serve the purpose of sharing (reducing) the bank's risk. Rather than generally supporting small businesses applying for loans, such schemes benefit from the insight that in addition to the characteristics of the borrowing business, the characteristics of the project play an important role in determining if the bank is willing to provide the funding needed. These schemes, therefore, are best directed to sound businesses that for various reasons have a relatively weak financial position (because they are young, or because they are using their resources to expand) and wish to pursue projects that involve risk. Unless the bank can share the risk, these projects are unlikely to receive bank financing.

3. The *moderately (un)attractive* category in the bottom left-hand corner have weak financial standings but do not wish to pursue risky projects. As with the *highly attractive* category, they benefit from economic policies ensuring low and stable interest rates. We do not know to what extent small businesses with weak financial standing self-select into this

category. If they are attentive of bank policies, they may be aware that they will only receive funding for their less risky projects. If this is the case, they too will benefit from the guarantee schemes and other policies mentioned above.

Our findings concerning the interaction of financial risk and collateral also have policy implications. Figure 7.3 showed that small businesses that were unable to provide collateral independent of the project were highly unattractive for all projects, irrespectively of the risk associated with the project. Guarantee schemes appear relevant for these businesses, because they may well take some of the risk away from banks, possibly making them more willing to lend money to these small businesses.

Implications for Scholars

This chapter has a number of important implications for scholars. First, we introduce the financial gap facing entrepreneurs looking to expand their businesses and offer a counterweight to the extensive body of research that has focused on the venture capital edge of that gap. We focus on the debt capital edge of the financial gap by hypothesizing and testing the criteria that loan officers use when assessing a small business for loan approval. This approach challenges the assumption that the finance gap is the same size for all small businesses.

Second, we complement the limited research work on debt capital for small businesses by using a decision making perspective to theorize and rigorously investigate the content, emphases, and complexity of loan officers' decision policies. It is understandable that scholars are most interested in those small businesses that are going to grow rapidly and provide a high rate of return for its investors. It is for this reason, in part, that there has been so much scholarly attention directed toward venture capital and venture capitalists' decision policies. However, most small businesses do not fit into this high growth category and therefore have been relatively ignored by previous research. In this chapter, we focus on debt funding and suggest that more scholarly work be directed at this form of small business funding.

Third, we extend the research on the decision policies of resource providers (venture capitalists and loan officers) by using a human capital perspective to explore differences between decision makers based on their general experiences, specific experiences, and education. This is an interesting avenue for future research. It does not suggest that understanding the decision policies of loan officers as a whole is not important: on the contrary, such general rules are highly useful for understanding decision outcomes, especially at the aggregate level of analysis. But we can gain additional insight by understanding the decision policies of subgroups and how those subgroups differ. We hope that scholars will use human capital theory as a basis for explaining differences in decision policies within other stakeholder groups and even across stakeholder groups (see for example, Choi and Shepherd, 2004). There are also likely other theoretical perspectives that form the basis of an a priori expectation of subgroup differences.

CONCLUSION

Loans from banks represent an important funding source for small business managers to grow their businesses. The majority of growth that occurs in an economy is derived from the less spectacular growth of the large number of small businesses. These businesses typically do not meet venture capitalists' screening criteria and are more likely to approach banks applying for loans to fund growth than to approach venture capitalists for an equity infusion. However, these businesses generally have difficulties obtaining bank loans, which in turn constrains the growth of many businesses. This financial gap can largely be attributed to information asymmetry between the small business manager and the bank representative. Consequently, it is essential that banks develop methods that reduce risk and uncertainty in the loans that they make. In this chapter we complemented the recent work on venture capital for gazelles and venture capitalists' decision policies (captured in the previous chapter), to investigate debt capital for small businesses and loan officers' decision policies.

We found that loan officers were more likely to provide a small business loan if that business's past performance had been high and/or the business's competence was related to the project for which funding was required. The findings also suggest that the relationship between project risk and the assessment of investment likelihood was moderated by other considerations. Specifically, project risk decreased the likelihood of a loan officer granting a loan for those businesses in weak financial standing but had little to no impact on those businesses in strong financial standing. Similarly, project risk decreased the likelihood of a loan officer granting a loan to those businesses with collateral independent of the success of the project but had little to no impact for those businesses that were able to offer collateral independent of project success (they were unlikely to receive a loan irrespective of the level of risk involved). Therefore, while a financing gap might exist for businesses, the gap is smaller from some than others. We also found that loan officers differed in their decision policies and those differences could be explained, in part, by differences in human capital.

Obtaining a loan may help the small business manager pursue desired projects but the outcomes are not always as expected. For example, by introducing new products there is the possibility of substantially increasing sales but there is also a possibility that the market does not react as expected, sales are disappointing and the small business manager is unable to repay the loan. Under these circumstances the business may become bankrupt and the small business manager must deal with his or her business's failure. In the next chapter, we address the emotional side of such an outcome and offer a process by which small business managers can learn from the experience and how educators can better prepare their students for this (highly likely) possibility.

APPENDIX: CONJOINT EXPERIMENT, VARIABLES, AND LEVELS

Conjoint Analysis

This study uses conjoint analysis, a technique that requires respondents to make a series of judgments based on a set of attributes from which the underlying structure of their decisions can be decomposed by means of hierarchical linear modeling. This method allows the researcher to examine how respondents process contingency relationships (Hitt and Barr, 1989; Priem and Harrison, 1994), without relying on the respondents' (generally inaccurate) introspection (Fischhoff, 1982; Priem and Harrison, 1994). Conjoint analysis and policy capturing have been used in hundreds of studies of judgment and decision making (Green and Srinivasan, 1990). These studies vary from research into consumer purchase decisions (Lang and Crown, 1993), manager's strategic decisions (Hitt et al., 2000; Priem, 1994) and venture capitalists' assessment of a portfolio company's return on investment (Zacharakis and Meyer, 2000), profitability (Shepherd et al., 2000), and survival (Shepherd, 1999). Conjoint analysis is particularly appropriate for this study because as a real time method it overcomes many of the potential research biases associated with post-hoc methods, such as self-reporting biases, retrospective reporting biases and difficulty collecting contingent decision data.

Experimental Design

Because a fully crossed factorial design for this study would require 256 (2^8) profiles, an orthogonal fractional factorial design was used to reduce the number of attribute combinations and thus make the decisionmaking task more manageable (Green and Srinivasan, 1990). In choosing an orthogonal fractional factorial design we followed the general rule of confounding effects of most interest with effects that are unlikely to be significant or, if they are significant, are unlikely to cause much bias in the parameters that are estimated (Louviere, 1988). We chose a design from Hahn and Shapiro (1966) which confounded the main effects and all two way interactions involving 'project risk' (the effects of most interest) with other two-way and all higher-order interactions (those effects of least interest); and therefore, it is unlikely that non-hypothesized higher-order effects biased this study's results (as higher-order interactions typically account for minuscule proportions of variance (Louviere, 1988)). Each of the profiles was fully replicated. We randomly assigned the 32 profiles and the order of attributes within a profile for four versions of the experiment to test for order effects. There was no significant difference across versions ($p > 0.10$) and therefore order effects are unlikely to have influenced the results. A practice profile was used at the start of the experiment to familiarize respondents with the experiment but was not used in the analysis. We pilot tested the instrument with six lending officers. Comments suggested that the instructions and definitions of attribute levels were clear and that the instrument appeared realistic (had face validity).

Experiment

In this conjoint experiment, loan officers were asked to evaluate a series of hypothetical profiles and decide on the likelihood that they would offer the business a loan. All hypothetical businesses were characterized as selling five products or services, having a market share of 5 per cent in a local market, competition being neither intense nor weak, situated in a city of 120 000 inhabitants, the five biggest customers generate 40 per cent of sales, cash flow matches the industry average, and the company wishes to borrow an amount equal to its equity. The instructions specified that all conditions, other than the attributes described in the profile, are to be considered constant across all profiles. This controlled for other possible confounding attributes.

Having assessed a hypothetical profile, the loan officers were asked to respond to the following question: 'How would you rate the probability that you would support this firm's credit request?' It was measured on a nine-point scale anchored in 'not at all likely' (scored one) and 'very likely' (scored nine). Eight attributes were used to construct the hypothetical profiles (scenarios). Six of the attributes correspond to our independent variables and two were included as control variables. The independent variables and their levels are:

1. Past performance: high – the company's profit is well above the industry average; low – the company's profit is well below the industry average.

2. Competence related to project: high – the new project is estimated to be profitable, in line with the firm's previous projects, and is highly related to the firm's proven knowledge; low – the new project is estimated to be profitable, but is considerably different from previous projects, and is only not related to the firm's proven knowledge.

3. Risk of project: high – the firm prefers high-risk projects that offer the chance of a very high return; low – the firm prefers low-risk projects that have a high probability to gain a small amount.

4. Financial position: high – the firm's liquidity and solvency is well above the industry average; low – the firm's liquidity and solvency is well below the industry average.

5. Independence of collateral: high – the firm offers collateral that is independent of the firm's success or failure in the project, such as bond, personal guarantee, private property; low – the firm offers collateral that is dependent on the firm's success or failure in the project, such as floating charge, receivables.

6. Share of investment: high – the firm finances 35 per cent of the capital requirements either through internally generated funds or by additional capital provided by the owner(s); low – the firm finances 5 per cent of the capital requirements either through internally generated funds or by additional capital provided by the owner(s).

Controls

The funding literature suggests that two further attributes are likely to impact loan officers' lending decisions. An important indicator of the future performance of the business at a particular task is the experience of the entrepreneur. This experience may lead to expertise in running an independent business (Wright et al., 1997) and provide benchmarks for judging the relevance of information (Cooper et al., 1995), which can enhance performance (Davidsson and Honig, 2003; Brüderl and Schüssler 1990). Longer tenure as a small business manager indicates more experience and this is controlled for by the following attribute: *CEO tenure*: High – the CEO started his/her position eight years ago, has a business education, and is regarded as honest and reliable. The CEO lacks previous experience in the industry and as a CEO. Low – the CEO started his/her position two years ago, has a business education, and is regarded as honest and reliable. The CEO lacks previous experience in the industry and as a CEO.

In evaluating a business, loan officers must evaluate the business's ability to develop appropriate strategies (cf. Berger 1997/1998). The business's business plan provides information to its reader about the ability of management to communicate its strategies to stakeholders (Sargent and Young, 1991) and the extent and cohesiveness of information contained within the plan is an indirect indicator of the quality of the management team (Sinkey, 1992). The following attribute was included as a control variable. *Comprehensiveness of Strategic Plan*: High – the firm has a comprehensive business plan which is documented and followed; low – the firm follows a distinct strategic line, but its plans for doing so are not documented.

Post-Experiment Survey

After completing the conjoint experiment, each loan officer completed a survey, the answers to which provided information about their human capital. We now detail the operationalization of each human capital variable.

- Lending experience: respondents were asked to state how many years they have worked as a lending officer.
- Relative experience with lending to small businesses: respondents were asked to self-report the percentage of the previous year's loans that were disbursed to (1) micro businesses, (2) small businesses and (3) medium sized businesses. To capture the emphasis on smaller businesses we summed the reported percentages for the amount of loans to micro and small businesses: the higher the percentage on this measure, the greater the relative experience with lending to small businesses over other types of businesses.
- Age: respondents were asked to state the year in which they were born. From this their current age was calculated.
- Education: respondents were asked to state their highest level of completed education using the following categories: junior secondary school; senior high school; some university; bachelor's degree; master's degree.

There were few loan officers in the first and last of these categories (nine of 114). We therefore dichotomized the education responses into those that have an undergraduate degree or more advanced degree as their highest level of education (dummy coded one; $n = 25$) and those that do not (dummy coded zero; $n = 89$).

NOTES

1. This chapter is based on a working paper: Bruns et al., (2004).
2. To the extent that there are bank policies on lending, these will be reflected in the loan officers' decision policies.
3. Curvilinear relationships for the human capital variables were also investigated and none were found to be significant.

8. Learning from small business failure[1]

INTRODUCTION

Previously in this book we have addressed how small businesses can improve their performance, increase growth rates, and receive outside funding from banks and venture capitalists in order to develop. In other words, we have largely focused on the positive side of operating a small business. In this chapter we acknowledge that not all attempts to launch and grow a business are successful – businesses do fail. In the literature, business failure has received relatively little attention (McGrath, 1999), but statistics show that it is a common phenomenon.[2] In 2001, there were 12 457 US businesses that ceased operations, only to have their assets liquidated with the proceeds remitted to creditors (a chapter 7 bankruptcy). That same year, the much smaller economy of Sweden had 7433 businesses that filed for bankruptcy. These statistics understate the number of business failures because they do not account for those businesses that are sold or merged with another firm to avoid bankruptcy. Business failure occurs when a fall in revenues and/or rise in expenses are of such magnitude that the firm becomes insolvent and is unable to attract new debt or equity funding; consequently, it cannot continue to operate under the current ownership and management. This chapter does not focus on how failure can be avoided – the careful reader should have identified several opportunities for improving performance by reading this book. Instead we turn our focus to how it is possible to learn from failure and possibly return to operating a business more successfully.

The idea that operating a failing business enhances the ability to start and manage a new one successfully is not totally new. Although reports vary, one study suggests that 51 per cent of all entrepreneurs in the USA have previous owner–manager experience (Schollhammer, 1991). Through the feedback obtained from these experiences the entrepreneurs' knowledge is enhanced (see Minniti and Bygrave, 2001), and this new knowledge can be highly useful in managing subsequent businesses. These experiences involve both successes and failures, but it has been suggested that more can be learned from failure than from success (Sitkin, 1992). Therefore, it may be possible to turn the managing of a failing small business into a valuable experience.

Losing a business due to failure can be very emotionally upsetting for the small business owner–manager because a business is often an extension of his or her personality. Failure therefore likely represents a personal loss, which in turn generates a negative emotional response. Negative emotions may impact the ability to learn from an event (Isen and Baron, 1991). Some researchers suggest that negative emotions enhance learning (Cyert and March, 1963; Kiesler and Sproull, 1982; Lant and Mezias, 1992; Lant et al., 1992; Morrison and Robinson, 1997) while others hold that they restrict learning (Barker and Mone, 1998; D'Aunno and Sutton, 1992; Ocasio, 1995; Staw et al., 1981; Sutton and D'Aunno, 1989). It appears that to gain a deeper understanding of learning from failure, we need to explore the role of negative emotions. Emotions are defined here as the personal displays of affected, or 'moved', 'agitated' states (Fineman, 1996: 546). An emotional response to an event involves feelings, moods, emotions and sympathetic nervous-system activity that people have experienced in relation to an event and subsequently associate with it (Eagly and Chaiken, 1998: 272).

This chapter utilizes the psychology literature on grief and emotions to gain a deeper understanding of the ability of the small business manager to learn from business failure. In doing so it makes a contribution to our understanding of entrepreneurial small businesses by acknowledging that the loss of a business can generate a negative emotional response and that this emotional response can interfere with the small business manager's ability to learn from the loss: learning from failure is not automatic or instantaneous. This chapter also offers new ideas to organizational research on emotions by explaining the problems associated with a certain type of learning – learning from failure – and how learning can be enhanced by a process of grief recovery. Specifically, we focus on information about why a business failed, how grief interferes with the processing of this information, and how the process of grief recovery can reduce emotional interference and thereby enhance an individuals' ability to learn from business failure. Finally, this chapter offers a challenge to educators to prepare their students better to regulate grief in the event that they manage a small business that fails.

THE SMALL BUSINESS MANAGER AND GRIEF

There appears to be an emotional relationship between small business managers and their businesses. For example, the motivation for managing one's own business is not simply one of personal profit but also includes loyalty to a product, loyalty to a market and customers, personal growth, and the need to prove oneself (Bruno et al., 1992). Similarly, Cova and Svanfeldt (1993: 297) propose that entrepreneurs '. . . create a product that flows from their own internal desires and needs. They create primarily to express subjective conceptions of beauty, emotion, or some aesthetic ideal.' For members of a family business, the firm may not only be a source of income but also a context for family activity and the embodiment of family pride and identity (Meyer and Zucker, 1989: 78). The above suggests that the loss of a business is likely to generate a negative emotional response from the small business manager, namely grief.[3]

Archer (1999) argues that even though we normally think of grief as occurring in the context of the death of a loved one, a broadly similar reaction can occur when a close relationship is ended through separation, or when a person is forced to give up some aspect of life deemed to be important. The authors have experienced this first hand. When Dean's family business failed, his father (John Shepherd) exhibited a number of worrying emotions. There was numbness and disbelief that this business he had created 20-odd years ago was no longer alive. There was some anger towards the economy, competitors and debtors. A stronger emotion than anger was that of guilt and self-blame. He felt guilty that he had caused the failure of the business, that it could no longer be passed on to Dean's brother, and that as a result he had failed not only as a business person but also as a father. These feelings caused him distress and anxiety. He felt the situation was hopeless, became withdrawn, and at times depressed. When Johan's mother (Maud Wiklund) sold the family business due to personal health problems, similar emotions arose. These are all symptoms of grief (Bonanno and Keltner, 1997; Janoff-Bulman, 1992; Klass, 1988; Middleton et al., 1997; Parkes, 1988; Shuchter, 1986; Williams and Moris, 1996). Therefore, we argue that it is typical for small business managers to feel grief, which is a negative emotional response to the loss of a business capable of triggering behavioral, experiential and physiological symptoms (Gross, 1998).

This chapter relies, in part, on the literature on grief over the loss of a loved one. Even though the loss of a loved one and the loss of a business may both generate grief, we do not want our approach to diminish the feelings involved with losing a loved one. Obviously, there are different levels of grief and those who have lost a loved one are likely to grieve differently from those that lose a business. For example, learning from the loss of a loved one is likely to be highly philosophical and existential whereas learning from the loss of a business can be more practical and constructive. Therefore, care must be taken in generalizing results of grief studies in one context into another. Additionally, just as the grief of losing a loved one is deeply personal, individuals who have lost a business will most likely differ from each other in their level of grief. Explaining why there are differences in the level of grief over the loss of a business is beyond the scope of this chapter; rather, our focus is to understand the relationship between grief, recovery from grief, and the ability of small business managers to learn from the loss of their business. Accordingly, we now turn our attention to exploring the relationship between grief and learning.

Learning from Business Loss

A person learns using the outcome of action (feedback) to revise one's belief system (Huy, 1999; Kim, 1993; Weick, 1979). For small business managers, learning from business failure occurs when they can use the information available about why the business failed (feedback information) to revise their existing knowledge of how to manage their own business effectively (small business knowledge); that is, to revise assumptions about the consequences of previous assessments, decisions, action and inaction. For example, Ravi Kalakota has learned a number of lessons from the loss of his small business, Hsupply.com, such as, 'don't let venture capitalists hijack your vision', 'don't rapidly burn through capital to achieve short-term growth', and 'don't under-estimate the speed with which others will imitate your products and services' (Gilbert, 2000). The amount of feedback information 'available' to be learned may vary independently of the level of grief; for example, there is more to be learned when the action or inaction of the small business manager caused the loss of the business than when an external, improbable event caused the loss of the business, such as an earthquake or a terrorist attack.

The entrepreneurship literature suggests that there is an opportunity for small business managers to process feedback information into small business knowledge, yet this literature has not sufficiently considered the role of grief in this learning process. Grief is a negative emotional response, and negative emotions have been found to interfere with individuals' allocation of attention in the processing of information (Mogg et al., 1990; Wells and Matthews, 1994). Such interference negatively impacts an individual's ability to learn from that negative event (Bower, 1992). For example, emotional events receive high priority in processing information (Ellis, et al., 1971; and see Ellis and Ashbrook, 1988, 1989). This can cause individuals not to process mentally the last few items preceding the emotional event (Bower, 1992). For small business managers, this could mean focusing attention on the day that the business closed (that is, dwelling on announcements to employees, buyers and suppliers, as well as handing over the office keys to a liquidator), rather than allocating sufficient attention on feedback information, such as previous action and/or inaction that caused the deterioration in business performance and ultimately the loss of the business.

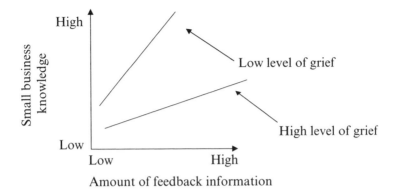

Figure 8.1   The moderating role of grief on the relationship between feedback information and small business knowledge

Thus, the interference of grief with the ability to learn from past events suggests that the level of grief affects how much a small business manager is able to learn from the feedback he or she receives from the failure. The nature of this relationship is illustrated in Figure 8.1 and is now stated.

Proposed relationship 8.1: *Individuals with high levels of grief learn less from information about the loss of a small business than individuals with low levels of grief.*

THE GRIEF RECOVERY PROCESS

An individual has recovered from grief when thoughts about the events surrounding, and leading up to the loss of the small business, no longer generate a negative emotional response. Those that feel grief over the loss of a small business will eventually recover from grief or will suffer chronic grief requiring professional psychological assistance (which is beyond the scope of this chapter). In the literature on grief over the loss of a loved one, there are two primary descriptions of the process of recovering from grief, classifiable as either loss-oriented or restoration-oriented. These two orientations are introduced and adapted to grief over the loss of a small business.

Loss Orientation

Loss orientation refers to working through, and processing, some aspect of the loss experience (Stroebe and Schut, 1999) and, as a result of this process, breaking emotional bonds to the object lost (Archer, 1999). Typical of the loss-oriented approach for grief over the loss of a loved one, Malkinson (1996: 155) states: 'Grieving is crucial, necessary, and unavoidable for successful adaptation' (p. 155). This process of constructing a series of accounts about the loss, gradually provides the loss with meaning and eventually produces a changed viewpoint of the self and the world (Archer, 1999). Changing the way that an event is interpreted can allow an individual to regulate emotions so that thoughts of the event no longer generate negative emotions (Gross, 1999).

Small business managers with a loss orientation might seek out friends, family or psychologists to talk about their grief. They may also focus their thoughts on the time spent in creating and nurturing the small business and may ruminate about the circumstances and events surrounding its loss. It appears that such thoughts could evoke a sense of yearning for the way things used to be or foster a sense of relief that the events surrounding the loss (such as arguing with creditors, explaining to employees, family and friends that the business has failed) are finally over. These feelings of relief and pain wax and wane over time, although Stroebe and Schut (1999) propose that in the early periods of grief over the loss of a loved one, painful memories are likely to dominate.

A number of scholars have raised a note of caution about whether 'grief work' is essential for the recovery from grief (Bonanno and Keltner, 1997; Prigerson et al., 1996; Stroebe and Schut, 1999; Wortman and Silver, 1989, 1992). Confrontation of the loss appears insufficient to explain the grief recovery process: 'Those who show the most evidence of working through the loss are those who ultimately have the most difficulty in resolving what has happened' (Wortman and Silver, 1987: 207). It appears that confrontation of the loss can make negative thoughts and memories more accessible and salient, and thereby slow the recovery process (Lyubomirsky and Nolen-Hoeksema, 1995; Nolen-Hoeksema et al., 1997). Suppression of feelings of loss and getting on with one's life also appears to be an approach to grief recovery. This alternative approach is referred to as restoration-orientation.

Restoration Orientation

Restoration orientation is based on both avoidance and proactiveness towards secondary sources of stress arising from the loss of the small business. For avoidance, it is possible that small business managers can distract themselves from thinking about the loss of the business to speed recovery from grief. For example, Cuisner et al. (1996) found that both a subsequent pregnancy and the birth of a new baby predicted lower levels of grief over the loss of a baby. New relationships enable individuals to distract themselves from loss related thoughts, which allows for the gradual fading of memories associated with the loss. Remarriage after the death of a spouse is another example of an action that can lead to speedier recovery (Shuchter, 1986). This might be because the new marriage replaces many of the features of the married state that are particularly missed; in essence, this highlights the distinction between the loss of a role and the loss of an individual. For small business managers, founding a new business might enhance recovery from grief over the loss of a previous business (although there is the possibility that the same mistakes are replicated because these individuals have not sufficiently learned from the loss).

A restoration orientation is not simply about avoidance, it also concerns the way that a person attends to other aspects of his or her life (such as coping with daily life, learning new tasks). It refers to being proactive towards secondary sources of stress instead of being concerned with the loss itself. Such activities enable individuals to distract themselves from thinking about the loss while simultaneously maintaining essential activities necessary for restructuring aspects of their lives (Archer, 1999). This may apply to small business managers, for whom the loss of the business itself generates a negative emotional response while causing the loss of income, social status and self-perception. For example, a small business manager must reorganize one's life to cope without the business. It might be necessary to apply for jobs, join the unemployment queue, and/or sell the house and move to a less expensive neighborhood (requiring the children to change school). There might also be other stressors such as responding to questions such as: 'What do you do for a living?' or 'How is your business going?' In addressing these secondary sources of stress, small business managers are able to reduce the negative emotions associated with thoughts of the events surrounding the loss of the business.

A Dual Process for Grief

Which process of grief recovery is the most effective? Stroebe and Schut (1999) have argued that recovery from grief over the loss of a loved one is not an 'either/or' choice between the two orientations. Both loss-oriented and restoration-oriented coping styles are likely to have different costs. A loss orientation involves confrontation, which is physically and mentally exhausting whereas a restoration orientation involves suppression, which requires mental effort and presents potentially averse consequences for health (Archer, 1999). Oscillation between the two models of coping behavior provides a central regulating mechanism enabling the person to obtain the benefits of each and to minimize the costs of maintaining one for too long. This dual process speeds the recovery process (see Stroebe and Schut, 1999). Speeding the recovery process is important because it reduces more quickly the emotional interference with learning. However, the benefits of this dual process might be greater than just speed.

Weick's (1990) investigation of the Tenerife air disaster provides an illustration of how negative emotions can both enable and inhibit adaptation. He argued that psychological stress (a result of negative emotion) triggers the autonomic nervous system, which can have a positive effect on adaptation because it alerts people to the importance of the event and therefore attention is allocated to processing information about it (Weick, 1990; see also Fineman, 1996; Frank, 1993; Hirshleifer, 1993; De Sousa, 1987), but if diagnosis and coping are not swift, arousal from the negative emotion begins to register in the consciousness and consume scarce information processing capacity, which decreases cognitive efficiency (Weick, 1990; see also Argyris, 1990; Elster, 1999; Staw et al., 1981). A process that utilizes negative emotions to focus an individual's attention on the event while simultaneously not allowing that focus to become cognitively inefficient could enhance learning from failure.

A dual process of grief recovery provides a regulating mechanism for a small business manager's grief such that it may lead to both a quicker recovery from grief, and, at a given level of grief, a more efficient processing of information about the loss of his or her business. Both enhance a small business manager's ability to learn from the loss of a business. For example, starting with a loss orientation provides a small business manager the ability to focus first on aspects of the loss experience and begin processing information about the business loss as well as breaking the emotional bonds to the business. When attention begins to shift focus from the event to aspects of the grief itself then learning is likely reduced by emotional interference and the small business manager should switch to a restoration orientation. Switching to a restoration orientation encourages individuals to think about other aspects of their life. It also breaks the cycle of continually thinking about the symptoms of grief; such thoughts can increase feelings of grief (Nolen-Hoeksema, 1991). This restoration orientation also provides the opportunity to address secondary causes of stress, which may reduce the emotional significance of the loss of the small business. When information processing capacity is no longer focused on the symptoms associated with grief, the small business manager can shift back to a loss orientation and use his/her information processing capacity to generate further meaning from the loss experience and also further reduce the emotional significance of the loss of the business. Oscillation should continue until the small business manager has recovered from grief. Thus,

Proposed relationship 8.2: *Grief over the loss of a small business is reduced by a loss orientation or a restoration orientation.*

Proposed relationship 8.3: *A dual process of grief recovery reduces grief more quickly than the exclusive use of either orientation. A speedier recovery allows small business managers to learn more quickly from information about the loss of a business.*

Proposed relationship 8.4: *At a given level of grief over the loss of a business, a dual process of grief recovery enhances a small business manager's ability to learn more from information about the loss of the business than the exclusive use of either orientation.*

DISCUSSION

Summary

Although grief from the death of a loved one is different from grief over the loss of a small business, the concepts of grief and grief recovery offer a useful framework for understanding the reaction of small business managers to business failure. The negative emotional response to the loss of a business represents grief that, while present, will diminish the small business manager's ability to learn from the events surrounding the loss, especially when there is considerable feedback information. We proposed that a dual process of grief recovery, one that involves oscillating between a loss and a restoration orientation, provides the speediest path to grief recovery. Recovery from grief allows learning to take place without interference from strong emotions. But even in the presence of grief, this dual process regulates information processing to minimize emotional interference and thereby enhances learning from the loss of a small business.

Implications of the Dual Process Model of Grief for the Self-Employed and their Family and Friends

Bill Lewis represents an example of someone who has experienced grief and recovered from it. He had founded eight businesses and been through two bankruptcies when he was interviewed by *Inc* magazine (Richman, 1990). He stated:

> [The business is] a child. . . . [Losing the business] was devastating. . . . The things that were going on in my life – I'd lost my company, lost my home, lost everything. I couldn't handle it. . . . There was a time . . . when I sat in my office

and cried, and then put a gun to my head. . . . When I finally got over all that [pain and anger associated with the loss of the business] was when I quit blaming other people. . . . It was my fault because I didn't plan far enough ahead. It was stupid as hell of me to sit there exposed like that. . . . Listen, this lesson was extremely expensive. I paid dearly, my family paid dearly. . . . Yeah, I learned a lot. . . . I'd be an incredible CEO for some company. I'm the best.

This article's model of the grief recovery process for the self-employed has a number of practical implications.

1. The knowledge that the feelings and reactions the individual is experiencing are normal for someone dealing with such a loss may help to reduce feelings of shame and embarrassment. This in turn might encourage the self-employed to articulate their feelings of grief, possibly speeding the recovery process.
2. There are psychological and physiological outcomes caused by the feelings of loss associated with grief. Realizing that these are 'symptoms' of grief can reduce secondary sources of stress and may also assist with the choice of treatment.
3. There is a process of recovery from grief, which offers the self-employed some comfort that the feelings of loss, sadness, helplessness, and so on that they now feel will eventually diminish. The recovery and learning process can be enhanced by some degree of oscillation between a loss and a restoration orientation.
4. Starting a new business can be a vehicle to recover from the grief associated with losing a business.
5. Recovery from grief offers the opportunity to increase one's knowledge of self-employment. This provides benefits to the individual and to society.
6. Business failure is common but not discussed much in the literature. Recovering from failure is an aspect that should be emphasized and taught in entrepreneurship programs. We return to this issue in more detail later in this chapter.

Learning from Failure: Categorizing Small Business Managers in terms of their Grief Recovery Process and the Amount of Available Feedback Information

Attempts to explain how much a small business manager will learn from failure based solely on the amount of available information that could be used as valuable feedback is unlikely to be successful unless we also consider the small business manager's ability to reduce his or her grief over the failure experience. We characterize this ability to reduce (and eventually

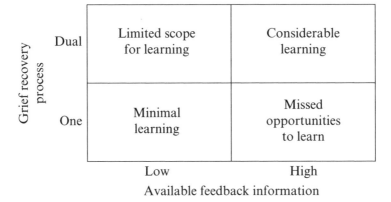

Figure 8.2   *Levels of learning from failure: four types of small businesses
          in terms of the grief recovery process and available feedback
          information*

eliminate) grief by the process that is used: a high ability is associated with
the use of a dual process model of grief recovery and low ability with the
exclusive use of either a loss orientation or a restoration orientation. That
is, without considering the grief recovery process used by the small business
manager, we are likely to overestimate the learning from failure that takes
place by small business managers, especially those that exclusively use
either a loss or a restoration orientation.

Based on the information in this chapter, we present a categorization of
small business managers in terms of the amount they learn from business
failure. Specifically, Figure 8.2 categorizes small business managers along
two dimensions; 'grief recovery process' represents one dimension, and
the 'amount of available feedback information' represents the other.
Depending on their position along these two dimensions, four types of
small businesses are identified.

1. Small business managers in the upper right quadrant have the oppor-
    tunity to learn a lot from the failure experience because considerable
    feedback information is readily available, or – if it is not readily avail-
    able – they actively search for information in order to understand
    why the business failed. They also use a grief recovery process that
    minimizes the interference grief creates and reduces the level of grief.
    These small business managers learn considerable new knowledge as a
    result of the small business failure. Although we believe that most small
    business managers do have the opportunity to learn a lot from the
    failure experience, we fear that few have the skills needed to oscillate

between a loss orientation and a restoration orientation as necessary for the dual process model of grief recovery. This belief is reflected in our emphasis throughout the chapter on increasing small business managers' ability to cope with the grief over the loss of a business.

2. The upper left quadrant contains the small business managers who have the ability to learn from the feedback provided by a business failure but find that there is little useful feedback information. We expect that business failures typically offer considerable feedback information that, when processed into new knowledge, can help small business managers run future businesses. But some small business managers may falsely claim that the failure outcome was completely beyond their personal control or blame it on other irrelevant causes because of attribution bias. Or they may choose not to attend to the information available. Situations are also conceivable where little in fact can be learnt from failure. For example, natural disasters, or legal changes that can make otherwise flourishing businesses fail, are causes beyond the control of the small business manager. In such situations, little can in fact be learnt from failure that is useful in successive business owner-management.

3. In the lower right quadrant are the small business managers who face an environment that is rich in feedback information about the loss experience but these small business managers have limited ability to capitalize on this information and learn from the experience because grief interferes in their processing of information and they have only limited ability to reduce that level of grief. We suspect that most small business managers of failed businesses fall into this category. Although information is plentiful, they may overemphasize the restoration-orientation trying to move on with their lives, thereby actively avoiding feedback information and the possibility of learning from this information. They may eventually recover from their grief but have learned little from the experience (other than maybe not to try again). It is this group of small business managers that represent our mission, our chance to do some good, because these small business managers need not face an extended period of emotional heartache and the resulting missed opportunities to learn. We hope to (and inspire others to) provide small business managers the ability to engage a dual process model of grief recovery and thereby move into the first (upper right) quadrant. We dig deeper into this issue in the next section of this chapter, which focuses on teaching small business management students about how to learn from business failure. Thereby we hope to prepare students to be in the first quadrant rather than this one.

4. In the lower left quadrant are the small business managers who have limited scope to learn and have limited ability to learn and therefore it is not surprising that they do not learn. As argued in the upper left quadrant above, it is only under extreme circumstances that there is limited scope to learn from failure and therefore there would be very few small business managers in this quadrant. Teaching these small business managers to use a dual process model of grief recovery rather than the exclusive use of a loss or a restoration orientation will move them to the upper left quadrant. What is the benefit of such a move when the learning outcome is the same – minimal learning? It is here that we step out of the strict interpretation of our 2×2 matrix to say that there are emotional benefits to a quicker recovery from grief and that these benefits are as important (and we think more important) than simply whether it helps small business managers learn from the failure experience or not.

Implications of the Dual Process Model for Scholars

Research on grief has the potential to help scholars in a number of ways. First, entrepreneurship research acknowledges the importance of learning from failure. This chapter argues that for small business managers, learning is not automatic or instantaneous and is dependent upon, in part, their grief and grief recovery process. Second, it has been argued that entrepreneurship is a context that generates considerable emotions (Baron, 1998). With few exceptions, for example feelings of regret (Baron, 2000), entrepreneurship scholars have not given sufficient attention to the role of emotions. Based on the emotions literature, this chapter proposes that the negative emotional response from the loss of a small business (grief) interferes with the ability to learn from the experience. A dual process of grief recovery can minimize this emotional interference, and recovery from grief removes it completely.

Finally, organizational scholars have investigated the role of negative emotions in the ability of organizations to learn and adapt, especially when the organization is in decline. But this research has rarely extended beyond the life of the organization and has, therefore relatively ignored the death of the organization, the negative emotion arising from that death, and the ability of small business managers to learn from this organizational failure.[4] This chapter investigated the negative emotional response by small business managers to the death of their business and provided some insight into the role of grief recovery in the learning of new 'small business knowledge'.

For the learning to be useful it must be applied to another business. However, the loss of a business likely lowers an individual's entrepreneurial self-efficacy and therefore the motivation to choose to be a small business manager again. Entrepreneurial self-efficacy refers to the strength of a person's belief that he or she is capable of successfully performing the various roles and tasks of entrepreneurship and influences the choice of whether to engage in an entrepreneurial career (Boyd and Vozikis, 1994; Chen, et al., 1998). From the psychology literature on the loss of a loved one, learning is believed to re-establish individuals' assumptions by offering an explanation for why the loss occurred, and in doing so, it helps individuals to establish a new set of assumptions about themselves (Parkes, 1975). Future research should investigate the relationships between the loss of a small business and entrepreneurial self-efficacy, as well as learning (during, and as a result of, the grief recovery process) and entrepreneurial self-efficacy.

LEARNING FROM FAILURE: IMPLICATIONS FOR EDUCATORS

Today, universities and other educators offer courses on various aspects of small business management, many of them related to the issues we have discussed in previous chapters. We are not aware, however, of any courses that explicitly deal with how to recover and learn from business failure. We therefore devote some space to outlining how this important element of small business management can be taught. Given the importance of a dual process model of grief recovery to learning from failure, we ask ourselves how students can be better prepared to learn from small business failure. It is to this educational challenge that we now turn our attention. For those readers less interested in the educational aspects of learning from business failure, we suggest that they skip the next section and proceed to the conclusion of this chapter.

Entrepreneurship and small business educators are well versed in increasing students' knowledge through lectures, by providing vicarious experiences through guest speakers and case studies, as well as by providing direct experiences through simulations. With this in mind, we now discuss how these methods and some new ones can be used to educate students about managing emotions associated with failure in order to minimize interference and maximize learning from the experience.[5]

Lectures

As with all lectures, the content is highly reliant on available theory. In Table 8.1, we propose the layout of a possible lecture. First, relying on entrepreneurship or small business management texts, the professor establishes the existence of an emotional relationship between small business managers and their businesses, offers statistics on the likelihood of business failure, and highlights the point that failure represents an opportunity to learn but also acknowledges the difficulty in doing so. Second, the professor utilizes theory from psychology on bereavement to explore processes of

Table 8.1   Theory lecture on how individuals can manage emotions associated with business failure in order to maximize learning from the experience

Stage 1	*Pre-readings*
(i)	A chapter from the course textbook on why people become entrepreneurs.
(ii)	A chapter from the existing course textbook on business failure and bankruptcy.
(iii)	Journal article(s) on grief over the loss of a loved one (for example, Nolen-Hoeksema, et al., 1997; Stroebe and Schutt, 1999) or trauma (chapters from Janoff-Buhlman, 1992).
(iv)	Journal article on entrepreneurs' grief over business failure (for example, Shepherd, 2003).
Stage 2	*Entrepreneurs and their businesses (approximately 10 minutes)*
(i)	Explain the reasons entrepreneurs start their own businesses.
(ii)	Use these reasons to highlight entrepreneurs' emotional attachment to their businesses.
(iii)	Point out the statistics on business failure.
(iv)	Separate the entrepreneur from the business: 'businesses fail: entrepreneurs learn'.
(v)	Relate back to entrepreneurs' attachment to their business and describe their emotions when a business is lost.
(vi)	Describe how emotions interfere with processing information and with learning.
Stage 3	*Grief and the recovery process (approximately 25 minutes)*
(i)	Introduce the grief literature to highlight how people feel when they lose a loved one.
(ii)	Describe the negative emotions and the physical, psychological, and physiological outcomes of grief.
(iii)	Describe the two dominant perspectives of coping with grief (the loss and restoration orientations) and the advantages and disadvantages of each.
(iv)	Talk through the dual process of recovering from grief over the loss of a business.
(v)	Bring together these two coping mechanisms and explain the dual process of grief recovery.

Table 8.1   (continued)

Stage 4   *Recovering from grief over business failure (approximately 40 minutes)*
  (i)   Reinforce the attachment of entrepreneurs to their businesses.
  (ii)   Generalize the negative emotions of grief over the loss of a loved one to grief over the loss of a business.
  (iii)   Detail how grief interferes with the process of learning from failure.
  (iv)   Talk through the dual process of recovering from grief over the loss of a business.
  (v)   Relate the recovery process to learning from failure and entrepreneurs' willingness to try again.

---

coping with, and recovering from, grief over the loss of a loved one. Finally, the professor moves from death of a loved one to business failure to explore the role of emotional management in maximizing one's ability to learn from small business failure.

Lecturing on emotions, while not necessarily an oxymoron, is likely to be very difficult because it is a topic that is less about what we think and more about how we feel. To provide students with insight into the emotions of business failure, lectures should be complemented with (or replaced by) methods that provide indirect and/or direct experiences of the emotions associated with failure. Next we offer suggestions for indirect (guest speakers and cases) and direct (reflections, role-plays, and simulations) experiences.

Indirect Experiences

Guest speakers
Guest speakers could be used in classes to articulate their insights into business failure and the means of coping with that failure. Ideally, one guest speaker of a recently failed business would talk about the negative emotions of business failure, and a second guest speaker would build upon this discussion to detail how he or she was able to cope with grief, recover, and then learn from the experience. However, there are a number of challenges in using this approach effectively. First, educators need to find small business managers of failed businesses, which itself can be a difficult task. Second, these small business managers must be prepared to talk about the emotions of business failure. Third, and the major challenge with guest speakers on this topic, is to overcome the possibilities of self-reporting and retrospective reporting biases.[6] For example, small business managers of failed businesses might be motivated to diminish the role of emotions in order to appear more 'rational'.

A third party observer may provide additional insights into a small business manager's emotions over business failure and the recovery process. Such experts might include accountants and lawyers who specialize in bankruptcy as well as financiers, such as venture capitalists. Family members of small business managers of failed businesses would likely also provide considerable information about how the small business manager felt, how the small business manager managed his or her emotions, and eventually how the small business manager learned from failure. These third party sources of information are likely to be less 'biased' than those reports directly from the small business manager.

Given the above discussion, guest speakers may provide only marginal insight into their personal emotional response to failure (although this depends on the individual guest speaker), but guest speakers are likely to provide less biased accounts on the emotions of failure at the organizational level. For example, a CEO could provide an account of project failure that details the norms and routines that are in place that allow the organization to monitor and attend to its members' emotions. The discussion can then explore questions such as 'How were such routines first developed?' and 'What (and how many) resources are allocated to this emotional management of project failures?'

Case studies
Existing case studies could be used as a springboard for a discussion on a small business manager's emotions and his or her ability to learn from a failure experience – even though these cases are only indirectly related to the emotional aspect of the situation. For example, Professor Myra Hart provides two Harvard Business School Press cases about an entrepreneur, Eric Wood. The first case, *Eric Wood A* (Hart, 1996a), 'describes the early career of an MBA who went to work in a small business, bought the company, and is now contemplating an acquisition to expand the business' (Harvard Business School Press website). This case could be used for its original purpose of educating students on growth management, but it could also be used to highlight the emotional relationship that entrepreneurs have with their businesses.

The second case, *Eric Wood B* (Hart, 1996b), 'describes Eric's purchase of the much larger Shaw Co. and describes the operating and financial problems that ensue, leaving Eric considering the option of bankruptcy. Issues include the overlap of business and personal finances, as well as the mechanics and implications of bankruptcy.' (Harvard Business School Press website). Again this case could be used for its original purpose of highlighting issues of bankruptcy, but it could also be used for a discussion of Eric Wood's likely negative emotional reaction to the decline of his business. The discussion could be extended further to speculate on his emotional state if the business were to fail, and explore ways in which Eric Wood could best deal with the negative emotions that are evoked when a business is lost so that he can learn from the experience.

With avoiding failure as a primary focus of entrepreneurship theory (McGrath, 1999), it is not surprising that cases stop before the organization goes out of business. But there is a need for some cases to focus on the emotions of a small business manager who has lost his or her business due to poor performance (or other reasons such as a terrorist act). Ideally, Professor Hart would write a part C to the above cases (if indeed the business did fail) and detail the emotions and the behaviors of Eric Wood. A hypothetical example of content from Eric Wood part C is offered in Appendix A. Such a case study would provide a more solid foundation for a discussion on the emotions of failure and the management of those emotions. We hope that case writers take up this challenge.

Direct Experiences

Despite obvious differences between educating people to 'deal with' death and educating students to deal with business failure, we explore the 'death education' literature for hints on effective methods for helping people learn about emotions and managing those emotions in the face of losing something important. One important difference is that most people will face the grief of losing a loved one, whereas in an entrepreneurship class only a subset will become entrepreneurs and only a subset of that will lose a business. We chose the 'death education' literature because it is based on solid psychological theories and methods and also has a strong practitioner perspective, that is, helping people deal with the emotions associated with the loss of a loved one. This literature suggests that reflections on grief, role-plays and simulations are effective educational methods (see Hutchison and Scherman, 1992; Ratner and Song, 2002). We now assess and adapt these methods for the entrepreneurial context.

Reflections on grief
Gould (1994) proposes a class structure that is used to develop students' understanding of grief over the loss of a loved one by making students become more attached to the material at an affective level. This educational method begins with something autobiographical through individual introspection, and then moves to a more general understanding of the phenomenon through group discussion. Adapting this method to failure would likely provide students the chance to see the commonalities between the feelings that they have experienced and those they will likely experience if

they were an entrepreneur of a failed business. They might feel empowered by the knowledge that they have coped with the loss of a loved one, that these skills are transferable to the loss of a business, and that these skills can be further improved. In Table 8.2 below, there is a version of Gould's (1994) educational method adapted for use in entrepreneurship classes.

Table 8.2 Approach to encourage reflections on loss and grief over business failure

Step	Activity
1.	Students prepare for the class by reflecting on their own experiences of losses and the associated feelings and behaviors. It is reinforced that these losses should be significant, such as the death of a loved one. Each student is asked to document these stories of loss and complete a grief awareness exercise (for example, Hogan et al., 2001) and be prepared to share one story with a small group of fellow students.
2.	In groups of three or four each student describes one story and the group compiles a list of the expressed feelings and behaviors. From this information, the groups are asked to define grief, prioritize symptoms, and prioritize coping behaviors. This information should be illustrated in a diagram which is presented to class. As a class, the teacher calls for and lists on one white board the symptoms of grief from which a definition of grief emerges. Questions, comments and examples are used to revise these generalizations. The teacher then calls for coping behaviors which are listed on the left of the board if the behavior is loss-oriented and on the right if it is restoration-oriented. The students are then asked what is common about the list on the left and what is common about the list on the right. Although the labels are likely to be different, the discussion emerges on a classification of loss-orientated and restoration-orientated behaviors.
3.	The teacher leads discussion back to the first board (list of symptoms and definition of grief) and asks students whether this definition and list symptoms applies to the loss of something really important even if that loss is not the death of a loved one. 'What are the feelings towards the *thing* lost that generates grief?' 'Do entrepreneurs feel this way about the businesses that they create?' 'Therefore are entrepreneurs likely to feel grief over the loss of their businesses?' From the discussion elicited by these questions, it is likely to emerge that losing a loved one is not the same as losing a business, but one may feel many of the same negative emotions. The student's definition can then be compared to the one offered in Shepherd (2003): 'a negative emotional response to the loss of a business capable of triggering psychological, behavioral, and physiological symptoms'.

Table 8.2 (continued)

Step	Activity
4.	Attention is then turned to the two lists of behavior labelled as something along the lines of loss orientation and restoration orientation. The students are then asked which is best and to justify their choice. Some students will argue for one approach and some will argue for the alternate approach and from this discussion the benefits and limitations of each will emerge. After the benefits and limitations of each have been sufficiently discussed, the teacher asks 'How can we get the benefits of both while also minimizing the associated weaknesses?' This question and subsequent discussion will lead to the notion that people can alternate between the two, and eventually speed up recovery. The teacher can offer and begin a discussion around the dual models of recovery from grief over the loss of a loved one (Stroebe and Schut, 1999) and the loss of a business (Shepherd, 2003).

Role-play

Role-plays ask students to imagine, think and behave as if they were someone else in a particular situation. It involves 'as if' experimentation (Mercado, 2000) and provides students with a unique opportunity for active learning in a safe and low risk environment (Brown, 1994; Egri, 1999; Lehman and Taylor, 1994). The environment is safe and low risk for students because they can separate themselves from the character they are playing. This can be a highly liberating experience (Mercado, 2000) and important when the role-play involves expressing emotions. For example, many of the inhibitions in expressing one's own emotions are eliminated or minimized with role-plays. Therefore role-plays are highly effective for students to learn about attitudes, behaviors and as the basis for experiencing different psychological contexts (Greenberg and Eskew, 1993). Hodgkinson (2000) provides an example of role-plays being used for post-graduate managers and there is evidence of its use to teach business ethics and accounting (Craig and Amernic, 1994). We now offer some examples of possible role-plays for individuals to experience the emotions of failure:

- *Role-play 1:* One student prepares and presents a speech as if s/he is a small business manager informing employees that her/his business has failed and will not be operating from tomorrow. The rest of the class can respond and ask questions as if they are devoted employees upset about losing their jobs.

- *Role-play 2:* In groups of two, one student can role-play a small business manager informing his/her spouse of the business' failure and the other student role-plays the shocked spouse's response and subsequent discussion.
- *Role-play 3:* In small groups, students co-role-play the interchange between a small business manager of a failed business expressing his/her negative emotions and a friend providing advice on how to best cope with the situation.
- *Role-play 4:* In small groups, students co-role-play the interchange between (1) a small business manager of a recently failed business who still feels negative emotions when thinking about the lost business, and (2) a small business manager of a failed business who has recovered from grief, learned from the experience and has started another business.

Simulations

Simulations offer numerous learning benefits to business school students (Petranek and Corey, 1992; Petranek, 2000). Simulations may be particularly useful in educating entrepreneurship and small business management students about grief and learning from business failure because, as Bredemeier and Greenblat (1981) point out, affective and behavioral learning is enhanced with simulations over traditional modes of learning. Simulations are currently used in entrepreneurship and strategy classes (see Hindle, 2002; Keys, 1997; Wolfe, 1997; Wolfe and Bruton, 1994). Students make decisions and track firm performance. Although companies may make losses in these simulations, few companies go bankrupt. For example, Paich and Sternman (1993: 1442) describe a simulation where students manage a new product over a ten-year period and 'subjects may lose as much money as they like without facing bankruptcy. The task is therefore more forgiving than reality since losses leading to bankruptcy in real life can in the game be offset by subsequent profits'. We point out this feature of most simulations, not to be critical of them, but to demonstrate that not all simulations are well suited to the purpose of providing students experience with the emotions of business failure. We speculate that the reason few simulations allow businesses to fail, is that these simulations have been created for strategic management classes and learning from business failure is not a primary objective of this pedagogy (see Knotts and Keys, 1997).

One exception is the 'Small business growth management flight simulator' (Bianchi, 2000) which simulates the management of a family business that is facing a number of economic problems. This simulation helps students gain a deeper understanding of the different aspects of the business, the environment and how one's decisions (primarily related to financial structure) can limit firm growth and put its survival in peril. The business can fail for a number of different reasons. For example:

> Company failure may be caused by a growth policy that is not sustainable because of excessive bank withdrawals aimed at increasing the family's quality of life, both in terms of current expenses and personal assets. Such a phenomenon is mainly caused by bias in profit and cash flow expectations and related distorted information, combined with entrepreneur's emotional involvement in coping with the business/family overlap. (Bianchi, 2000: 217)

Active participation in simulations provides students the opportunity to unconsciously process all types of information including emotions, strategies, and feelings (Petranek and Corey, 1992). Specifically, by being actively involved in a failure, students likely unconsciously process information about the negative emotions they feel, strategies to try and recover from this position, and how those strategies worked. To maximize learning from playing the simulation, Petranek and Corey (1992) propose the complementary use of oral debriefings and keeping a written journal.

Oral Debriefings

Teachers can engage in a class discussion designed for students to reflect upon their emotional experiences evoked by the simulation. To structure this discussion, Petranek and Corey (1992) propose that the debriefing revolves around events, emotions, empathy and explanations. In Table 8.3, we offer questions that could be used to start the discussion for each of these categories.

Writing a journal
The final phase requires students to record their perceptions of the simulation by writing a journal. This, unlike the oral debriefing proposed above, represents a personal and private communication with the professor (Wollman-Bonilla, 1989). Students are more likely to record feelings of pain, humiliation and anger than they are willing to express it verbally to the whole class. Writing a journal encourages greater reflection and introspection (Petranek, 2000). The student also has the opportunity to reflect on others' expressed interpretations of the events, emotions about those events and empathy toward the journal writer. Keeping a journal (as well as oral debriefings) provides students with the opportunity to integrate theories of grief, emotional management, and failure into the experience of the simulation, which encourages a higher level of analytical learning (see

Table 8.3 *Questions to stimulate discussion in each stage of simulation debriefing*

Stage of debriefing	Questions to stimulate discussion
Events	Describe the events surrounding the business failure.
	Describe the events that happened to you after the business failed.
Emotions	How did you feel when you realized the business was going to fail?
	What were the emotions that you felt after the business had failed and everyone in the class knew about it?
Empathy	For those entrepreneurs whose business did not fail, what were your feelings towards those that did have businesses fail?
	How would you have felt and acted if you were in their shoes?
Explanation	How does this experience relate to the saying 'Businesses fail: entrepreneurs learn'?
	Do real-life entrepreneurs of failed businesses feel this way?

Petranek, 2000). In summarizing research on the learning benefits from journal writing, Wollman-Bonilla (1989: 113) states that:

> . . . journals validate self-expression and personal response, encourage understanding, imaging, speculation, questioning and the shaping of ideas and provide students with information relevant to their concerns and problems in the content of their own entries and teacher's response.

The Next Steps for Entrepreneurship Educators

1. Maintain currency with theoretical advancements on topics of (a) the emotions of failure, (b) the role of emotions in causing failure, (c) the process of learning from failure and (d) other work on emotional intelligence and emotional capability that could be applicable to aspects of the entrepreneurial process.
2. Use information gained in step one to supplement the content of current lectures and/or as the basis for new lectures.
3. Seek out potential guest speakers who (a) manage an organization that experiences project failures as a result of a conscious strategy of pursuing 'high risk' projects, (b) have considerable emotional capability, and (c) can articulate the organizational norms and routines that the organization uses to manage the emotions of its employees and how

this impacts organizational learning. If such a guest speaker is found, then use him or her in class.

4. Re-analyse cases that have previously been used as part of your pedagogy (and/or look for new cases) that can be used to stimulate discussion on the emotions surrounding failure and the importance of learning from the experience (at the individual and/or organizational level). Adapt existing teaching notes to highlight this new dimension of the case to encourage class discussion and learning.

5. Experiment with the proposed methods of 'reflections' and role-play. Such experimentation could first involve using one of these methods to explore previously covered content. Once confident with the new method, it should be used for the proposed new content.

6. Choose and use simulations to evoke emotions (preferably around the experience of small business failure) and then use oral debriefings and require students to keep a journal account of the simulation to maximize the educational benefits of students' emotional experiences.

7. Be entrepreneurial. With increased knowledge of current theories and the motivation to improve one's pedagogy, educators will likely be willing to experiment with pedagogies that provide students emotional experiences (at first with failure and then other aspects of the entrepreneurial process) and the opportunity to learn how to better manage these emotions.

The Next Step for Education Researchers

1. Include in entrepreneurship textbooks new theoretical advancements on the emotions of failure, the role of emotions in causing failure, the process of learning from failure, and other work on emotional intelligence and emotional capability that could be applicable to aspects of the entrepreneurial process.

2. Write new cases (or put a 'new spin' on old cases) that provide the basis for student analysis and discussion on emotion and learning from failure.

3. Create more simulations (and/or adapt existing simulations) that allow businesses to fail but an individual's opportunity to participate in the simulation is not automatically terminated, rather the students of failed businesses have the opportunity to learn from the failure and apply this new knowledge by creating a new small business.

4. Research the educational benefits of the proposed changes in pedagogy. To conduct such research requires further work on adapting and refining existing measures for use with students in an entrepreneurial context; for example, anxiety or emotional regulation.

5. Test the impact of proposed changes to pedagogy on students' motivations to pursue a career as a small business manager.
6. Distinguish between pedagogies to determine the most effective approach for students to learn how to best manage emotions (after failure and/or to avoid failure).

CONCLUSION

Failure is rarely mentioned as an aspect of business life, and when it is, it largely concerns how to avoid failure. In this chapter we have chosen a different tack and address how business failure can be turned into a valuable experience. Most small business owner–managers have a close personal relationship with their business and losing the business because of failure often arouses strong negative emotions such as grief. But failing as an owner–manager might not be the end of the world. It is possible to learn from the experience and to return into business with greater knowledge and the potential to build a fledging business. One important feature for being able to learn from failure is to have a sound grief recovery process. In this chapter we suggest that the best thing to do is to have a deliberate grief recovery process that oscillates between loss orientation and restoration orientation. This means that from time to time it is valuable to think about what went wrong and grieve about the past (loss orientation). But it is important not to get stuck in grief and also move on to organize life without the business and diminish memories of it by starting a new one (restoration orientation).

We develop a model showing that, in addition to oscillating between these modes of recovery, addressing substantial amounts of feedback information from the failure is important for the learning process. Sometimes large amounts of information are readily available. In such situations, the important thing for the owner manager is to evaluate his or hew own role critically and not just blame failure on causes beyond his or her control. In other situations, the owner–manager might have to actively search for information in order to understand what went wrong. There may be a risk that processing information from the past can lead to a loss orientation. Therefore, we again emphasize that both recovery orientations should be in place.

While failure is not a centerpiece of the literature, it has attracted some attention. The same cannot be said for education. We are unaware of any education that emphasizes how business failure can be a route to subsequent success. Therefore we have developed some guidelines and examples of how this element can be introduced into entrepreneurship teaching.

Taken together, we believe that what we propose in this chapter can make those small business owner–managers who fail less devastated and offer them ways to learn from their failures which can be important in their future careers. We also hope that prospective small business managers will be better prepared by understanding that business failure is common, that it does not represent personal failure, that there are ways to overcome the grief typically associated with business failure, and that business failure provides an excellent and unique learning opportunity. This provides benefits to individuals as well as to society.

APPENDIX: A HYPOTHETICAL EXAMPLE OF A CASE STUDY ON THE EMOTIONS OF BUSINESS FAILURE

Case Study

After his business failed, Eric felt anger, guilt, distress and anxiety. He knew that he had to get out of this current emotional state. He tried to think through the sequence of events leading up to the failure of the business so that he could learn from his mistakes but every time he thought about the business it made him feel even more depressed. He thought it would likely make him feel better if he simply distracted himself from the whole event by focusing on other aspects of his life, like finding a job, and finding a new house and a new school for the children. While this was attractive in the short term, would this be detrimental to his recovery efforts in the long run and to being able to learn from the failure? Is there anything Eric can do to improve his emotional state, reorganize his life and also learn from the experience?

Discussion

From such a case, some students might suggest that Eric should immediately start another business because this would help him overcome grief over the loss of the previous business. However, students will soon realize that there has been no opportunity for learning and the same mistakes could be made again. Attention will turn to speeding recovery. Some will advocate 'grief work' in which Eric should bear the emotional pain and focus his attention on the events surrounding the business – processing this information will help with recovery and learning from the experience. Others will argue that distractions are the best approach and work on the secondary causes of stress. This discussion will bring out the advantages and disadvantages of the two coping mechanisms (which can be recorded and labeled on a white board). The professor can then ask: 'Is there any way that Eric could get the advantages of both without their corresponding disadvantages?' This discussion will highlight the benefits of a recovery process that alternates between the two coping mechanisms.

NOTES

1. This chapter is based on Shepherd (2003) and Shepherd (2004).
2. McGrath (1999) argues that there is a tendency to view failure negatively, which introduces a pervasive bias in entrepreneurship theory and research. An anti-failure bias by entrepreneurs can be considered a reasonable emotional reaction to the loss of something important. The concern is that such a response will interfere with people's (and organizations') ability to make sense out of the experience (McGrath, 1999; Shepherd, 2003).
3. Interviews with employees of organizations that have closed reveal negative emotions such as those associated with grief (Sutton, 1983; Harris and Sutton, 1986).
4. A possible exception is research on employees' emotion surrounding the death of an organization (Harris and Sutton, 1986; Sutton, 1983), although this research focuses on how management can best manage these emotions to ensure a realization that the organization has died. This chapter focused on the self-employed and the process of learning from failure.
5. This chapter does not offer a review of the literature of emotion, information processing, or failure, rather it builds on recent theoretical advancements to explore possible changes to entrepreneurship pedagogy necessary for the delivery of this content and to explore the implications of these proposed changes.
6. In a research setting, Huber and Power (1985) and Golden (1992) propose that retrospective reports provide data that have errors and biases due to respondents' motivation to bias the results (Cannell and Henson, 1974; March and Feldman, 1981) and there are also issues related to the perceptual and cognitive limitations of respondents (Duncan, 1979; Fischhoff, 1982; Nisbett and Ross, 1980).

9. Conclusion

In this book we have taken a resource-based perspective to provide a deeper understanding of the growth and performance of entrepreneurial small businesses. This section provides us the opportunity to summarize each chapter's key findings and reflect upon them.

Concerning the empirical analyses presented in this book, a consistent strategy has been to analyse bundles of resources and their interaction with other variables in predicting important small business outcomes, such as growth, performance, entrepreneurial activity, or the chance of receiving debt or equity capital. The resource variables we have examined range from aspects of the human capital of the small business manager, such as length of education, or prior experience of business start-ups, over social capital variables, to firm-level resources, such as access to financial capital, or competence. Our overarching argument is that while resources may be valuable, it is essential that the small business has the processes that facilitate the manipulation of resources into value creating strategies. For example, we found that the education of the small business manager had no direct effect on growth. But when the growth aspirations of the small business manager were taken into account, those with more education were better at executing the strategies needed to fulfill their growth aspirations.

We believe that this is a useful approach in utilizing the resource-based perspective within the small business context. We and others find that resources are important to small business outcomes, but we argue that increased understanding is obtained by considering how these resources interact with other aspects of the small business. Suitable resource variables can be sought within various literature, including human capital theory, social capital theory as well as resource-based theories of strategy (RBV). The same goes for variables that moderate the relationship between resources and outcomes – there are several literatures that identify such variables.

Rather than reaching the conclusion that 'more is better', this approach has allowed us to tease out the conditions under which certain resources are particularly valuable to small businesses as well as the conditions under which these and other resources are less valuable. Based on these findings, we have also created a number of taxonomies of small businesses that can be useful for categorization as well as for future research. With this, we turn to a more detailed summary of the findings obtained within each individual chapter.

Summary of Findings

After an introductory chapter, Chapter 2 focused on the small business manager's motivation to grow his or her business. We concluded that motivation does matter such that the stronger the aspiration for growth the more likely it occurs *but* the strength of this relationship differs depending on the small business manager's resources. Growth aspirations are more closely related to actual growth for those small business managers who are more highly educated, have more related experience (experience with start-ups, management, and with rapidly growing organizations), are in more dynamic environments and have superior access to financial resources. This chapter emphasized the importance of small business managers' human capital, access to financial resources, and environmental dynamism in explaining the nature of the relationship between motivation and small business growth.

In the next chapter we continued to investigate the resources of small business managers, specifically their human and social capital. Rather than explaining growth, Chapter 3 focused on who was most likely to engage in entrepreneurial activity and, of those that do, how they chose to pursue this opportunity. We concluded that the small business managers most likely to pursue entrepreneurial opportunities (subsequent new entries) are those who are more highly educated, have more start-up experience, have more developed business networks and have greater contact with government support agencies (higher relational density). We also concluded that not all small business managers that pursue an entrepreneurial opportunity do so by creating a new organization, some prefer to do so using their existing small business. Those small business managers with start-up experience are more likely to create a new organization while those without such experience are more likely to use their existing small business. This chapter pointed out that the resources of the small business manager not only helped explain which small business managers are more likely to engage in entrepreneurial action but also helped explain the choice of organization mode used to exploit the discovered opportunities.

Moving from Chapter 3 to Chapter 4 required a change in the level of analysis from the resources of the individual to the resources of the firm. We concluded that a small business's knowledge-based resources applicable to the discovery and exploitation of opportunity are positively related to performance *and* that a small business's entrepreneurial orientation is positively related to performance *but* our explanation of small business performance is increased by recognizing that EO enhances the positive relationship that a bundle of knowledge-based resources has with small business performance. The major implication was that having a small business with considerable knowledge-based resources is likely to help improve firm performance but these resources will be underutilized unless the small business also has an entrepreneurial orientation. The flipside of the same argument applies; that is, an EO is likely to improve the performance of a small business but its full potential of that orientation will not be reached unless the small business also has considerable knowledge-based resources.

While Chapter 4 highlighted the importance of the interdependent relationship between entrepreneurial orientation and the internal resources of the small business, Chapter 5 extended this relationship to include consideration of the external environment. Again we concluded that entrepreneurial orientation has a positive association with small business performance but our explanation of performance is improved by concomitant consideration of entrepreneurial orientation, access to capital, and environmental dynamism. Of greatest interest was the finding that small businesses that benefit most from EO are those facing severe constraints in terms of limited access to finance and a stable environment. In this way entrepreneurial orientation can be used to overcome environmental and financial constraints.

Rather than analyse the resources possessed by the small business and/or its manager, Chapter 6 and 7 focused on how small business managers can access resources from venture capitalists and banks, respectively. Chapter 6 first used a resource-based perspective to explain how venture capitalists assess the attractiveness of entrepreneurial businesses and then provided advice to managers on how to develop this important relationship further. We concluded that venture capitalists value more highly those businesses with highly proprietary technology, considerable market familiarity in fast growing markets and with managers who have considerable leadership experience. In fact, venture capitalists value leadership experience more for those businesses in large markets, that face weak competitors and that face many competitors. In the venture capitalist's eyes, small businesses can somewhat compensate for minimal leadership experience if the team has some previous start-up experience. We also concluded that for those small businesses that secure venture capital backing, the management must work to build trust with the venture capitalists by signaling commitment to the relationship, instituting procedures that are 'fair', making adjustments to maintain a 'good fit' and communicating openly and frequently.

Although much attention has been focused on venture capitalists, bank loans are a more common source of funding for small business growth. Loan officers use different assessment criteria than venture capitalists. In

Chapter 7 we concluded that the probability that lending officers will support a loan request by a small business is higher when that business has performed well in the past, is very competent for the proposed project, is willing to share the risk, is in a strong financial position, offers collateral that is independent of the project being funded and has a request based on a low risk project. Although loan officers are concerned about the riskiness of a project that concern can be somewhat alleviated when the small business has a strong financial position and/or can offer independent collateral.

Chapter 8 recognizes that some (many) entrepreneurial businesses will fail and that this failure typically generates a negative emotional response (grief) that has adverse psychological and physical outcomes as well as hindering the small business manager's ability to learn from the event. In this chapter we offered a process that enhances grief recovery, which in turn enhances the small business manager's ability to learn from the event. This process involves oscillating between two grief orientations to benefit from each orientation while also not bearing the costs of maintaining one orientation over an extended period of time. This chapter concluded with a challenge to scholars and educators to better prepare future, and existing, small business managers for the emotional consequences of small business failure and the opportunity to learn from the experience.

Implications for Policymakers

One important observation that the careful reader may have made by reading the preceding chapters is that not all small businesses are the same. There is sometimes a tendency to view small business as one homogeneous group and contrast it with larger firms. This is often not the case. The studies analysed in this book cover some small businesses that are very innovative and entrepreneurial and others that are conservative. Some businesses are bound for rapid growth, while others wish to remain at a small scale. Further, classifications of small businesses based on tangible variables such as industry or location do not seem highly meaningful because key characteristics that influence performance, innovativeness and growth appear to cut across such simple classifications. For example, we find high performing, entrepreneurial, and growing small businesses across industries.

However we do believe that classifications can be helpful and throughout the book we have provided a number of taxonomies of small businesses. We have also indicated that suitable policy measures likely differ depending on the type of small businesses targeted. Reviewing these typologies and policy measures recommended across the chapters, some common themes surface. The first one we wish to point out is related to the aspirations of the small business owner–manager. For example, there are great differences among small businesses in their aspirations to expand their businesses or to seek external equity capital as well as debt capital. The provision of public assistance to small businesses that does not take this into account is likely to be very inefficient. Depending on the objectives of support programs we believe that small businesses at all aspiration levels can be targeted, but the content and approach of programs must be different.

Our consistent findings of the benefits of an entrepreneurial orientation speak to the relevance for policymakers of attempting to instill an entrepreneurial spirit in society. We are not only referring to encouraging an increased number of people to start their own business, but wish to emphasize that it appears valuable if existing small businesses become more entrepreneurial in their outlook. If small business managers with limited aspirations for development can be motivated to attempt to expand their businesses, to innovate and to be proactive, there are substantial benefits for society as well as for the small businesses themselves.

It appears that entrepreneurial small businesses are entrepreneurial in the way that they approach funding. That is, they are better able to solve their funding needs than are less entrepreneurial small businesses. We also found that small businesses that for various reasons have a relatively weak financial position (because they are young, or because they are using their resources to expand, or similar) are less likely to receive bank loans for risky projects. Also, previous research suggests that developing funding schemes to small businesses is a relatively effective policy measure (Storey, 1994). This suggests that a relevant public policy for small business funding could be to target funding schemes to small businesses that wish to become more entrepreneurial, or to make such schemes conditional on an entrepreneurial orientation of the small firm seeking this type of funding.

Finally, a revised attitude to business failure is needed in society. We point to ways in which small business managers can overcome the grief associated with business failure and learn from the experience. We have also developed some guidelines and examples of how lessons learned from business failure can be introduced into entrepreneurship teaching as a route to subsequent success. At present we are aware of no courses working in this area and one role of public policy could be to introduce such pedagogies. We believe that not only can such educational changes lead to failing small business managers recovering from failure more quickly, but it could also encourage more people to become entrepreneurs if they realize that they are equipped with the skills to cope with the negative consequences of business failure.

The European Union has recently published a green paper on entrepreneurship followed by an action plan for entrepreneurship. The action plan focuses on fostering entrepreneurial mindsets, tackling the negative effects of business failure and improving the flow of finance. As detailed throughout the book, we agree that these are important public policy areas. We also believe that this book presents empirical evidence in support of such policies as well as several measures that can be taken to achieve these objectives. This should be of value to policymakers within and outside the European Union.

We conclude the book the way it started – entrepreneurial small businesses are important. Entrepreneurial small businesses are important for most national economies and to their owner–managers. We hope that this book has inspired you to conduct research that extends the topics of the preceding chapters, educate small business managers for success and prepare them for failure, grow your own, or help others grow their small business, and/or become an entrepreneur. Good luck in pursuing one or more of these opportunities.

Dean Shepherd and Johan Wiklund

References

Abernathy, W.J. and J. Utterback (1978), 'Patterns of industrial innovation', *Technological Review*, **80** (7), 40–7.

Acs, Z.J. (1992), 'Small business economics: a global perspective', *Challenge*, **35**, 38–44.

Afua, A. (2003), 'Redefining firm boundaries in the face of the Internet: Are firms really shrinking?', *Academy of Management Review*, **28**, 34–54.

Ajzen, I. (1988), *Attitudes, Personality, and Behavior*, Chicago, IL: Dorsey Press.

Ajzen, I. (1991), 'The theory of planned behavior', *Organizational Behavior and Human Decision Processes*, **50**, 179–211.

Ajzen, I. and B.L. Driver (1992), 'Contingent value measurement: On the nature and meaning of willingness to pay', *Journal of Consumer Psychology*, **1** (4), 297–316.

Aldrich, H. (1999), *Organizations Evolving*, London: Sage Publicatications.

Altman, E. (1983), *Corporate Financial Distress: A Complete Guide to Predicting, Avoiding and Dealing with Bankruptcy*, New York: John Wiley and Sons.

Alvarez, S. and L.W. Busenitz (2001), 'The entrepreneurship of resource-based theory', *Journal of Management*, **27**, 755–76.

Amit, R., L. Glosten and E. Muller (1990), 'Entrepreneurial ability, venture investments, and risk sharing', *Management Science*, **38** (10), 1232–45.

Amit, R., E. Muller and I. Cockburn (1995), 'Opportunity costs and entrepreneurial activity', *Journal of Business Venturing*, **10**, 95–107.

Amit, R. and P. Schoemaker (1993), 'Strategic assets and organizational rent', *Strategic Management Journal*, **24**, 33–46.

Ammann, M. (2001), *Credit Risk Valuation: Methods, Models, and Applications*, Berlin: Springer-Verlag.

Andersson, P. (2001), *Expertise in Credit Granting – Studies on Judgment and Decision-Making Behavior*, PhD thesis, Stockholm School of Economics.

Andrews, K.R. (1987), *The Concept of Corporate Strategy*, Homewood, IL: Irwin.

Aragon, L. (2001), 'How to rate a venture capital firm', *Red Herring*, 16 April.

Archer, J. (1999), *The Nature of Grief: The Evolution and Psychology of Reactions to Loss*, New York: Routledge.

Ardishvili, A., S. Cardozo, S. Harmon and S. Vadakath (1998), *Towards a theory of new venture growth*, paper presented at the 1998 Babson Entrepreneurship Research Conference, Ghent, Belgium.

Argyris, C. (1952), *Personality Fundamentals for Administrators: An Introduction for the Layman*, New Haven, CT: Yale University Labor and Management Center.

Argyris, C. (1990), *Overcoming Organizational Defenses: Facilitating Organizational Learning*, Boston, MA: Allyn and Bacon.

Bagozzi, R. and P.R. Warshaw (1992), 'An examination of the etiology of the attitude–behavior relation for goal-directed behaviors', *Multivariate Behavioral Research*, **27** (4), 601–34.

Baird, I.S. and H. Thomas (1985), 'Toward a contingency model of strategic risk taking', *Academy of Management Review*, **10**, 230–43.

Baker, D.D. and J.B. Cullen (1993), 'Administrative reorganization and configurational context: The contingent effects of age, size, and change in size', *Academy of Management Journal*, **36** (6), 1251–77.

Bamberg, S., I. Ajzen and P. Schmidt (2003), 'Choice of travel mode in the theory of planned behavior: The roles of past behavior, habit, and reasoned action', *Basic and Applied Social Psychology*, **25** (3), 175–87.

Barker, V.L. III, and M.A. Mone (1998), 'The mechanistic structure shift and strategic reorientation in declining firms attempting turnarounds', *Human Relations*, **51**, 1227–58.

Barney, J. (1991), 'Firm resources and sustained competitive advantage', *Journal of Management*, **17**, 99–120.

Barney, J. (1995), 'Looking inside for competitive advantage', *Academy of Management Executive*, **9**, 49–61.

Barney, J., L. Busenitz, J. Fiet and D. Moesel (1996), 'New venture teams' assessment of learning assistance from venture capital firms', *Journal of Business Venturing*, **11** (4), 257–72.

Baron, R. (1998), 'Cognitive mechanisms in entrepreneurship: why and when entrepreneurs think differently than other people', *Journal of Business Venturing*, **13**, 275–94.

Baron, R. (2000), 'Counterfactual thinking and venture formation: The potential effects of thinking about "What might have been"', *Journal of Business Venturing*, **15**, 79–91.

Bates, T. (1990), 'Entrepreneur Human Capital Inputs and Small Business Longevity', *Review of Economics and Statistics*, **72** (4), 551–9.

Bates, T. (1995), 'Self-employment entry across industry groups', *Journal of Business Venturing*, **10**, 143–56.

Baum, J.A.C. and C. Oliver (1992), 'Institutional linkages and organizational mortality', *Administrative Science Quarterly*, **36** (X), 187–218.

Baum, J.A.C. and C. Oliver (1996), 'Toward an institutional ecology of organizational founding', *Academy of Management Journal*, **39** (5), 378–1427.

Baumol, W. (1993), *Entrepreneurship, Management and the Structure of Payoffs*, Cambridge, MA: MIT Press.

Beaulieu, P.R. (1994), 'Commercial lenders' use of accounting information in interaction with source credibility', *Contemporary Accounting Research*, **10**, 557–85.

Beaulieu, P.R. (1996), 'A note on the role of memory in commercial loan officers' use of accounting and character information', *Accounting, Organizations and Society*, **21** (6), 515–28.

Becker, G.S. (1975), *Human Capital*, Chicago, IL: Chicago University Press.

Bédard, J. (1991), 'Expertise and its relation to audit decision quality', *Contemporary Accounting Research*, **8**, 198–223.

Bellu, R.R. and H. Sherman (1995), 'Predicting business success from task motivation and attributional style: a longitudinal study'. *Entrepreneurship and Regional Development*, **XX**, 349–63.

Berger, A.N. and G.F. Udell (2003), 'Small business and debt finance', in Z.J. Acs and D.B. Audretsch (eds), *Handbook of Entrepreneurship Research, Vol. 1*, Boston, MA: Kluwer, pp. 299–300.

Berger, H.S. (1997/1998), 'One risk manager's approach', *Commercial Lending Review*, **13** (1), 72–4.

Bianchi, C., (2000), 'Commercial and financial policies in family firms: the small business growth management flight simulator', *Simulation and Gaming*, **31** (2), 197–230.

Binks, M.R., C.T. Ennew and G.V. Reed (1992), 'Information asymmetries and the provision of finance to small firms', *International Small Business Journal*, **11** (1): 35–46.

Birch, D. (1977), *The Job Generating Process*, Cambridge, MA: MIT Program on Neighborhood and Regional Change.

Bird, B. (1989), *Entrepreneurial Behavior*, Lenview, IL: Scott, Foresman and Company.

Birley, S. (1985), 'The role of networks in the entrepreneurial process', *Journal of Business Venturing*, **1** (1), 107–17.

Birley, S. and P. Westhead (1990), 'Growth and performance contrasts between "types" of small firms', *Strategic Management Journal*, **2**, 535–57.

Birley, S. and P. Westhead (1994), 'A comparison of new businesses established by "novice" and "habitual founders" in Great Britain', *International Small Business Journal*, **12**, 38–60.

Black, J.A. and K.B. Boal (1994), 'Strategic resources: Traits, configurations and paths to sustainable competitive advantage', *Strategic Management Journal*, **15**, 131–48.

Bolton, J.E. (1971), *Small Firms: Report of the Committee of Inquiry on Small Firms*, London: Her Majesty's Stationery Office.

Bonanno, G.A. and D. Keltner (1997), 'Facial expression of emotion and the course of conjugal bereavement', *Journal of Abnormal Psychology*, **106**, 126–37.

Bourgeois, L.J. (1981), 'On the measurement of organizational slack', *Academy of Management Review*, **6**, 29–39.

Bowden, R. (1994), 'Bargaining, size and return in venture capital funds', *Journal of Business Venturing*, **9**, 307–30.

Bower, G.H. (1992), 'How might emotions affect learning?', in S. Christianson (ed) *The Handbook of Emotion and Memory: Research and Theory*, Hillsdale, NJ.: Lawrence Erlbaum, pp. 3–31.

Boyd, B. and G.S. Vozikis (1994), 'The influence of self-efficacy on the development of entrepreneurial intentions and actions', *Entrepreneurship: Theory and Practice*, **18**, 63–77.

Bredemeier, M. and C. Greenblat (1981), 'The educational effectiveness of simulation games', *Simulations & Games*, **12**, 307–31.

Brown, K.M. (1994), 'Using role-play to integrate ethics into the business curriculum: A financial management example', *Journal of Business Ethics*, **13**, 105–10.

Brown, S.L. and K.M. Eisenhardt (1995), 'Product development: past research, present findings, and future directions', *Academy of Management Review*, **20**, 342–78.

Brown, T. (1996), *Resource Orientation, Entrepreneurial Orientation and Growth: How The Perception of Resource Availability Affects Small Firm Growth*, Newark, NJ: Rutgers University.

Brown, T.E., P. Davidsson and J. Wiklund (2001), 'An operationalization of Stevenson's conceptualization of entrepreneurship as opportunity-based firm behavior', *Strategic Management Journal*, **22**, 953–68.

Brüderl, J. and R. Schüssler (1990), 'Organisational mortality: The liability of newness and adolescence', *Administrative Science Quarterly*, **35**, 530–47.

Bruno, A.V., E.F. McQuarrie and C.G. Torgrimson (1992), 'The evolution of new technology ventures over 20 years: patterns of failure, merger, and survival', *Journal of Business Venturing*, **7**, 291–302.

Bruns, V., J. Wiklund and D. Shepherd (2004), 'Loan officers' decision policies towards small businesses', working paper.

Brush, C.G., P.G. Greene and M.M. Hart (2001), 'From initial idea to unique advantage: The entrepreneurial challenge of constructing a resource base', *Academy of Management Executive*, **15** (1), 64–78.

Brush, C.G. and P.A. Vander Werf (1992), 'A comparison of methods and sources for obtaining estimates of new venture performance', *Journal of Business Venturing*, **7** (2), 157–70.

Burgelman, R.A. (1983), 'Corporate entrepreneurship and strategic management: insights from a process study', *Management Science*, **29**, 1349–64.

Burt, R.S. (1992), *Structural Holes: The Social Structure of Competition*, Cambridge, MA: Harvard University Press.

Burt, R.S. (1997), 'The contingent value of social capita', *Administrative Science Quarterly*, **42** (2), 339–65.

Burt, R.S., S.M. Gabbay, G. Holt and P. Moran (1994), 'Contingent organization as a network theory: the culture–performance contingency function', *Acta Sociologica*, **37** (4), 345–70.

Busenitz, L. and J. Barney (1997), 'Differences between entrepreneurs and managers in large organizations: Biases and heuristics in strategic decision-making', *Journal of Business Venturing*, **12**, 9–30.

Butler, J. (1991), 'Towards understanding and measuring conditions of trust: Evolution of a conditions of trust inventory', *Journal of Management*, **17**, 643–63.

Bygrave, W. and J. Timmons (1991), *Venture and Risk Capital: Practice and Performance, Promises and Policy*, Boston, MA: Harvard Business School Press.

Cable, D.M. and S. Shane (1997), 'A prisoner's dilemma approach to entrepreneur–venture capitalist relationships', *Academy of Management Review*, **22** (1), 142–76.

Camerer, C.F. and E.J. Johnson (1991), 'The process-performance paradox in expert judgment: How can experts know so much and predict so badly?', in K. Anders Ericsson and J. Smith (eds), *Toward a general theory of expertise: Prospects and limits*, New York: Cambridge University Press, pp. 195–217.

Cameron, K. (1978), 'Measuring organizational effectiveness in institutions of higher education', *Administrative Science Quarterly*, **23** (X), 604–32.

Cameron, R. (2003), *Small Business Research Report*, Cameron Research Group, www.cameronresearch.com.au.

Cannell, C.F. and R. Henson (1974), 'Incentives, motives and response bias', *Annals of Economic and Social Measurement*, **3** (2), 307–17.

Carpenter, M.A., W.G. Sanders and H.B. Gregersen (2001), 'Building human capital with organizational context: the impact of international assignment experience on multinational firm performance and CEO pay', *Academy of Management Journal*, **44**, 493–512.

Castrogiovanni, G. (1991), 'Environmental munificence: A theoretical assessment', *Academy of Management Review*, **16** (3), 542–65.

Chandler, G.N. and S.H. Hanks (1993), 'Measuring the performance of emerging businesses: a validation study', *Journal of Business Venturing*, **8**, 391–408.

Chandler, G.N. and S.H. Hanks (1994), 'Founder competence, the environment, and venture performance', *Entrepreneurship Theory and Practice*, **18** (3), 77–89.

Chase, W. and H. Simon (1973), 'Perception in chess', *Cognitive Psychology*, **XX**, 55–81.

Cheah, H.B. (1990), 'Schumpeterian and Austrian entrepreneurship: unity within duality', *Journal of Business Venturing*, **5**, 341–8.

Chen, C.C., P.C. Greene and A. Crick (1998), 'Does entrepreneurial self-efficacy distinguish entrepreneurs from managers?', *Journal of Business Venturing*, **13** (4), 295–316.

Chi, M.T.H. and Koeske, R.D. (1983), 'Network representation of a child's dinosaur knowledge', *Developmental Psychology*, **19** (1), 29–39.

Choi, Y.R. and D.A. Shepherd (2004), 'Entrepreneurs' decisions to exploit opportunities', *Journal of Management*, **30**, pp. 377–95.

Choi, Y. and D.A. Shepherd (forthcoming), 'Stakeholder perceptions of newness', *Journal of Management*.

Choo, F. and K. Trotman (1991), 'The relationship between knowledge structure and judgments for experienced and inexperienced auditors', *The Accounting Review*, July, 464–85.

Clark, K.B. (1985), 'The interaction of design hierarchies and market concepts in technological evolution', *Research Policy*, **14**, 235–51.

Cockburn, I.M., R.M. Henderson and S. Stern (2000), 'Untangling the origins of competitive advantage', *Strategic Management Journal*, **21**, 1123–45.

Coff, R. (1999), 'When competitive advantage doesn't lead to performance: the resource-based view and stakeholder bargaining power', *Organization Science*, **10**, 119–33.

Cohen, J. and P. Cohen (1983), *Applied Multiple Regression/Correlation Analysis for the Behavioral Sciences*, Hillsdale, NJ: Lawrence Erlbaum Associates.

Cohen, W.M. and D.A. Levinthal (1990), 'Absorptive capacity: A new perspective on learning and innovation', *Administrative Science Quarterly*, **35**, 128–52.

Coleman, J. (1988), 'Social capital in the creation of human capital', *American Journal of Sociology*, **97**, 95–120.

Conner, K. (1991), 'A historical comparison of resource-based theory and five schools of thought within industrial organization economics: do we have a new theory of the firm?', *Strategic Management Journal*, **17**, 121–55.

Conner, K.R. and C.K. Prahalad (1996), 'A resource-based theory of the firm: knowledge versus opportunism', *Organization Science*, **7**, 477–501.

Cooper, A.C. (1995), 'Challenges in predicting new venture performance', in I. Bull, H. Thomas and G. Willard (eds), *Entrepreneurship: Perspectives on Theory Building*, 109–27, London: Elsevier Science.

Cooper, A.C. and W. Dunkelberg (1986), 'Entrepreneurship and paths to business ownership', *Strategic Management Journal*, **7**, 53–68.

Cooper, A.C., T.B. Folta and C. Woo (1995), 'Entrepreneurial information search', *Journal of Business Venturing*, **10** (2), 107–20.

Cooper, A.C., F.J. Gimeno-Gascon and C.Y. Woo (1994), 'Initial human and financial capital as predictors of new venture performance', *Journal of Business Venturing*, **9** (5), 371–95.

Cova, B. and C. Svanfeldt (1993), 'Societal innovations and the postmodern aestheticization of everyday life', *International Journal of Research in Marketing*, **10**, 297–310.

Covin, J.G. and D.P. Slevin (1989), 'Strategic management of small firms in hostile and benign environments', *Strategic Management Journal*, **10**, 75–87.

Covin, J.G. and D.P. Slevin (1990), 'New venture strategic posture, structure, and performance: an industry life cycle analysis', *Journal of Business Venturing*, **5**, 123–35.

Covin, J.G. and D.P. Slevin (1991), 'A conceptual model of entrepreneurship as firm behavior', *Entrepreneurship Theory and Practice*, **12**, 7–25.

Covin, J.G. and D.P. Slevin (1997), 'High growth transitions: theoretical perspectives and suggested directions', in D. Sexton and R. Smilor (eds), *Entrepreneurship 2000*, Chicago: Upstart Publishing Company.

Covin, J.G., D.P. Slevin and T.J. Covin (1990), 'Content and performance of growth-seeking small firms in high- and low-technology industries', *Journal of Business Venturing*, **5**, 391–412.

Craig, R. and J. Amernic (1994), 'Role-playing in a conflict resolution setting: description and some implications for accounting', *Issues in Accounting Education*, **9** (1), 28–45.

Creed, W. and R. Miles (1996), 'Trust in organizations: A conceptual framework linking organizational forms, managerial philosophies, and the opportunity costs of controls', in R. Kramer and T. Tyler (eds), *Trust in organizations: Frontiers of theory and research*, Thousand Oaks, CA: Sage, pp. 16–38.

Cromie, S., S. Birley and I. Callaghan (1994), 'Community brokers: their role in the formation and development of business ventures', in J.M. Veciana (ed.), *SMEs: Internationalization, Networks and Strategy*, Hampshire, U.K.: Avebury.

Cuisner, M., H. Janssen, C. Graauw, S. Bakker and C. Hoogduin (1996), 'Pregnancy following miscarriage: Curse of grief and some determining factors', *Journal of Psychometric Obstetrics and Gynecology*, **17**, 168–74.

Cyert, R.M. and J.G. March (1963), *A Behavioral Theory of the Firm*, Englewood Cliffs, NJ: Prentice-Hall.

Dahlqvist, J., P. Davidsson and J. Wiklund (2000), 'Initial conditions as predictors of new venture performance: a replication and extension of the Cooper et al. study', *Enterprise and Innovation Management Studies*, **1** (1), 1–17.

Das, T. and B. Teng (1998), 'Between trust and control: Developing confidence in partner cooperation in alliances', *Academy of Management Review*, **23** (3), 491–512.

D'Aunno, T. and R.I. Sutton (1992), 'The responses of drug abuse treatment organizations to financial adversity: a partial test of the threat-rigidity thesis', *Journal of Management*, **18**, 117–31.

Davidsson, P. (1989a), *Continued Entrepreneurship and Small Firm Growth*, Stockholm: Stockholm School of Economics.

Davidsson, P. (1989b), 'Entrepreneurship – and after? A study of growth willingness in small businesses', *Journal of Business Venturing*, **4**, 211–26.

Davidsson, P. and B. Honig, (2003), 'The role of social and human capital among nascent entrepreneurs', *Journal of Business Venturing*.

Davidsson, P. and B. Honig (2003), 'The role of social and human capital among nascent entrepreneurs', *Journal of Business Venturing*, **18**, 301–32.

Davidsson, P., L. Lindmark and C. Olofsson (1994), *Dynamiken i svenskt näringsliv (Business Dynamics in Sweden)*, Lund, Sweden: Studentlitteratur.

Davidsson, P., L. Lindmark and C. Olofsson (1996), *Näringslivsdynamik under 90-talet*, Stockholm: NUTEK.

DeCarolis, D.M. and D.L. Deeds (1999), 'The impact of stocks and flows of organizational knowledge on firm performance: an empirical investigation of the biotechnology industry', *Strategic Management Journal*, **20**, 953–68.

Delmar, F. (1996), *Entrepreneurial Behavior and Business Performance*, Stockholm: Stockholm School of Economics.

Delmar, F. (1997), 'Measuring growth: Methodological considerations and empirical results', in R. Donckels and A. Miettinen (eds), *Entrepreneurship and SME Research: On its Way to the Next Millennium*, Aldershot, VA: Avebury, pp. 190–216.

De Sousa, R. (1987), *The Rationality of Emotion*, Cambridge, MA: MIT Press.

Dess, G.G. and D.W. Beard (1984), 'Dimensions of organizational task environments', *Administrative Science Quarterly*, **29**, 52–73.

Dess, G.G., G.T. Lumpkin and J.G. Covin (1997), 'Entrepreneurial strategy making and firm performance: Tests of contingency and configurational models', *Strategic Management Journal*, **18** (9), 677–95.

Dess, G.G. and H.C. Picke (1999), *Beyond Productivity: How Leading Companies Achieve Superior Performance By Leveraging Their Human Capital*, New York: Amacon Books.

Dierickx, I. and K. Cool (1989), 'Asset stock accumulation and sustainability of competitive advantage', *Management Science*, **35**, 1504–11.

Dixon, J.R. and M.R. Duffey (1990), 'The neglect of engineering design', *California Management Review*, **32**, 9–23.

Doll, J. and I. Ajzen (1992), 'Accessibility and stability of predictors in theory of planned behavior', *Journal of Personality and Social Psychology*, **63** (5), 754–6.

Dollinger, M.J. (1999), *Entrepreneurship: Strategies and Resources*, Upper Saddle River, NJ: Prentice Hall.

Doty, D.H., W.H. Glick and G.P. Huber (1993), 'Fit, equifinality, and organizational effectiveness: a test of two configurational theories', *Academy of Management Journal*, **36**, 1196–251.

Douglas, E. and D.A. Shepherd (2000), 'Entrepreneurship as a utility maximizing response', *Journal of Business Venturing*, **15** (5), 393–410.

Drucker, P. (1985), *Innovation and Entrepreneurship*, New York: Harper and Row.

Duncan, R. (1979), *Strategic Management: A New View of Business Policy and Planning*, Boston, MA: Little, Brown.

Eagly, A.H. and S. Chaiken (1998), 'Attitude structure and function', in D.T. Gilbert, S.T. Fiske and G. Lindsey (eds), *Handbook of Social Psychology, Vol. 2*, Boston: McGraw-Hill, pp. 269–322.

Egri, C.P. (1999), 'The environmental round table exercise: The dynamics of multi-stakeholder decision making processes', *Journal of Management Education*, **23** (1), 95–112.

Eisenhardt, K.M. and J.A. Martin (2000), 'Dynamic capabilities: What are they?', *Strategic Management Journal*, **21** (X), 1105–21.

Elliott, M.A., C.J. Armitage and C.J. Baughan (2003), 'Drivers' compliance with speed limits: an application of the theory of planned behavior', *Journal of Applied Psychology*, **88** (5), 964–72.

Ellis, N.R. and P.W. Ashbrook (1988), 'Resource allocation model and the effects of depressed mood states on memory', in K. Fiedler and J. Forgas (eds), *Affect, Cognition and Social Behaviour*, Toronto, CA: Hogreff.

Ellis, N.R. and P.W. Ashbrook (1989), 'The state of mood and memory research: A selective review', *Journal of Social Behavior and Personality*, **4** (2), 1–22.

Ellis, N.R., D.K. Detterman, D. Runcie, R.B. McCarver and E.M. Craig (1971), Amnesic effects in short-term memory', *Journal of Experimental Psychology*, **84**, 357–61.

Elster, J. (1999), *Alchemies of the Mind*, Cambridge: Cambridge University Press.

Evans, D.S. and L.S. Leighton (1989), 'Some empirical aspects of entrepreneurship', *The American Economic Review*, **79**, 519–35.

Fiet, J. (1995), 'Risk avoidance strategies in venture capital markets', *Journal of Management Studies*, **324**, 551–75.

Fineman, S. (1996), 'Emotion and organizing', in S.R. Clegg, C. Hardy and W.R. Nord (eds), *Handbook of Organization Studies*, London: Sage, pp. 543–64.

Fischhoff, B. (1982), 'For those condemned to study the past: Heuristics and biases in hindsight', in D. Kahneman, P. Slovic and A.Tversky (eds), *Judgment Under Uncertainty: Heuristics and Biases*, New York: Cambridge University Press, pp. 335–51.

Fisher, J. and V. Govindarajan (1992), 'Profit center management compensation: An examination of market, political and human capital factors', *Strategic Management Journal*, **13** (3), 205–17.

Folger, R. and M. Konovsky (1989), 'Effects of procedural and distributive justice on reactions to pay raise decisions', *Academy of Management Journal*, **32**, 115–30.

Fombrun, C.J. and S. Wally (1989), 'Structuring small firms for rapid growth,' *Journal of Business Venturing*, **4**, 107–22.

Frank, R.H. (1993), 'The strategic role of the emotions', *Rationality and Society*, **5**, 160–94.

Frederick, D. (1991), 'Auditors' representation and retrieval of internal control knowledge', *The Accounting Review*, **66** (April), 240–58.

Frederick, D.M. and Libby, R. (1986), 'Expertise and auditors' judgments of conjunctive events', *Journal of Accounting Research*, Autumn, 270–90.

Gabarro, J. (1978), 'The development of trust influence and expectations', in A. Athos and J. Gabarro (eds), *Interpersonal behavior: Communication and understanding in relationships*, Englewood Cliffs, NJ: Prentice Hall, pp. 290–303.

Gaglio, C.M. and J.A. Katz (2001), 'The psychological basis of opportunity identification: entrepreneurial alertness', *Small Business Economics*, **16**, 95–112.

Galunic, D.C. and S. Rodan (1998), 'Resource combinations in the firm: Knowledge structures and the potential for Schumpeterian innovation', *Strategic Management Journal*, **19**, 1193–201.

Gibson, B. (1993), 'The alternative to assuming rational use of financial information within small firms', *Journal of Small Business Finance*, **22**, 163–74.

Gilbert, A. (2000), 'Lessons learned from failure', *Information Week*, **817**, 111.

Gimeno, J., T.B. Folta, A.C. Cooper and C.Y. Woo (1997), 'Survival of the fittest? entrepreneurial human capital and the persistence of under performing firms', *Administrative Science Quarterly*, **42**, 750–83.

Gobbo, C. and Chi, M. (1986), 'How knowledge is structured and used by expert and novice children', *Cognitive Development*, **1**, 221–37.

Golden, B.R. (1992), 'The past is the past – or is it? The use of retrospective accounts as indicators of past strategy', *Academy of Management Journal*, **35**, 848–60.

Goll, I. and A. Rasheed (1997), 'Rational decision-making and firm performance: The moderating role of environment', *Strategic Management Journal*, **18** (7), 583–91.

Gomez-Mejia, L., D. Balkin and T. Welbourne (1990), 'Influence of venture capitalists on high tech management', *The Journal of High Technology Management Research*, **1**, 103–18.

Goold, M. and A. Campbell (1987), *Strategies and Styles: The Role of the Centre in Managing Diversified Corporations*, Oxford: Basil Blackwell.

Gorman, M. and W. Sahlman (1989), 'What do venture capitalists do?', *Journal of Business Venturing*, **4**, 231–48.

Gould, J.B. (1994), 'A picture is worth a thousand words: a strategy for grief education', *Death Studies*, **18** (1), 65–74.

Granovetter, M. (1985), 'Economic action and social structure: the problem of embeddedness', *American Journal of Sociology*, **91** (3), 481–510.

Grant, R.M. (1991), 'The resource-based theory of competitive advantage: implications for strategy formulation', *California Management Review*, **33** (3), 114–35.

Green, R. and V. Srinivasan (1990), 'Conjoint analysis in marketing: New developments and directions', *Journal of Marketing*, **54**, 3–19.

Greenberg, J. and D.E. Eskew (1993), 'The role of role-playing in organizational research', *Journal of Management*, **19** (2), 221–41.

Greene, P. and T. Brown (1997), 'Resource needs and the dynamic capitalism typology', *Journal of Business Venturing*, **12**, 161–73.

Gross, J.J. (1998), 'Antecedent- and response-focused emotion regulation: divergent consequences for experience, expression, and physiology', *Journal of Personality and Social Psychology*, **74**, 224–37.

Gross, J.J. (1999), 'Emotion regulation: past, present, future', *Cognition and Emotion*, **13**, 551–73.

Gupta, A. and V. Govindarajan (2000), 'Knowledge flows within multinational corporations', *Strategic Management Journal*, **21**, 473–96.

Hahn, G. and S. Shapiro (1966), *A Catalogue and Computer Program for the Design and Analysis of Orthogonal Symmetric and Asymmetric Fractional Factorial Designs*, Schenectady, NY: General Electric Corporation.

Hambrick, D.C. and L.M. Crozier (1985) 'Stumblers and stars in the management of rapid growth', *Journal of Business Venturing*, **1**, 31–46.

Hamel, G. (2000), *Leading the Revolution*, Cambridge, MA: Harvard University Press.

Hamel, G. and C.K. Prahalad (1989), 'Strategic intent', *Harvard Business Review*, **67**, 63–76.

Hamel, G. and C.K. Prahalad (1990), 'The core competence of the corporation', *Harvard Business Review* (May–June), 75–84.

Hanks, S.H., C.J. Watson, E. Jansen and G.N. Chandler (1993), 'Tightening the life cycle construct: A taxonomic study of growth stage configurations', *Entrepreneurship Theory and Practice*, **18** (2), 5–30.

Harris, S.G. and R.I. Sutton (1986), 'Functions of parting ceremonies in dying organizations', *Academy of Management Journal*, **29**, 5–30.

Hart, M. (1996a), *Eric Wood A*, Cambridge, MA: Harvard Business School Press.

Hart, M. (1996b), *Eric Wood B*, Cambridge, MA: Harvard Business School Press.

Hart, S.L. (1992), 'An integrative framework for strategy-making processes', *Academy of Management Review*, **17** (2), 327–51.

Hayek, F.A. (1945), 'The use of knowledge in society', *American Economic Review*, **35**, 519–30.

Heckman, J. (1979), 'Sample selection bias as a specification error', *Econometrica*, **47**, 153–61.

Heide, J.B. and G. John (1992), 'Do norms matter in marketing relationships?', *Journal of Marketing*, **56** (2), 32–44.

Helfat, C.E. (2000), 'Guest editor's introduction to the special issue: the evolution of firm capabilities', *Strategic Management Journal*, **21** (X), 955–9.

Hindle, K. (2002), 'A grounded theory for teaching entrepreneurship using simulation games', *Simulation & Gaming*, **33** (2), 236–42.

Hirshleifer, J. (1993), 'The affections and the passions: their economic logic', *Rationality and Society*, **5**, 185–202.

Hitt, M.A. and S.H. Barr (1989), 'Managerial selection decision models: examination of configural cue processing', *Journal of Applied Psychology*, **74**, 53–61.

Hitt, M.A. and B.B. Tyler (1991), 'Strategic decision models: Integrating different perspectives', *Strategic Management Journal*, **12**, 327–51.

Hitt, M.A., R.D. Ireland and R.E. Hoskisson (1999), *Strategic Management: Competitiveness and Globalization*, Cincinatti, OH: South-Western College Publishing.

Hitt, M, M.T. Dacin, E. Levitas, J. Arregle and A. Borza (2000), 'Partner selection in emerging and developed market contexts: resource-based and organizational learning perspectives', *Academy of Management Journal*, **43** (3), 449–67.

Hodgkinson, M. (2000), 'The role of higher education in facilitating organization learning: with HRD managers', *Human Resource Development International*, **3** (3), 361–75.

Hoffman, H. and J. Blakey (1987), 'You can negotiate with venture capitalists', *Harvard Business Review* (March–April), 6–24.

Hogan, N.S., D.B. Greenfield and L.A. Schmidt (2001), 'Development and validation of the Hogan Grief Reaction Checklist', *Death Studies*, **25**, 1–32.

Hrebiniak, L.G. and W.F. Joyce (1985), 'Organizational adaptation: Strategic choice and environmental determinism', *Administrative Science Quarterly*, **30**, 336–49.

Huber, G.P. (1991), 'Organizational learning: The contributing processes and the literatures', *Organization Science*, **2**, 88–115.

Huber, G.P. and D.J. Power (1985), 'Retrospective reports of strategic-level managers: Guidelines for increasing their accuracy', *Strategic Management Journal*, **6**, 171–80.

Hughes, A. (1996), 'Finance for SMEs. What needs to change?', in R. Cressy, B. Gandemo and C. Olofsson (eds), *Financing Small and Medium Sized Businesses – A Comparative Perspective*, Stockholm: NUTEK, pp. 13–42.

Hutchison, T. and A. Scherman (1992), 'Didactic and experiential death and dying training: Impact upon death anxiety', *Death Studies*, **16**, 317–30.

Huy, Q.N. (1999), 'Emotional capability, emotional intelligence, and radical change', *Academy of Management Review*, **24**, 325–45.

Inkpen, A. and N. Choudhury (1995), 'The seeking of a strategy where it is not: towards a theory of strategy absence', *Strategic Management Journal*, **16**, 313–23.

Ireland, R. and M.A. Hitt (1999), 'Achieving and maintaining strategic competitiveness in the 21st century: The role of strategic leadership', *Academy of Management Executive*, **13**, 43–57.

Isen, A.M. and R.A. Baron (1991), 'Positive affect as a factor in organizational behavior', in B.M. Staw and L.L. Cummings (eds), *Research in organization behavior, Vol. 13*, Greenwich, CT: JAI Press, pp. 1–53.

Janoff-Bulman, R. (1992), *Shattered Assumptions: Towards a New Psychology of Trauma*, New York: Free Press.

Jennings, E. (1971), *Routes to The Executive Suite*, New York: McGraw-Hill.

Jennings, P. and G. Beaver (1997), 'The performance and competitive advantage of small firms: A management perspective', *International Small Business Journal*, **15** (2), 63–75.

Johannisson, B. (2000), 'Networking and entrepreneurial growth', in D. Sexton and H. Landström (eds), *The Blackwell Handbook of Entrepreneurship*, Oxford, MA: Blackwell, pp. 26–44.

Johnson, J., J. Cullen, T. Sakano and H. Takenouchi (1997), 'Setting the stage for trust and strategic integration in Japanese–U.S. cooperative alliances', in P. Beamish and J. Killing (eds), *Cooperative Strategies: North American perspectives, Vol. 1*, San Francisco, CA: New Lexington Press, pp. 227–54.

Johnson, P.E., K. Jamal and R.G. Berryman (1991), 'Effects of framing on auditor decisions', *Organizational Behavior and Human Decision Processes*, **50**, 75–106.

Johnson-George, C. and W. Swap (1982), 'Measurement of specific interpersonal trust: construction and validation of a scale to assess trust in a specific other', *Journal of Personality and Social Psychology*, **43**, 1306–17.

Kam, V. (1990), *Accounting Theory*, Singapore: John Wiley and Sons.

Katz, J.A. (1994), 'Modeling entrepreneurial career progressions: Concepts and considerations', *Entrepreneurship: Theory and Practice*, **19**, 23–40.

Keasey, K. and P. McGuiness (1990), 'Small new firms and the return to alternative sources of finance', *Journal of Small Business Economics*, **2**, 213–22.

Keats, B.W. and J.S. Bracker (1988), 'Toward a theory of small firm performance: a conceptual model', *American Journal of Small Business*, **14**, 41–58.

Ketchen, D.J.J., J.B. Thomas and C.C. Snow (1993), 'Organizational confirgations and performance: a comparison of theoretical approaches', *Academy of Management Journal*, **36** (6), 1278–304.

Keys, B.J. (1997), 'Strategic management games: a review', *Simulation & Gaming*, **28** (4), 395–423.

Kiesler, C.A., and L.S. Sproull (1982), 'Managerial responses to changing environments: Perspectives on problem sensing from social cognition', *Administrative Science Quarterly*, **27**, 548–70.

Kim, D.H. (1993), 'The link between individual learning and organizational learning', *Sloan Management Review*, **35** (Fall), 379–500.

Klass, D. (1988), *Parental Grief: Solace and Resolution*, New York: Springer.

Kline, S.J. and N. Rosenberg (1986), 'Overview of innovation', in R. Landau and N. Rosenberg (eds), *The Positive Sum Strategy*, Washington, DC: National Academy Press, pp. 275–305.

Knight, G.A. (1997), 'Cross-cultural reliability and validity of a scale to measure firm entrepreneurial orientation', *Journal of Business Venturing*, **12**, 213–25.

Knotts, U.S. and B.J. Keys (1997), 'Teaching strategic management with a business game', *Simulation & Gaming*, **28** (4), 377–95.

Kogut, B. and U. Zander (1992), 'Knowledge of the firm, combinative capabilities, and the replication of technology', *Organization Science*, **3**, 383–97.

Kolvereid, L. (1992), 'Growth aspirations among Norwegian entrepreneurs', *Journal of Business Venturing*, **7**, 209–22.

Kolvereid, L. and E. Bullvåg (1996), 'Growth intentions and actual growth: the impact of entrepreneurial choice', *Journal of Enterprising Culture*, **4** (1), 1–17.

Komorita, S., J. Hilty and C. Parks (1991), 'Reciprocity and cooperation in social dilemmas', *Journal of Conflict Resolution*, **35** (3), 494–518.

Konovsky, M. and R. Cropanzano (1991), 'Perceived fairness of employee drug testing as a predictor of employee attitudes and job performance', *Journal of Applied Psychology*, **78**, 698–707.

Korsgaard, A., D. Schweiger and H. Sapienza (1995), 'Building commitment, attachment and trust in strategic decision-making teams: the role of procedural justice', *Academy of Management Journal*, **38**, 60–84.

Lang, J.Q. and E.M. Crown (1993), Country-of-origin effect in apparel choices: A conjoint analysis, *Journal of Consumer Studies and Home Economics*, **17** (March), 87–98.

Lant, T.K. and S.J. Mezias (1992), 'An organizational learning model of convergence and reorientation', *Organizational Science: A Journal of the Institute of Management Sciences*, **3** (1), 47–72.

Lant, T.K., F.J. Milliken and B. Batra (1992), 'The role of managerial learning and interpretation in strategic persistence and reorientation: an empirical exploration', *Strategic Management Journal*, **13**, 585–608.

Larson, A. (1992), 'Network dyads in entrepreneurial settings: a study of the governance of exchange relationships', *Administrative Science Quarterly*, **37**, 76–104.

Lawless, M.W. and L. Finch (1989), 'Choice and determinism: a test of Hrebiniak and Joyce's framework on strategy–environment fit', *Strategic Management Journal*, **10**, 351–65.

Leff, N.H. (1979), 'Entrepreneurship and economic development: the problem revisited', *Journal of Economic Literature*, **17**, 46–64.

Lehman, C.M. and S. Taylor (1994), 'A role-playing exercise for analyzing inter-cultural communication', *Bulletin of the Association of Business Communication*, **57** (2), 23–32.

Leifer, R. and P.K. Mills (1996), 'An information processing approach for deciding upon control strategies and reducing control loss in emerging organizations', *Journal of Management*, **22**, 113–37.

Lesgold, A. (1988), 'Problem solving', in R.J. Sternberg and E.E. Smith (eds), *The Psychology of Human Thought*, Cambridge: Cambridge University Press, pp. 188–213.

Levinthal, D. and J.G. March (1981), 'A model of adaptive organizational search', *Journal of Economic Behavior and Organization*, **2**, 307–33.

Lewicki, R.J., D.J. McAllister and R.J. Bies (1998), 'Trust and distrust: new relationships and realities', *Academy of Management Review*, **23**, 438–59.

Lin, N., W. Ensel and J. Vaughn (1981), 'Social resources and strength of ties: structural factors in occupational status attainment', *American Sociological Review*, **46** (4), 393–405.

Lindell, M.K. and D.J. Whitney (2001), 'Accounting for common method variance in cross-sectional research designs', *Journal of Applied Psychology*, **86**, 114–21.

Locke, E.A. (1991), 'Introduction to special issue', *Organizational Behavior and Human Decision Making*, **50**, 151–3.

Logan, G.D. (1990), 'Repetition priming and automaticity: common and underlying mechanisms?', *Cognitive Psychology*, **22**, pp. 1–35.

Louviere, J.J. (1988), *Analyzing Decision Making: Metric Conjoint Analysis*, Newbury Park, CA: Sage Publications.

Low, M.B. and I.C. MacMillan (1988), 'Entrepreneurship: past research and future challenges', *Journal of Management*, **14**, 139–61.

Lumpkin, G.T. and G.G. Dess (1996), 'Clarifying the entrepreneurial orientation construct and linking it to performance', *Academy of Management Review*, **21**, 135–72.

Lyubomirsky, S. and S. Nolen-Hoeksema (1995), 'Effects of self-focused rumination on negative thinking and interpersonal problem solving', *Journal of Personality and Social Psychology*, **69**, 176–90.

MacMillan, I.C., R. Seigel and P.N. Subba Narasimha (1985), 'Criteria used by venture capitalist to evaluate new venture proposals', *Journal of Business Venturing*, **1**, 119–28.

Macrae, D.J.R. (1992), 'Characteristics of high and low growth small and medium sized businesses', *Management Research News*, **15** (2), 11–17.

Madhok, A. (1995), 'Revisiting multinational firms' tolerance for joint ventures: a trust-based approach', *Journal of International Business Studies*, **26**, 117–37.

Madhok, A. (1996), 'The organization of economic activity: Transaction costs, firm capabilities and the nature of governance', *Organization Science*, **7**, 577–90.

Madhok, A. (1997), 'Cost, value and foreign market entry mode: The transaction and the firm', *Strategic Management Journal*, **18**, 39–61.

Madhok, A. and S.B. Tallman (1998), 'Resources, transactions and rents: Managing value through interfirm collaborative relationships', *Organization Science*, **9** (3), 326–40.

Malkinson, R. (1996), 'Cognitive behavioral grief therapy', *Journal of Rational-Emotive and Cognitive-Behavior Therapy*, **14**, 155–71.

March, J.G. (1991), 'Exploration and exploitation in organizational learning', *Organization Science*, **2**, 71–87.

March, J.G. and M.S. Feldman (1981), 'Information in organizations as signal and symbol', *Administrative Science Quarterly*, **26** (2), 171–86.

March, J.G. and H. Simon (1963), *Organizations*, New York: Wiley.

Mata, F., W. Fuerst and J. Barney (1995), 'Information technology and sustained competitive advantage: a resource-based analysis', *MIS Quarterly*, **19** (4), 487–505.

McAllister, D. (1995), 'Affect- and cognition-based trust as foundations for interpersonal cooperation in organizations', *Academy of Management Journal*, **38**, 2449–XX.

McEvily, S.K. and B. Chakravarthy (2002), 'The persistence of knowledge-based advantage: an empirical test for product performance and technological knowledge', *Strategic Management Journal*, **23**, 285–305.

McGrath, R. (1999), 'Falling forward: real options reasoning and entrepreneurial failure', *Academy of Management Review*, **24** (1), 13–30.

McGrath, R.G. (2001), 'Entrepreneurship, small firms, and wealth creation: a framework using real options reasoning', in A.M. Pettigrew, H. Thomas and A. Whittington (eds), *Handbook of Strategy and Management*, London: Sage Publications.

McGrath, R.G. (2001), 'Exploratory learning, innovative capacity, and managerial oversight', *Academy of Management Journal*, **44**, 118–31.

McGrath, R., M. Tsai, S. Venkataraman and I. MacMillan (1996), 'Innovation, competitive advantage and rent: a model and test', *Management Science*, **42**, 389–403.

Mercado, S.A. (2000), 'Pre-managerial business education: a role for role-plays?', *Journal of Further and Higher Education*, **24** (1), 117–25.

Meyer, A.D., A.S. Tsui and C.R. Hinings (1993), 'Configurational approaches to organizational analysis', *Academy of Management Journal*, **36** (6), 1175–95.

Meyer, M.W. and L.G. Zucker (1989), *Permanently Failing Organizations*, Newbury Park, CA: Sage.

Middleton, W., P. Burnett, B. Raphael and N. Martinek (1997), 'Psychological distress and bereavement', *Journal of Nervous and Mental Disease*, **185**, 447–53.

Miller, D. (1983), 'The correlates of entrepreneurship in three types of firms', *Management Science*, **29**, 770–91.

Miller, D. (1986), 'Configurations of strategy and structure: towards a synthesis', *Strategic Management Journal*, 7, 233–50.

Miller, D. (1987), 'The structural and environmental correlates of business strategy', *Strategic Management Journal*, **8**, 55–76.

Miller, D. (1988), 'Relating Porter's business strategies to environment and structure: analysis and performance implications', *Academy of Management Journal*, **31** (2), 280–308.

Miller, D. (1990), 'Organizational configurations: cohesion, change, and prediction', *Human Relations*, **43** (8), 771–89.

Miller, D. (1996), 'Configurations revisited', *Strategic Management Journal*, **17**, 505–12.

Miller, D. and P.H. Friesen (1978), 'Archetypes of strategy formulation', *Management Science*, **24**, 921–33.

Miller, D. and P.H. Friesen (1982), 'Innovation in conservative and entrepreneurial firms: Two models of strategic momentum', *Strategic Management Journal*, **3**, 1–25.

Miller, D. and P.H. Friesen (1984), *Organizations – A Quantum View*, Englewoods Cliffs, NJ: Prentice Hall.

Miller, D. and J. Shamsie (1996), 'The resource-based view of the firm in two environments: the Hollywood film studios from 1936 to 1965', *Academy of Management Journal*, **39** (3), 519–43.

Mincer, J. (1997), 'The production of human capital and the life cycle of earnings: variations on a theme', *Journal of Labor Economics*, **15**, S26–48.

Miner, J.B., N.R. Smith and J.S. Bracker (1994), 'Role of entrepreneurial task motivation in the growth of technologically innovative businesses: interpretations from follow-up data', *Journal of Applied Psychology*, **79** (4), 627–30.

Minniti, M. and W. Bygrave (2001), 'A dynamic model of entrepreneurial learning', *Entrepreneurship Theory and Practice*, **25**, 5–16.

Mintzberg, H. (1984), 'The simple structure', in J.B. Quinn, H. Mintzberg and J.M. James (eds), *The Strategy Process: Concepts, Contexts and Cases*, Englewood Cliffs, NJ: Prentice Hall, pp. 532–9.

Mogg, K., A. Mathews, C. Bird and R. MacGregor-Morris (1990), 'Effects of stress and anxiety on the processing of threat stimuli', *Journal of Personality and Social Psychology*, **59**, 1230–37.

Mok, A.L. and H. van den Tillaart (1990), 'Farmers and small business-men: a comparative analysis of their careers and occupational orienta-tion', in R. Donckels and A. Miettinen (eds), *New Findings and Perspectives in Entrepreneurship*, Aldershot, VA: Avebury.

More, G. (1999), Presentation at Babson College, March.

Morrison, E.W., and S.L. Robinson (1997), 'When employees feel betrayed:

a model of how psychological contract violation develops', *Academy of Management Review*, **22**, 226–56.

Muzyka, D., S. Birley and B. Leleux (1996), 'Trade-offs in the investment decisions of European venture capitalists', *Journal of Business Venturing*, **11** (4), 273–88.

Myers, S. and N.S. Majluf (1984), 'Corporate financing and investment decision when firms have information that investors do not have', *Journal of Financial Economics*, **3**, 187–221.

Namen, J.L. and D.P. Slevin (1993), 'Entrepreneurship and the concept of fit: A model and empirical tests', *Strategic Management Journal*, **14**, 137–53.

Nisbett, R. and L. Ross (1980), *Human Interferences: Strategies and Shortcomings of Social Judgment*, Englewood Cliffs, NJ: Prentice Hall.

Nolen-Hoeksema, S. (1991), 'Responses to depression and their effects on the duration of the depressive episode', *Journal of Abnormal Psychology*, **100**, 569–82.

Nolen-Hoeksema, S., A. McBride, and J. Larson (1997), 'Rumination and psychological distress among bereaved partners', *Journal of Personality and Social Psychology*, **72**, 855–62.

Nonaka, I. and H. Takeuchi (1995), *The Knowledge Creating Company: How Japanese Companies Create the Dynamics of Innovation*, New York: Oxford University Press.

Nosofsky, R. (1987), 'Attention and learning processes in the identification and categorization of integral stimuli', *Journal of Experimental Psychology: Learning, Memory and Cognition*, **13** (1), 87–108.

Nunnally, J.C. and I.H. Bernstein (1994), *Psychometric Theory*, New York, NY: McGraw-Hill.

Nunnally, J.C. (1967), *Psychometric Theory*, New York: McGraw-Hill.

Ocasio, W. (1995), 'The enactment of economic diversity: A reconciliation of theories of failure-induced change and threat-rigidity', in L.L. Cummings and B.M. Staw (eds), *Research in Organizational Behavior, Vol. 17*, Greenwich, CT: JAI Press, pp. 287–331.

Olson, J.M. and M.P. Zana (1993), 'Attitudes and attitude change', *Annual Review of Psychology*, **44**, 117–54.

Paich, M. and J.D. Sterman (1993), 'Boom, bust, and failures to learn in experimental markets', *Management Science*, **39** (12), 1439–59.

Parkes, C.M. (1975), 'What becomes of redundant world models? A contribution to the study of adaptation to change', *British Journal of Medical Psychology*, **48**, 131–7.

Parkes, C.M. (1988), 'Bereavement as a psychological transition: Processes of adaptation to change', *Journal of Social Issues*, **44**, 53–65.

Penrose, E. (1959), *The Theory of the Growth of the Business*, Oxford: Oxford University Press.

Peteraf, M.A. (1993), 'The cornerstones of competitive advantage: a resource based view', *Strategic Management Journal*, **14**, 179–91.

Petranek, C.F. (2000), 'Written debriefing: The next vital step in learning with simulations', *Simulation & Gaming*, **31** (1), 108–19.

Petranek, C.F. and S. Corey (1992), 'Three levels of learning in simulations: Participating, debriefing, and journal writing', *Simulation & Gaming*, **23** (2), 174–86.

Pettigrew, A.M. (1987), 'Context and action in the transformation of the firms', *Journal of Management Studies*, **24**, 649–70.

Pettit, R.R. and R.F. Singer (1985), 'Small business finance: A research agenda', *Journal of Financial Management Association*, **14** (3), 47–60.

Petty, R.E., D.T. Wegener and L.R. Fabrigar (1997), 'Attitudes and attitude change', *Annual Review of Psychology*, **48**, 609–47.

Porter, M. (1980), *Competitive Strategy: Techniques for Analyzing Industries and Competitors*, New York: The Free Press.

Portes, A. (1998), 'Social capital', *Annual Review of Sociology*, **23**, 1–24.

Powell, W. (1990), 'Neither market nor hierarchy: network forms of organization', in B. Staw and L. Cummings (eds), *Research in Organizational Behavior*, Greenwich, CT: JAI Press, pp. 293–336.

Priem, R.L. (1994), Executive judgment, organizational congruence, and firm performance. *Organizational Science*, **5**, 421–37.

Priem, R.L. and D.A. Harrison (1994), 'Exploring strategic judgment: methods for testing the assumptions of prescriptive contingency theories', *Strategic Management Journal*, **15**, 311–24.

Prigerson, H.G., M.K. Shear, J.T. Newson, E. Frank, C.F. Reynolds, P.K. Maciejewski, P.R. Houck, A.J. Bierhals and D.J. Kupfer (1996), 'Anxiety among widowed elders: is it distinct from depression and grief?', *Anxiety*, **2**, 1–12.

Quinn, J. (1980), *Strategies for Change: Logical Incrementalism*, Homewood, IL: Irwin.

Ratner, E.R. and J.Y. Song (2002), 'Education for the end of life', *Chronicle of Higher Education*, **48** (39), B12.

Rauch, A. and M. Frese (2000), 'Human capital of small scale business owners and business success: a longitudinal study of moderators and mediators', paper presented at the ICSB World Conference 2000, Brisbane, 16–18 June.

Richman, T. (1990), 'The lessons of bankruptcy', *Inc Magazine*, December (http://inc.com/incmagazine).

Ring, P. and A. Van de Ven (1994), 'Developmental processes of cooperative interorganizational relationships', *Academy of Management Review*, **19**, 90–118.

Robinson, J.P., P.R. Shaver and L.S. Wrightsman (1991), 'Criteria for scale selection and evaluation', in J.P. Robinson, P.R. Shaver and L.S. Wrightsman (eds), *Measures of Personality and Social Psychological Attitudes*, San Diego, CA: Academic Press, pp. 1–16.

Robinson, S. and D. Rousseau (1994), 'Violating the psychological contract: not the exception but the norm', *Journal of Organizational Behavior*, **15**, 245–59.

Robson, P.J.A. and R.J. Bennett (2000), 'Central government support to SMEs, compared to business link, business connect and business shop and the prospect for the small business service', *Regional Studies*, **33**, 779–97.

Romanelli, E. (1987), 'New venture strategies in the microcomputer industry', *California Management Review*, **30**, 160–75.

Rosenberg, N. (1982), *Inside The Black Box: Technology and Economics*, New York: Cambridge University Press.

Rosenberg, N. (1994), *Exploring The Black Box*, New York: Cambridge University Press.

Roure, J.B. and M.A. Madique (1986), 'Linking prefunding factors and high-technology venture success: an exploratory study', *Journal of Business Venturing*, **1** (3), 295–306.

Rousseau, D.M. (1995), *Psychological Contracts in Organizations: Understanding Written and Unwritten Agreements*, Thousand Oaks, CA: Sage.

Rousseau, D.M., S.B. Sitkin, R.S. Burt and C. Camerer (1998), 'Not so different after all: A cross-discipline view of trust', *Academy of Management Review*, **23** (3), 393–404.

Ruth, G. (1987), *Commercial Lending*, Washington, DC: American Bankers Association.

Sahlman, W. (1990), 'The structure and governance of venture-capital organizations', *Journal of Financial Economics*, **27**, 473–521.

Sapienza, H.J. and C.M. Grimm (1997), 'Founder characteristics, start-up process, and strategy/structure variables as predictors of shortline railroad performance', *Entrepreneurship: Theory and Practice*, **20** (Fall), 5–24.

Sapienza, H. and M.A. Korsgaard (1996), 'Procedural justice in entrepreneur-investor relations', *Academy of Management Journal*, **39** (3), 544–74.

Sargent, M. and J.E. Young (1991), 'The entrepreneurial search for capital: a behavioural science perspective', *Entrepreneurship and Regional Development*, **3**, 237–52.

Sartori, A.E. (forthcoming), 'An estimator for some binary-outcome selection models without exclusion restrictions', *Political Analysis*.

Scherr, F.C., T.F. Sugrve and J.B. Ward (1993), 'Financing the small firm start-up: determinants of debt use', *The Journal of Small Business Finance*, **3** (1), 17–36.

Schifter, D.E. and I. Ajzen (1985), 'Weight loss: intention, perceived control, and weight loss: an application of the theory of planned behavior', *Journal of Personality and Social Psychology*, 49 (3), 843–51.

Schollhammer, H. (1991), 'Incidence and determinants of multiple entrepreneurship', *Frontiers of Entrepreneurship Research*, Wellesley, MA: Babson College, 11–24.

Schumpeter, J. (1934), *The Theory of Economic Development*, Cambridge, MA: Harvard University Press.

Sexton, D.L. and N.B. Bowman-Upton (1991), *Entrepreneurship: Creativity and Growth*. New York: Macmillan.

Shane, S. (2000), 'Prior knowledge and the discovery of entrepreneurial opportunities', *Organization Science*, **11**, 448–69.

Shane, S.A. and S. Venkataraman (2000), 'The promise of entrepreneurship as a field of research', *Academy of Management Review*, **25** (1), 217–26.

Shapiro, A.C. (1990), *Modern Corporate Finance*, New York, Macmillan.

Sharma, P. and J.J. Chrisman (1999), 'Toward a reconciliation of the definitional issues in the field of corporate entrepreneurship', *Entrepreneurship Theory and Practice*, **24**, 11–27.

Shepherd, D.A. (1999), 'Venture capitalists' assessment of new venture survival', *Management Science*, **45** (5), 621–32.

Shepherd, D.A. (2003), 'Learning from business failure: Propositions about the grief recovery process for the self-employed', *Academy of Management Review*, **28**, 318–29.

Shepherd, D.A. (2004), 'Educating entrepreneurship students about emotion and learning from failure,' *Academy of Management Learning and Education*, **3** (3), 274–88.

Shepherd, D.A., E.J. Douglas and M. Shanley (2000), 'New venture survival: ignorance, external shocks, and risk reduction strategies', *Journal of Business Venturing*, **15**, 393–410.

Shepherd, D.A. and D. DeTienne (2004), 'Prior knowledge, potential financial reward, and opportunity identification', *Entrepreneurship, Theory and Practice*, **29** (1), 91–112.

Shepherd, D.A., R. Ettenson and A. Crouch (2000), 'New venture strategy and profitability: A venture capitalist's assessment', *Journal of Business Venturing*, **15** (5), 449–67.

Shepherd, D.A. and M. Shanley (1998), *New Venture Strategy: Timing, Environmental Uncertainty and Performance*, London: Sage Publications.

Shepherd, D.A. and A. Zacharakis (2001), 'The venture capitalist–entrepreneur relationship: control, trust and confidence in cooperative behavior', *Venture Capital: An International Journal of Entrepreneurial Finance*, **3** (2), 129–50.

Sheppard, B. and D. Sherman (1998), 'The grammers of trust: a model and general implications', *The Academy of Management Review*, **23** (3), 422–37.

Sheppard, B. and M. Tuchinsky (1996), 'Micro-OB and the network organization', in R. Kramer and T. Tyler (eds), *Trust in organizations: Frontiers of theory and research*, Thousand Oaks, CA: Sage, pp. 140–65.

Shuchter, S.R. (1986), *Dimensions of Grief: Adjusting to the Death of a Spouse*, New York: Jossey-Bass.

Simon, H. (1985), 'What we know about the creative process', in R. Kuhn (ed.), *Frontiers in Creative and Innovative Management*, Cambridge, MA: Ballinger, pp. 3–20.

Singh, J.V., D.J. Tucker and R.J. House (1986), 'Organizational legitimacy and the liability of newness', *Administrative Science Quarterly*, **31** (2), 171–93.

Sinkey, J.F., Jr (1992), *Commercial Bank Financial Management – In the Financial Services Industry*, New York: MacMillan.

Sitkin, S.B. (1992), 'Learning through failure: the strategy of small losses', *Research in Organizational Behavior*, **14**, 231–66.

Sitkin, S. (1995), 'On the positive effect of legalization on trust', in R. Bies, R. Lewicki and B. Sheppard (eds), *Research on Negotiation in Organizations, Vol. 5*, Greenwich, CT: JAI Press, pp. 185–217.

Sitkin, S. and N. Roth (1993), 'Explaining the limited effectiveness of legalistic remedies for trust/distrust', *Organization Science*, **4**, 367–92.

Smallbone, D., R. Leigh and D. North (1995), 'The characteristics and strategies of high growth SMEs', *International Journal of Entrepreneurial Behavior and Research*, **1** (3), 44–62.

Smart, D.T. and J.S. Conant (1994), 'Entrepreneurial orientation, distinctive marketing competencies and organizational performance', *Journal of Applied Business Research*, **10**, 28–38.

Snell, S.A. and J.W. Dean (1992), 'Integrated manufacturing and human resource management: a human capital perspective', *Academy of Management Journal*, **35** (3), 467–504.

Stanworth, J. and C. Grey (1991), *Bolton 20 Years On: A Review and Analysis of Small Business Research in Britain 1971–91*, London: Small Business Research Trust.

Starr, J.A. and W.D. Bygrave (1992), 'The second time around: the outcomes, assets and liabilities of prior start-up experience', in S. Birley and I. MacMillan (eds), *International Perspectives on Entrepreneurship Research*, London: Elsevier, pp. 340–63.

Staw, B.M., L.E. Sandelands and J.E. Dutton (1981), 'Threat rigidity effects in organizational behavior: a multilevel analysis', *Administrative Science Quarterly*, **26**, 501–24.

Steier, L. and R. Greenwood (1995), 'Venture capitalists relationships in the deal structuring and post-investment stages of new firm creation', *Journal of Management Studies*, **32**, 337–57.

Stevenson, H.H. (1983), 'A perspective on entrepreneurship', working paper 9-384-131, Harvard Business School.

Stevenson, H.H. (1984), 'A perspective of entrepreneurship', in H.H. Stevenson, M.J. Roberts, and H. Grousebeck (eds), *New Business Venture and the Entrepreneur*, Boston, MA: Harvard Business School Press.

Stevenson, H.H. and D.E. Gumpert (1985), 'The heart of entrepreneurship', *Harvard Business Review*, **85** (2), 85–94.

Stevenson, H.H. and J.C. Jarillo (1986), 'Preserving entrepreneurship as companies grow', *Journal of Business Strategy*, **6**, 10–23.

Stevenson, H.H. and J.C. Jarillo (1990), 'A paradigm of entrepreneurship: entrepreneurial management', *Strategic Management Journal*, **11**, 17–27.

Stiglitz, J.E. and A. Weiss (1981), 'Credit Rationing in Markets with Imperfect Information', *The American Economic Review*, **71** (3), 393–410.

Stinchcombe, A.L. (1965), 'Social structure and organizations', in J.D. March (ed.), *Handbook of Organizations*, Chicago, IL: Rand McNally, pp. 142–93.

Storey, D.J. (1994), *Understanding the Small Business Sector*, London: Routledge.

Storey, D.J. (1996), *The Ten Percenters*, London: Deloitte and Touche.

Stroebe, M.S. and H. Schut (1999), 'The dual process of coping with bereavement: rationale and description', *Death Studies*, **23**, 197–224.

Sutton, R.I. (1983), Managing organizational death, *Human Resource Management*, **22**, 391–412.

Sutton, R.I. and T. D'Aunno (1989), 'Decreasing organizational size: untangling the effects of money and people', *Academy of Management Review*, **14**, 194–212.

Sweeting, R. (1991), 'UK venture capital funds and the funding of new technology-based businesses: processes and relationships', *Journal of Management Studies*, **28**, 601–22.

Teece, D.J., G. Pisano and A. Shuen (1997), 'Dynamic capabilities and strategic management', *Strategic Management Journal*, **18**, 509–33.

Thomas, J. and L. Trevino (1993), 'Information processing in strategic alliance building: a multiple-case approach', *Journal of Management Studies*, **30**, 779–814.

Thorne, J.R. (1989), 'Alternative financing for entrepreneurial ventures', *Entrepreneurship Theory and Practice*, **X**, 7–9.

Thurik, A.R. and A.R.M. Wenneker (2004), 'Entrepreneurship, small business and economic growth', *Journal of Small Business and Enterprise Development*, **11** (1), 140–49.

Timmons, J. and W. Bygrave (1986), 'Venture capital's role in financing innovation for economic growth', *Journal of Business Venturing*, **1**, 161–76.

Toivanen, O. and R. Cressy (2000), *Lazy Entrepreneurs or Dominant Banks? An Empirical Analysis of the Market for SME Loans in the UK*, Entrepreneurial Finance Workshop, Jönköping, Jönköping International Business School.

Tsai, W.M.H., I.C. MacMillan and M.B. Low (1991), 'Effects of strategy and environment on corporate venture success in industrial markets', *Journal of Business Venturing*, **6** (1), 9–28.

Tushman, M.L. and P. Anderson (1986), 'Technological discontinuities and organizational environments', *Administrative Science Quarterly*, **31**, 439–65.

Uzzi, B. (1996), 'The sources and consequences of embeddedness for the economic performance of organization: the network effect', *American Sociological Review*, **61**, 674–98.

Van de Ven, A.H., R. Hudson and D. Schroeder (1984), 'Designing new business startups: entrepreneurial, organizational, and ecological considerations', *Journal of Management*, **10** (1), 87–107.

Venkataraman, S. (1997), 'The distinctive domain of entrepreneurship research: an editor's perspective', in J. Katz and J. Brockhaus (eds), *Advances in Entrepreneurship, Business Emergence, and Growth*, Greenwich, CT: JAI Press, pp. 119–38.

Venkatraman, N. (1989), 'Strategic orientation of business enterprises: the construct, dimensionality, and measurement', *Management Science*, **14**, 942–62.

Venkatraman, N. (1989b), 'Strategic orientation of business enterprises: the construct, dimensionality, and measurement', *Management Science*, **14**, 942–62.

Venture Economics (2000a), 'US venture-backed IPOs escalate to 271 in 1999', news release, 1 July.

Venture Economics (2000b), Venture Xpert Database.

Von Hippel, E. (1988), *The Sources of Innovation*, New York: Oxford University Press.

Von Hippel, E. (1994), ' "Sticky information" and the locus of problem solving: implications for innovation', *Management Science*, **40**, 429–39.

Walker, D.A. (1989), 'Financing the small firm', *Small Business Economics*, **1**, 285–96.

Weber, R. (1980), 'Some characteristics of free recall of computer controls by EDP auditors', *Journal of Accounting Research*, **18**, pp. 214–41.

Weick, K. (1979), *The Social Psychology of Organizing*, Reading, MA: Addison-Wesley.

Weick, K. (1990), 'The vulnerable system: an analysis of the Tenerife air disaster', *Journal of Management*, **16** (3), 571–94.

Wells, A. and G. Matthews (1994), *Attention and Emotion: a Clinical Perspective*, Hove, UK: Lawrence Erlbaum Associates Ltd.

Wernerfelt, B. (1984), 'A resource based view of the firm', *Strategic Management Journal*, **5**, 171–80.

Westhead, P. and M. Wright (1998), 'Novice, portfolio, and serial founders: Are they different?', *Journal of Business Venturing*, **13** (3), 173–204.

Whitener, E., S. Brodt, A. Korsgaard and J. Werner (1998), 'Managers as initiators of trust: an exchange relationship framework for understanding managerial trustworthy behavior', *Academy of Management Review*, **23** (3), 513–30.

Wiklund, J. (1998), *Small Firm Growth and Performance: Entrepreneurship and Beyond*, doctoral dissertation, Jönköping: Jönköping International Business School.

Wiklund, J. (1999), 'The sustainability of the entrepreneurial orientation–performance relationship', *Entrepreneurship Theory and Practice*, **24**, 37–48.

Wiklund, J., P. Davidsson and F. Delmar (2003), 'What do they think and feel about growth? An expectancy-value approach to small business managers' attitudes toward growth', *Entrepreneurship: Theory and Practice*, **27**, 247–71.

Wiklund, J., P. Davidsson, F. Delmar and M. Aronsson (1997), 'Expected consequences of growth and their effect on growth willingness in different samples of small firms', in P.D. Reynolds, W.D. Bygrave, N.M. Carter, P. Davidsson, W.B. Gartner, C.M. Mason and P.P. McDougall (eds), *Frontiers of Entrepreneurship Research*, Wellesley, MA: Babson College.

Wiklund, J. and D.A. Shepherd (2003a), 'Aspiring for, and achieving growth: the moderating role of resources and opportunities', *Journal of Management Studies*, **40** (8): 1919–42.

Wiklund, J. and D.A. Shepherd (2003b), 'Knowledge-based resources, entrepreneurial orientation, and the performance of small and medium sized businesses', *Strategic Management Journal*, **24**, 1307–14.

Wiklund, J. and D.A. Shepherd (2005), 'Entrepreneurial orientation and small business performance: a configurational approach', *Journal of Business Venturing*, **20** (1), 71–91.

Williams, D.G. and G.H. Moris (1996), 'Crying, weeping or tearfulness in British and Israeli adults', *British Journal of Psychology*, **87**, 479–505.

Winborg, J. and H. Landström (2000), 'Financial bootstrapping in small businesses: Examining small business managers' resource acquisition behaviors', *Journal of Business Venturing*, **16**, 235–54.

Wold, H. and K.G. Jöreskog (1982), 'The ML and PLS techniques for modeling with latent variables: historical and comparative aspects', *Systems Under Indirect Observation: Causality, Structure, Prediction*, Amsterdam: North-Holland, 263–70.

Wolfe, J. and G. Bruton (1994), 'On the use of computerized simulations for entrepreneurship education', *Simulation & Gaming*, **25** (3), 405–18.

Wolfe, J. (1997), 'The effectiveness of business games in strategic management course work', *Simulation & Gaming*, **28** (4), 360–76.

Wollman-Bonilla, J.E. (1989), 'Reading journals: invitations to participate in literature', *The Reading Teacher*, 112–20.

Womack, J.P., D.T. Jones and D. Roos (1990), *The Machine that Changed the World: Based on the Massachusetts Institute of Technology 5-million dollar 5-year Study on the Future of the Automobile*, New York: Rawson Associates.

Wortman, C.B. and R.C. Silver (1987), 'Coping with irrevocable loss', in G.R. Van de Bos and B.K. Bryant (eds), *Cataclysims, Crises and Catastrophes: Psychology in Action*, Washington, DC: American Psychological Association, pp. 189–235.

Wortman, C.B. and R.C. Silver (1989), 'The myths of coping with loss', *Journal of Consulting and Clinical Psychology*, **57**, 349–57.

Wortman, C.B. and R.C. Silver (1992), 'Reconsidering assumptions about coping with loss: An overview of current research', in L. Montada, S.H. Filipp and M.S. Lerner (eds), *Life crises and experiences of loss in adulthood*, Hillsdale NJ: Erlbaum, pp. 341–65.

Wright, M., K. Robbie and C. Ennew (1997), 'Venture capitalists and serial entrepreneurs', *Journal of Business Venturing*, **12** (3), 227–49.

Zacharakis, A. and G.D. Meyer (1998), 'A lack of insight: Do venture capitalists really understand their own decision process?', *Journal of Business Venturing*, **13** (1), 57–76.

Zacharakis, A. and G.D. Meyer (2000), 'The potential of actuarial decision models: Can they improve the venture capital investment decision?', *Journal of Business Venturing*, **15** (4), 323–47.

Zacharakis, A. and D.A. Shepherd (2001), 'The nature of information and venture capitalists' overconfidence', *Journal of Business Venturing*, **14** (6), 311–32.

Zacharakis, A. and D.A. Shepherd (2005), 'Entrepreneurs' leadership ability and venture capitalists' assessment of likely success: a contingent approach', *European Journal of Operational Research*, **162** (3), 673–90.

Zahra, S. (1991), 'Predictors and financial outcomes of corporate entrepreneurship: An explorative study', *Journal of Business Venturing*, **6**, 259–85.

Zahra, S. (1993a), 'A conceptual model of entrepreneurship as firm behavior: A critique and extension', *Entrepreneurship Theory and Practice*, **16**, 5–21.

Zahra, S. (1993b), 'Environment, corporate entrepreneurship, and financial performance: a taxonomic approach', *Journal of Business Venturing*, **8**, 319–40.

Zahra, S. and J. Covin (1995), 'Contextual influence on the corporate entrepreneurship-performance relationship: a longitudinal analysis', *Journal of Business Venturing*, **10**, 43–58.

Zajac, E.J., M. Kraatz and R. Bresser (2000), 'Modeling the dynamics of strategic fit: a normative approach to strategic change', *Strategic Management Journal*, **21**, 429–53.

Zucker, L. (1986), 'Production of trust: Institutional sources of economic structure, 1840–1920', in B. Staw and L. Cummings (eds), *Research in Organizational Behavior, Vol. 8*, Greenwich, CT: JAI Press, pp. 53–111.

Index